Reminiscences of

Captain Thomas H. Dyer

U.S. Navy (Retired)

U.S. Naval Institute

Annapolis, Maryland

1986

Preface

During the course of an oral history, the interviewer gains some interesting insights into the personality and character of the interviewee. Such was the case in this memoir of Captain Thomas Dyer. He revealed himself to be a friendly and charming man, one endowed with a wry sense of humor, a justified feeling of pride in his accomplishments, a willingness to admit mistakes, and a great deal of honesty in talking about the people and events he encountered in the course of a naval career. He was not hesitant to talk about those whom he felt had acted in self-interest rather than the interest of the Navy and the nation, but he also leavened the discussion with a light touch. He frequently gave the impression when he talked that he had a perpetual twinkle in his eye.

From a historical standpoint, this memoir is of considerable value because of Captain Dyer's enormous contribution in breaking Japanese communications codes during World War II. The role of codebreaking in the pivotal U.S. victory at the Battle of Midway has long been acknowledged. Captain Dyer here presents an insider's account of the conditions which prevailed in the subterranean code-breaking room at Pearl Harbor and the jealousies and feuds which followed as various groups sought to claim credit. Dyer has been termed an "unsung hero" for his contributions to the victory at Midway and many other successes in World War II. Here he explains what went into the various feats. He acknowledges the vital role of Captain Joseph Rochefort as a skilled analyst--able to look at decoded fragments of Japanese radio messages and to divine the enemy's intentions. Dyer takes for himself the credit as the best pure codebreaker in the outfit--the man who provided those fragments from which Rochefort worked.

Dyer's recollections provide a good deal of evidence to substantiate his claim that the best codebreakers often had offbeat personalities. In part, his abilities were a natural gift, just as a fine athlete has innate abilities which enable him to excel in sports. But Dyer also had a large measure of persistence and dedication which enabled him to make the most of his natural abilities. He was a stubborn man, which didn't always endear him to his co-workers, but that stubbornness also was a valuable attribute when wrestling with a code which did not yield its secrets readily.

The portrait of Thomas Dyer reveals him as a devoted family man, a religious person, and a student with wide-ranging interests. His abilities as a codebreaker were almost his undoing as a naval officer, because he was more interested in using his talents to best advantage in unraveling the mysteries of Japanese crypto systems rather than fitting into the rigid mold typically expected for U.S. naval officers of his era. Fortunately, his talents were recognized by those who mattered. The Navy was the beneficiary of his codebreaking efforts, and now we are the beneficiaries of his willingness to record his memories near the end of his life.

Captain Dyer died before he had the opportunity to correct the transcripts for the interviews. He did make inputs on the transcript of the first interview while still alive. His daughter, Ann L. Dyer, who works as a writer and editor, has made a substantial contribution to the final form of the transcript by editing to transform the record of the spoken word into a readable account in written form. She has also compiled the excellent index to the volume. Deborah Reid of the Naval Institute did the transcribing and smooth typing.

The Naval Security Group and National Security Agency reviewed the transcript to ensure that it contained no still-classified material. Captain Dyer himself was quite judicious in that regard, with the result that very little of what he said had to be removed from the final version. In those few instances, the omitted portions are indicated by X's.

During the more than 80 years of his life, Thomas H. Dyer left behind a great many solid achievements. This record of those achievements also stands as part of his legacy.

                                        Paul Stillwell
                                        Director of Oral History
                                        U.S. Naval Institute
                                        December 1986

CAPTAIN THOMAS H. DYER, U.S. NAVY (RETIRED)

PERSONAL DATA

    Born: 23 May 1902, Osawatomie, Kansas
    Parents: Thomas Henry Dyer (deceased) and Belle Jamison Dyer (deceased)
    Married: 25 June 1930 to Edith B. Miller in Forest Grove, Oregon
    Children: Thomas Edward Dyer, born 26 October 1935; Ann Leilani Dyer,
        born 27 February 1940
    Education: U.S. Naval Academy (Class of 1924)

PROMOTIONS

    Ensign: June 1924
    Lieutenant (junior grade): June 1927
    Lieutenant: June 1932
    Lieutenant Commander: June 1939
    Commander: July 1942
    Captain: July 1943

DECORATIONS AND MEDALS

    Distinguished Service Medal
    Navy Unit Commendation
    American Defense Service Medal with Base Clasp
    Asiatic-Pacific Campaign Medal with Star
    World War II Victory Medal
    National Defense Service Ribbon

CHRONOLOGICAL TRANSCRIPT OF SERVICE

July 1924-February 1925: Assistant Radio Officer, USS New Mexico (BB-40)

February 1925-April 1926: Assistant Communications Officer, Battleship Division Four

April-June 1926: Antiaircraft Control Officer, USS New Mexico (BB-40)

July-August 1926: Student, Submarine School, New London, Connecticut

August 1926-September 1927: Watch and Division Officer, USS Antares (AG-10)

June-September 1927: Under instruction, Office of Naval Communications

October 1927-May 1928: Assistant Communications Officer, Battleship Divisions

May 1928-May 1929: Assistant Communications Officer, Battle Fleet

August 1929-May 1930: Assistant Communications Officer, U.S. Fleet

May-June 1930: First Lieutenant, USS Pruitt (DD-347)

June 1930-May 1931: Communications and Commissary Officer, USS Badger (DD-126)

May 1931-May 1933: Officer in Charge, Research Desk, Office of Naval Communications

May 1933-June 1936: Gun Turret Officer, USS Pennsylvania (BB-38)

July 1936-December 1945: 14th Naval District, Fleet Radio Unit Pacific (classified duty)

February 1946-June 1949: Commander Support Activity (classified duty)

June 1949-September 1952: Armed Forces Security Agency (classified duty)

October 1952-January 1954: National Security Agency, Far East, Tokyo (classified duty)

February 1954-January 1955: National Security Agency, Washington, D.C. (classified duty)

1 February 1955: Retired from active duty

Authorization

The U.S. Naval Institute is hereby authorized to make available to individuals, libraries, and other repositories of its choosing the transcripts of six oral history interviews concerning the life and career of the late Captain Thomas H. Dyer, U.S. Navy (Retired), following a security clearance from the Naval Security Group and/or the National Security Agency. The six interviews were conducted on 15, 22 and 29 August, and 6, 14, and 20 September 1983 in collaboration with Paul Stillwell for the U.S. Naval Institute.

Acting on behalf of the estate of the late Captain Dyer, the undersigned does hereby release and assign to the U.S. Naval Institute all right, title, restriction, and interest in the six interviews. The copyright in both the oral and transcribed versions shall be the sole property of the U.S. Naval Institute. The tape recordings of the interviews are and will remain the property of the U.S. Naval Institute.

Signed and sealed this ___25th___ day of ___June___ 1985.

Ann L Dyer
Ann Dyer

This oral history transcript of the interview with Captain
Thomas H. Dyer, United States Navy, Retired (Deceased) has
been reviewed jointly by the Naval Security Group Command
and the National Security Agency. Some excisions have been
made. In this form the transcript satisfies all security
requirements pertaining to the protection of classified
matter. The document is certified to be unclassified per
Part 3, E. O. 12356.

Commander, Naval Security Group Command

(GHD/ _IGN_)   27 February 1986

Interview Number 1 with Captain Thomas H. Dyer, U.S. Navy (Retired)

Place: Captain Dyer's cottage, Sykesville, Maryland

Date: Monday, 15 August 1983

Subject: Biography

Interviewer: Paul Stillwell

Q: Captain, in telling your life story I think the appropriate place to begin is to mention when and where you were born and something about your forebears.

Captain Dyer: I was born in Osawatomie, Kansas, on the 23rd of May in 1902. My father was from Kentucky, and his ancestry went back to the early days of Virginia. But no one has ever had energy enough to trace the genealogy very accurately. My mother was from Missouri. Osawatomie itself was famous as the site of John Brown's first exploits.* I had two older brothers; Lowell was seven years older, and Charlie was four years older than I was.

My childhood and youth were relatively uneventful--all the usual things in the life of a small-town boy in the early days of the Boy Scouts. I was a Boy Scout in a rather disorganized troop for a couple of years. I stayed in Osawatomie until I had completed grammar school, and in 1916 my family moved to Kansas

---

*John Brown (1800-1859) was noted for his strong antislavery stands in the mid 19th century; he advocated abolishing slavery by force. In August 1856, he made a heroic stand at Osawatomie, Kansas, against a raid by proslavery forces from Missouri.

City, Missouri.

Q: What had led them to settle in Osawatomie before that?

Captain Dyer: I never knew for sure. It just happened.

Q: What was your father's profession or business?

Captain Dyer: Most of my childhood he was employed by the Missouri Pacific Railroad. Part of that time he worked for the state of Kansas in the state mental hospital which was also there. I'm not too sure just what he did for the railroad. He had a variety of positions but none of any distinguished character.

Q: I take it your mother had her hands full with three boys.

Captain Dyer: She had her hands full with three boys. On moving to Kansas City, she and my father purchased a small hotel which they operated during their entire stay in Kansas City.

I attended high school in Kansas City--the Manual Training High School. I don't know that my high school career was particularly eventful. During my freshman year I became a member of the high school cadets. I was on the staff of the yearbook and in my senior year I was editor of the yearbook. It was on the staff of the yearbook that I met my future wife, who was also a member of the staff.* She was a year ahead of me in high school, so that it was during my junior year that we became acquainted and dated. Then our paths separated, and it was not until some nine years later that we remet.

My entry into the Navy was indirectly connected with my service on the yearbook. During my junior year a friend of mine had taken the competitive examination for West Point--he said more to see how he made out than with any firm hope of getting it. The following year I was sitting in the room which we used as an office for the yearbook with the faculty advisor and reading the weekly school newspaper when I encountered an article concerning a competitive examination for the Naval Academy. More in the way of making conversation than with any other motive, I said, "I think I will go down like Bill Epperson did and take that."

Q: How well had Bill done on that exam?

Captain Dyer: Quite high but not high enough. That year there were some 83 candidates for a single appointment. Had I been left to my own devices, that would probably have been the end of

---
*Edith Beatrice Miller, whom Dyer married in 1930.

Dyer #1 - 4

the matter. But after my idle threat the faculty advisor kept harassing me to go take the exam, with the result that I did go down. In late 1919, a year after the war to end all wars had ended and things military being at a rather low ebb, there were only seven candidates. I was fortunate enough to beat out the other six.

Up to that time, it had been my firm intention to endeavor to go to college and medical school and to become a doctor, but when the congressman offered me the appointment, it seemed too good a thing to turn down without trying it.

Q: How good a student were you in high school?

Captain Dyer: I was a really good student. They had a system of honor pins there, and I received an honor pin for scholarship my last two years. I had essentially an "A" average.

Q: Were you in any other outside activities other than the yearbook? In sports?

Captain Dyer: No. The Cadet Corps was about the only other activity; I was the major of the cadet unit in my senior year.

Q: Was this part of the patriotic program brought on by World War I?

Captain Dyer: No. As a matter of fact, the Cadet Corps had shrunk by my senior year. I joined in early 1917, several months before we entered the war.

Q: What did the cadets do? Drilling, marching, maneuvers?

Captain Dyer: We did close-order drill; we had various things like wall-climbing, and we had sand tables, map games. In one sense, after the first year there was somewhat of a decline in the efficiency of the cadet organization. Originally there had been a captain in the regular Army and two sergeants who were in charge of the Cadet Corps in the four Kansas City high schools. But with the advent of the war, they had other fish to fry. At one time the gym teacher and coach was head of the Cadet Corps-- another year, the biology teacher. They went somewhere and took a three-week course in how to do it. But it didn't have a great deal of depth, actually.

Q: How large a group was it in your school?

Captain Dyer: I suppose we had about 100 until the last year; it shrunk to probably about 50.

Q: Was that useful leadership training for you?

Dyer #1 - 6

Captain Dyer: It was fairly good, although when I went to the Naval Academy, I very modestly refrained from telling them that I knew even how to do right face.

Q: Why was that?

Captain Dyer: I don't know. But there were several classmates who had gone to prep school at Marion down in Alabama. It had some military training, and they seemed to think that they knew all there was to know about close-order drill. I rather enjoyed being ignorant and laughing at them.

Q: Did your parents have you work in the family business at all?

Captain Dyer: Not really. I worked part of the time in high school for the YMCA, originally for a subsidiary organization called the Kansas City Boys Club which catered to newsboys and others of that kind. Later I was the assistant secretary in the boys department of the YMCA proper. I guess I worked there about two and a half out of my four years in high school. My last year I gave it up. During my last summer vacation in high school, together with three friends, I left immediately after school was out to go out and help harvest the Kansas wheat crop. That in itself was quite an experience.

Q: Why don't you describe that, please?

Captain Dyer: We were a little bit hesitant about bumming rides on trains, so we did take enough money to pay our fare. We went down to the southern part of Kansas around Anthony and Harper. We were split up there, and I succeeded in getting a job with a farmer who had about 2,000 acres of wheat. I was one of the first people he hired, there was another man. I have no idea what his name was, even now. We were lucky; we were given a room in the house to sleep in. The next four or six that were hired slept out in various sheds.

When the harvest started, we were in the field by about 7:30 in the morning and had to wait until the dew was off the grain. We worked about a 12-hour day at what at that time was the huge salary of 50 cents an hour.

Q: That was pretty good pay.

Captain Dyer: Plus, of course, room and board, as it were.

Q: Was this a horse-drawn combine or threshing machine?

Captain Dyer: That particular year there had been a lot of rain at the wrong time, and the heads of the wheat were down to where they had to cut it with an old-fashioned binder, which was horse-drawn. My job was to follow along behind the binder, shocking the wheat, that is putting it into shocks, little piles, which got rather tiresome in a 12-hour day.

Q: Did you have to tie them also?

Captain Dyer: Oh no, the binder did that. A binder cut the wheat, the straw, close to the ground and put it into bundles and tied a string around it. So you just had to pick them up and stand them up.

Q: So you were probably pretty robust by the time you finished that.

Captain Dyer: I stayed on for a while after the harvest was completed. They had about a three or four-day respite. I was put to work hoeing fence posts. In that part of Kansas no trees grow naturally. So this farmer had some saplings planted so he could have fence posts. We cleaned the weeds and things like that out, and then the threshing started. He had a rather large building, a storage building, that he filled up first with wheat to hold it for a better price. Another person and I were given the job, when a load of wheat was driven up, of getting into the wagon and throwing the wheat with a big scoop shovel out into the storage shed. That was fine when you were throwing it down, but as you filled up the shed, you put boards in front of the door higher and higher until finally you were throwing the wheat up. And you'd think, "Now, two more minutes and this wagon will be empty, and I'll get a chance to relax." In about one more minute, the next wagon would drive up. So you climbed out of one wagon into the other. And that was really work, which made the harvesting itself seem almost like a vacation. But finally the storage building was full, and I got promoted to driving a pair of mules to take the wheat into the elevator in town. That really wasn't bad at all.

Q: Did you have some objective in mind that you were saving your money for?

Captain Dyer: Not particularly. Of course, at that time I hoped to be going to college and medical school, and I was going to need money. I would not want to mislead anyone--I did not come from a wealthy family. I sometimes think when I read the papers nowadays that if they had a poverty line at that time we might have been below it. But we didn't know it, so we didn't realize it. We always had a place to sleep and enough to eat.

Q: What stimulated your interest in going to medical school?

Captain Dyer: I don't know. It was persistent from early childhood. When I was about seven or eight years old, the family doctor asked me what I was going to be when I grew up, and I said, "I'm either going to be a doctor or a preacher. Which one makes the most money?"

And his reply was that I'd better be a preacher because while a doctor made more, the preacher got it.

Anyway, when I was in grammar school, I borrowed books from the doctor. I read all of Gray's *Anatomy* and a couple of other standard texts.

Q: Did you enjoy reading?

Captain Dyer: Yes, I read most of my life, except when I was in the Naval Academy.

Q: Did you have any hobbies or outside interests in your growing-up years?

Captain Dyer: Not specifically, no.

Q: Did you have the usual games and so forth with your brothers?

Captain Dyer: I was too little. I had to find my playmates on my own, more my own age. I had a number of friends. I was never very good in athletic games. I played baseball a little bit--not really, not to the extent that one should. I'd rather go off and read.

Q: Did you enjoy science and math during those years?

Captain Dyer: I always liked math, arithmetic and so on. When I was in the seventh grade, I think, I was about 15 or 20 pages ahead of the class in working the problems in the arithmetic textbook just because I enjoyed it.

Q: What adjustments did you have to make in moving from Osawatomie to the much bigger city of Kansas City?

Captain Dyer: There really wasn't any particular adjustment. The hotel was right downtown. I don't know, it just seemed perfectly natural.

Q: How much awareness did you have of the Navy during those years in the Midwest?

Captain Dyer: I knew nothing about it. When it finally looked as if I was going to get the appointment to Annapolis, I went right up to the public library which was a couple of blocks from where I lived, got a book about the Naval Academy, and read it. It was the first that I had read.

I was pretty well versed in Army terminology, ranks, and so

forth because my two brothers had served in World War I in the same regiment with President Truman.* The younger brother, Charlie, was originally in the National Guard and went to the Mexican border in 1916 with Pershing.** When he came back, he got his older brother Lowell to join up, too. When they got down to Fort Sill, Camp Donovan, Lowell was selected to go to Officer Training School. He became a 90-day wonder officer. And Charlie said, "Eight months ago I was teaching him how to do right and left face, and now I have to salute the so-and-so." Lowell was Truman's first lieutenant for a while, in the same battery. It was an artillery regiment.

I had no idea when I arrived in Annapolis how you told one naval officer from another or what the different ranks were.

Q: Did you have any idea at that point of making the Navy a career?

Captain Dyer: It was completely an open option. I thought, "I'll go and see how I like it. If I don't like it, I can probably get out after a year or two years." At least I had the idea that I could probably transfer most of my credits and I

---
*Harry S Truman served as a field artillery officer in France during World War I and rose to the rank of captain.
**Major General John J. Pershing, USA, commanded an expeditionary force to Mexico in 1916 in pursuit of bandit leader Francisco ("Pancho") Villa. In 1917, Pershing became commander in chief of the American Expeditionary Force in France.

wouldn't be losing any real time or anything else. But I got there and I found that I did like it. So I decided to stay.

Q: Since you had already passed the exam, you didn't have to spend any time in prep school, did you?

Captain Dyer: Well, the exam I passed was just a local thing. I had taken it around Christmastime, and it was along in January when I found out that I had the appointment. It still had to take the regular entrance examination in April. But it did not seem the better part of wisdom to break up my last year in high school when I was editor of the yearbook. It just didn't make any sense to go to prep school.

By chance, my high school English teacher was a West Point graduate of the class of '06, or somewhere back there, maybe even farther back than that. He offered to coach me in English. One of the math teachers volunteered to spend some time with me on math. I sent away to somebody named Feldmeyer in Annapolis and got some copies of old exams.

I passed the exam with very good marks except in geometry. I didn't think that I had passed. They asked some things that I didn't remember too well. But whether it was courtesy or not--I think my other marks ran around 3.4, 3.5, 3.6--geometry was 2.5; they accepted me.

Q: Was it a considerable honor in that era to get an appointment to the Naval Academy?

Captain Dyer: Some people thought so, and some people didn't even know what it was. My hometown paper in Osawatomie had a little piece, a squib, about how I was going to the Naval Training School in "Indianapolis."

Q: How much contact had you had with the congressman about getting the appointment?

Captain Dyer: None. As a matter of fact, to get back to this English teacher of mine, he had been chairman of the examining committee. I don't think that had anything to do with my marks, but they had a committee from the four high schools to conduct the examination. He kept asking me, "Have you heard anything from the congressman?" Finally he got me after class and he said, "I don't know whether I ought to do this or not, but I think you ought to know you will probably have to take an entrance examination in April." This was in February, I think. He said, "A congressman can do what he pleases with the results of the competitive examination. If somebody puts enough pressure on him, he can give the appointment to somebody who never took the examination. But I think you ought to know that you did stand number one."

Dyer #1 - 15

As I later found out, the congressman had two vacancies that year. I got one principal appointment, and a stranger got the other. The other six were alternates, three for each appointment. The other principal appointment didn't stay; he didn't last.

Q: Did you finish the school year and graduate?

Captain Dyer: I finished the school year, but the night of my graduation I was sitting on the front steps of what was then called the Peggy Stewart Inn, across from the main gate of the Naval Academy, waiting to go in the next morning and take my physical examination.

Q: How did you stand in your high school class?

Captain Dyer: They never calculated the standing, but I was in the top 10%, probably the top 5%.

Q: Had you been away from home at all before you went to Annapolis?

Captain Dyer: No, other than the Kansas wheat field or casual trips. That's all.

Dyer #1 - 16

Q: Then could you describe your arrival at the Naval Academy, checking in, and so forth?

Captain Dyer: On the way to Annapolis a couple of boys my age approached me on the train, looking for somebody to play cards with. We finally got to exchanging confidences, as it were, and discovered we were all headed to the same place, not surprisingly, when you consider it. The family of one of them was very close to the congressman from their district, so they were met at the Washington station by the congressman's wife and daughter. I tagged along, and she took us up to the hotel, the Harrington Hotel on Pennsylvania Avenue, and we got a room. She picked us up and took us sight-seeing in Washington, over to the Capitol and so on. We must have arrived there on Tuesday. On Wednesday at her recommendation we took a trip to Mount Vernon. Wednesday night we went to Annapolis.

Thursday morning we reported to the Naval Academy and were taken over and put through the physical examination. At that time they did not have this business of a million plebes entering at one time. I suppose there were around 30 of us. And, of course, the military type physical examination was all new to us. But I passed without any difficulty. They said, "All right, goodbye. Come back in the morning."

And we came back the following morning and reported to the Superintendent's office. The clerks there, smart bunch of so-and-sos, said, "If you have any cigarettes, you better put them in this box." So they could smoke them. I did not smoke at that time really, but I did have a pack of cigarettes. I had smoked maybe the equivalent of one pack of cigarettes in my life.

We went in before the admiral and held up our right hand and swore. They took us over to Bancroft Hall and lined us up and said, "You want to take French or Spanish?" At that time half the class took French and half Spanish. That was the means by which the regimental organization was divided--four battalions, two of each. Somebody indicated to me that maybe I ought to take Spanish, and a boy I had met the night before said, "How about us rooming together?"

I said, "Okay." They took us down to the midshipmen's store and loaded us up with two laundry bags full of clothes. Finally we got up to our assigned room. Some old salts who'd probably been there all of two or three days now came around and explained the ropes to us, how to mark our clothes and how to store our clothes and this, that, and the other thing.

The rest of entering day is more or less a blur, except I think it was that first night that I was out in the passageway and an officer came by, and I gave him a snappy salute and caught hell. Of course, I didn't have a hat on, and he told me that you did not salute uncovered in the Navy.

Q: Who was your roommate?

Dyer #1 - 18

Captain Dyer: He was also from Missouri, the name of Wallar.* He lasted only until September. He decided it was too much for him, and he resigned.

Q: Did your time with the cadets prepare you for the sort of discipline that you were coming into?

Captain Dyer: Reasonably so. It prepared me for the discipline but not for the blisters you get rowing a cutter. Shortly, we went out and were introduced to rowing a cutter, and it seemed like those oars were like telephone poles.

Q: Especially in the Annapolis summer.

Captain Dyer: Yes. We had a very pleasant summer, on the whole. It was difficult, a lot of new things to learn. I spent quite a bit of time out at the rifle range and a lot of time with close order drill, a lot of time in gym and in various kinds of boats, marlinspike seamanship and what have you. Everything was new and different.

Q: How did you like it as you came to learn about it?

---
*Midshipman Leroy Wallar, USN.

Dyer #1 - 19

Captain Dyer: I liked it, except the blisters. You learned how to sail boats and things like that. That was fun.

Q: Was there any hazing from the upperclassmen?

Captain Dyer: There weren't any upperclassmen there. They were all on the midshipmen cruise. They had--I don't know how many now--four or eight fresh-caught ensigns from the class that had just graduated, and they acted as company officers that summer. One of them, also from Kansas, was very young. He had entered the Academy at 16, into the class of '21, a wartime class which was divided into two halves. The first half graduated early, in three years.

Q: So he was '21A.

Captain Dyer: He was '21A. He was just 19. Well, one of the lads there, who was very small, and who later did become one of my roommates, was just barely under the wire of 20 when he entered. This ensign came by inspecting one day and said, "How old are you, son?"

And he said, "Twenty, sir." We all knew the ensign was only 19. Try to keep your face straight.

But it was an interesting summer. On the first of September the upper classes came back from the cruise and immediately left on a month's leave. On the first of October they came back and the academic year started. That was, again, a bit different. Academically I got off on a pretty good foot. In high school I'd had second year algebra. The first course we had in math was algebra. So it was very easy for me. I'd had a pretty rigorous two years of mechanical drawing in high school, so the drawing seemed very elementary to start with. Without going into a lot of other courses, English--I'd studied *Hamlet* in high school, and they had *Hamlet* again. That made that a lot easier. So I got off academically to a pretty good start.

Q: Is this why you say you didn't have to do so much reading at the Naval Academy?

Captain Dyer: Well, no. I didn't do much reading, because there you did have to read some of your texts. In plebe year I got tangled up in two extracurricular activities. In the first place, I got involved with the electrical gang of the theatrical organization. I don't know whether they still do it or not, but we used to put a great big electric sign on the front of the tower of Mahan Hall for the annual show.

Q: I haven't seen that recently.

Captain Dyer: Probably they don't do it anymore. Of course, we had to build the sign from scratch. Most of my plebe year I ran the movies every Saturday night. The other activity was as a typist on the *Log* staff. I spent every evening study hour from 7:30 to 9:30 working in the *Log* office. And both of those organizations did me a little dirt. That year the first class were the only ones who were allowed to smoke, and then only after dinner in the evening in Smoke Hall. That's where it gets its name. It still has the name, but I doubt if anyone knows the whys and wherefores. It wasn't official, but the first class on the staff were allowed to smoke in the *Log* office. Well, since that accounted for smoking in the *Log* office, everybody on the staff smoked.

It was a little less formal over at Mahan Hall with the electrical gang. In the first place, we didn't have any first classmen that year. But the upper class smoked, the plebes smoked, everybody smoked. It was a privilege. Here was a privilege that I could enjoy; it was illegal, but I could get by with it. So I smoked. And I'll tell you, if smoking had been permitted, I don't know whether I would ever have started. But I did start and smoked for more than 30 years; then I quit.

Q: You said they did you dirt. How did you mean that?

Captain Dyer: That's what I mean. By extending an illegal privilege to me, it got me into a bad habit. But, of course, if

I was in the Log office in the evening, I was completely away from any upperclassman who could in any way harass me.

Q: The Log is the midshipman magazine. Was that an outgrowth of your journalistic experience in high school?

Captain Dyer: Not entirely, because I was just a typist. I was one of the few who seemed to know how to run a typewriter fairly well--not that I was an expert, but I had typed for years. That's what they put out, an appeal for any plebes who knew how to type. I responded. As I say, it got me out of an awful lot of grief with the upper class. An upperclassman around the end of my plebe year said, "Dyer, you've gotten by with more as a plebe than anyone has since Admiral Mahan," which wasn't true, I don't think.*

Q: You mentioned movies. Did the Naval Academy have movies separate from the ones in town?

Captain Dyer: Oh, yes. Over in Mahan Hall every Saturday night, they had a show. Later they switched it to the armory to accommodate a larger audience. And then, I think in my youngster year they had a civilian employee who ran them. But my plebe

---

*Alfred Thayer Mahan, noted naval historian and strategist, was in the Naval Academy class of 1859.

Dyer #1 - 23

year, if a midshipman didn't run them, there wasn't any show.

Q: So these were free movies? Did Hollywood supply them to the Academy?

Captain Dyer: I haven't any idea. They were not the very latest releases, I can assure you.

Q: Did you get Charlie Chaplin and Tom Mix and some of those?

Captain Dyer: Some Westerns I know. The projector we had at that time was not even motor-driven. You had to hand-crank it, a carbon arc light. It wasn't extensive, but I had had some experience with that type of projector before. It wasn't all new to me.

Q: One of the upperclassmen you encountered in your electrical gang experience was Ruthven Libby, who was in the class of '22. What did that lead to?*

Captain Dyer: My youngster year they were having a series of shows put on by the various battalions. One of the first classmen in my battalion who was connected with the show asked me

---
*Midshipman Ruthven E. Libby, USN, who eventually retired as a vice admiral. His oral history is included in the Naval Institute collection.

Dyer #1 - 24

to do something about the lights for the show. I said, "Sure." And I did, and I didn't consult with Libby. He was a little bit irate, to say the least. He informed me that he didn't appreciate it, and if I was going to run the juice gang, he would get out, and if he was going to run it, I'd better get out. So I did.

Q: Did you wind up in something else instead?

Captain Dyer: I transferred. I didn't want to give up the Masqueraders completely--the stage theatrical outfit. So I became a stagehand. And along in the spring of 1922, about March, I guess, we were getting ready for a Navy Relief show. One of my classmates went up the ladder with a 15-pound sash weight to send down some lines. Just as he got to the top, the sash weight got away from him and came down and hit me on top of my head. I think the thing that actually saved me was that it did strike the ladder maybe two or three feet above my head. If it hadn't, maybe it would have missed me completely, but then--anyway, it knocked me down. I don't think I was unconscious, but I got up and I went to feel the bump on my head and put my hand up there, and blood was dropping off my elbow. The wife of one of the officers who was there in connection with the show had her car. She took me over to Bancroft Hall, assisted by none other than Ruth Libby.

Q: Your nemesis.

Captain Dyer: At that time we had a rather odd character on the medical staff. He had the duty; he got me up there, got the story of what happened, and then said, "Mr. Dyer, how many foot-pounds of force did that hit you with?" I don't know what I responded.

He picked up a quart bottle of iodine and poured it on top of my head, so it came down and dripped off my chin. It was strong enough that it took some of the skin off my chin and cheeks. Then he bandaged me up and sent me to the hospital. I had a very pleasant three weeks in the hospital and got ready to go back to duty. The morning I was supposed to go back to duty, I had a cough and a sore throat. So they decided to keep me in the hospital. They transferred me to another ward and took my tonsils out.

The upshot of that was that it led to my having the highest standing I ever had in a single course, the highest mark, because at that time the rule was that if you did not have two recitations during the month, you did not have to take the monthly examination. I was gone for a complete month, which was the entire period, really, that they had on stereographic projections. But I did have to take the final, which became my mark for the course. I studied real hard and got a 3.8 or 3.9. I've forgotten where I stood--one, I think.

Q: How much of a challenge scholastically was the Naval Academy to you?

Captain Dyer: Very little except for Spanish. Foreign languages--Latin in high school, Spanish at the Naval Academy--were my most difficult subjects, which may seem strange considering my subsequent vocation.

Q: Yes, it does.

Captain Dyer: But Spanish is probably the thing that kept me from graduating with distinction, because my final average was something on the average of 3.39 with about a 2.6 in Spanish.

Q: How was your grease mark?*

Captain Dyer: Not amongst the best.

Q: Why was that?

Captain Dyer: Partly bad luck. Partly, I think, because I have to admit that I don't think I was ever a prepossessing military figure and such things as--for example, jumping ahead to our

---

*This was the score for conduct and military aptitude.

first class cruise, we were in Greenock, Scotland. On Sunday a friend of mine and I went down to Gourock, which is on the streetcar line, practically at the end of the line, to visit some people he had met. We had a wonderful time down there. We had high tea, and they asked us to stay for supper, too, so we stayed. Liberty was supposed to be up on the dock at 10:00 o'clock. Probably along towards 9:00 o'clock, we said, "Well, we better be starting back." And then we found out that on Sunday in Scotland the streetcars stopped running at 6:00 o'clock. There was only one means of getting from there to the dock in Greenock, about eight miles. We were a little late getting back.

We tried to explain. I don't like to say this about some of my classmates, but some of them weren't bothering to come back from liberty at all and weren't getting caught. Here we were trying to be honest and we were caught. We got 20 demerits and lost liberty in Lisbon and in Gibraltar. That affected the grease mark for the summer, which had a profound bearing on the first appointments for officer positions in the fall.

Q: Just a matter of bad luck.

Captain Dyer: Just bad luck. Nobody's fault. Probably just as well. But then I don't know; I think that I made a reasonable effort to do what was right. I didn't go out of my way to try to impress the company officer or anything of that kind.

Q: How would you characterize the quality of the instruction, the education you got?

Captain Dyer: I think it was very good. The system, particularly in that day--I think it's changed considerably now--was one where you didn't have teachers; you had referees. The normal procedure in practically every subject was that you were given an assignment that you had to read. In the classroom the instructor would say, "Any questions? Draw slips." He would have some questions on cut-up slips of paper on his desk. You would go up and draw one and go to the board and write the answer. Then as time remained, he would read it and criticize or comment. But when you come down to it, there was very little that corresponded to instruction, little lecturing, very little instruction and discussion. But it worked. I had no complaint about it at the time. Later, when I was teaching at the University of Maryland, I found no way of using such a system.

Q: Are there any of the professors you particularly recall?

Captain Dyer: Not too many. C. Alphonso Smith was greatly loved. He was head of the English department. And Captain Garrison, who headed the math department, was very well respected.*

---
*Captain Daniel M. Garrison, USN.

Dyer #1 - 29

Q: "Slipstick Willie" was sort of an institution, wasn't he?

Captain Dyer: "Slipstick Willie" was an institution.* I never had him as an instructor, but I met up with him during the war out in Pearl Harbor. I don't know how it is now, but one difficulty was that you changed instructors every month. As a result, unless someone was extremely good or extremely bad, or at least very much of a character, you didn't remember him. For instance, I remember the Spanish instructor, Tony the Bootblack. He was the brother of Mayor La Guardia of New York.**

I knew Royal Pease in the English department, both as an instructor and as the coach for the dramatic part of the theatrical organization. In fact, he was still doing that when my son was there in the class of '57. I can probably think of a few more. A number of them were officers--about half and half, I guess.

Q: Did you make any friendships with your classmates or other midshipmen that lasted over the years?

Captain Dyer: Oh, yes. Moving ahead a little bit, when the

---
*"Slipstick Willie" was the nickname given Professor Earl W. Thomson because of his prowess with a slide rule. He taught at the Naval Academy from 1919 to 1959.
**C.G.B. La Guardia was the brother of Mayor Fiorello La Guardia.

staff for our yearbook was formed, I became assistant manager. The manager and I were quite good friends, and the editor, and the associate editor. The editor and associate editor are both dead. The roommate whom I had practically the entire four years and I were pretty good friends, but unfortunately he wound up in a mental hospital. I used to go see him at St. Elizabeth's in the early Thirties when I was in Washington, but it took so much out of me that I didn't even attempt to renew it when I came back to Washington after the war. I didn't think I was doing him any good, and I was tearing myself up pretty badly.

There are some other people, but they're not all men who go back to when I was a midshipman. We still attended class luncheons up until about the time we moved up here. We had a stag luncheon once a month for classmates, and once a quarter we had what we called the coed luncheon. The stag luncheon dwindled down to a low number and was discontinued, but some of them are getting together even less formally. I had some old-time friends in the class and some relatively new friends. I was secretary and treasurer of the Washington group for about, I guess, 12 or 13 years and sent out monthly notices about where the luncheon would be and collected the reservations.

But I don't know, I have never been a person to look back. I can be good friends with somebody when we're shipmates or something, but I have no real interest in continuing the friendship by voluminous correspondence afterwards. Some people

Dyer #1 - 31

do. So whether it's Naval Academy classmates or people I met later, I form friendships. I retired from the service after spending about ten years at Nebraska Avenue.* I never went back there until several years later when they asked me to come back and read a couple of historical things.

Q: So you don't dwell on the past at all.

Captain Dyer: No point in it. When I ceased being a naval officer and became a college teacher, I was a college teacher. I tried to find my associations and friendships at the university.

Q: You mentioned your first class cruise already. Do you want to cover the two that preceded that?

Captain Dyer: The first cruise, the youngster cruise, I had never been aboard a large ship of any kind. I had never seen the ocean. And so there was a lot of new experiences. We departed right after graduation. They divided the regiment alphabetically, and with a name beginning with "D," I should have been on the Connecticut. But the Log staff had managed to get some key people, including a couple of typists, assigned to the Minnesota. So that's where I was assigned. Also assigned to the

---
*The Naval Security Station on Nebraska Avenue in Washington, D.C.

Minnesota were some of the people who were "unsat." Some of my friends who didn't know me very well, I think, concluded that I was on the Minnesota because I was "unsat."

We had 19 days at sea. I was working as compartment cleaner in one of the forward compartments on the Minnesota when we got out of Chesapeake Bay and on the ocean. I couldn't have been in a worse place in the ship. I promptly got really seasick. But I recovered. I lived.

We went around the north of Scotland through Pentland Firth and almost experienced the "land of the midnight sun" there. I had watch one night on a sunset that never got so dark that you couldn't read without light on deck. In the Christiania Fjord--it was Christiania in those days, not Oslo--we arrived on midsummer's day, the 21st of June, which is a holiday and there were dozens of sailboats on the fjord. A beautiful sight.

Innocent midshipmen that we were, we were shocked--a rowboat came by with a couple of girls in it, and a man swimming alongside with not a stitch of clothes on. How he managed to swim in that water later puzzled me, because I could hardly stand to help scrub down the decks in the morning. But we found that that wasn't so uncommon up there. That was the first big surprise we had, though. We had a very pleasant stay in Christiania.

We would go ashore and engage some English-speaking Norwegian in conversation, and he would ask what ship we were on. I would say, "The Minnesota."

"Ah, the Minnesota. I have a cousin in Minnesota, maybe you know him." Then try to explain.

After 19 days at sea, the food was wonderful.

Q: How was the food on board ship?

Captain Dyer: That part of the cruise, it wasn't too bad, but it wasn't too good. It got a lot worse.

Q: What did you wind up eating?

Captain Dyer: We had eggs about two or three days a week for breakfast. The eggs got so bad that the only way they could serve them was in a Spanish omelet. The beef was so bad that about the only thing you could eat was the gravy. As far as the potatoes and things like that were concerned, they kept body and soul together pretty well.

Q: Was the food spoiled? Was that the problem?

Captain Dyer: Well, they were breaking sides of beef out of a refrigerator, and one of my classmates slipped and went down. His hand went into the side of beef up to his wrist. A little mushy, but we survived.

I, politician that I was, had learned in high school, among other things, how to set type and how to be a printer. I got down around the print shop, and the key printer found out I could set type. They were putting out a special edition of the newspaper that had a lot of type to set. He went to the executive officer and got me detailed down there. I got out of about 10 or 20 days in the fireroom. Theoretically, we had 40 days on deck and 40 days in the engineering force. It should have been ten days in the fireroom, ten days in the engine room, ten days in the electrical department, and so on. But with the plebes it was 40 days in the fireroom. So I had my share. I got out of having more than my share, as it were, but I never felt very guilty about it.

Q: Did you enjoy being at sea?

Captain Dyer: Yes, very much, after I got used to it. Sleeping in a hammock was a novel experience, learning how to stretch a hammock so that you could sleep in it.

Q: Did you stand deck watches?

Captain Dyer: Yes. Somewhere up in North Sea I had a lookout watch up in the searchlight platform. I had on two pairs of pants, two pairs of socks, and so forth, and I nearly froze to death. Now I don't know what kinds of watches we stood. We got rotated through various and sundry things.

Q: The Minnesota was one of the victims of the Washington Naval Disarmament Conference.* What was the reaction at the Naval Academy to the move toward naval disarmament?

Captain Dyer: We didn't question so much discarding the Minnesota and the Kansas and the Connecticut and so on, but we did question the wisdom of scrapping six battle cruisers and the battleships and so forth. Of the six battle cruisers, two of them were converted to carriers and the other four were scrapped. I don't know. Naturally, the midshipmen were not too enthusiastic about it.

There were repercussions in the Academy. There was a great deal of doubt raised about the class of '22, whether they would all be commissioned or not. They were encouraged to resign. Finally, all of them who didn't resign were commissioned, but it looked for a long time as if maybe they would just have to draw the line so that half would get commissioned and half wouldn't, as did happen later, in '33.

---

*The Washington naval treaty of 1922 set tonnage ratios for the key nations. The United States scrapped the unfinished battleship Washington (BB-47) and a number of older battleships. Battle cruisers Lexington and Saratoga were converted to aircraft carriers; the rest of the planned class of six was either scrapped or not begun.

Let's finish up on the cruise. We left Copenhagen and went to Lisbon for two weeks. While we were there, we were moored in the Tagus River, and the mooring swivel on the Minnesota fouled and stuck. When we got ready to leave, we had two anchor chains twisted around each other many, many times. So the other three ships left us there, and we departed almost 24 hours after they did. The captain decided that, if he possibly could, he was going to catch up with them. So we were ordered to make all the speed we could, with some kind of an offer that the watch that made the best distance in the run to Gibraltar would get some privilege. I don't know what it was now. We did get them in sight just as we were out of Gibraltar. We had four days in Gibraltar and came back and stopped in Guantanamo for a couple or three days, and then back to Annapolis. On that cruise I haven't any idea where or when we coaled ship, except I remember it was a horrible ordeal.

Q: How did you get the anchor chains unfouled when you were at Lisbon?

Captain Dyer: We had to unshackle one of them and kind of dip it down and around. They didn't encourage onlookers at the operation.

Q: And you didn't particularly want to volunteer either.

Captain Dyer: I didn't want to volunteer. That was a big chain and really something to handle. The second cruise was a very limited cruise, really. I was assigned to the <u>Delaware</u>. We went first to Panama and went up the locks to Gatun Lake, the idea being that the period in fresh water kills your barnacles, and postpones for a little bit the dry-docking and scraping of barnacles. We coaled ship in Christobal from the pier there and started out with them furnishing the labor. We didn't have much to do, so some people got ants in their pants and we had to work. The next day was field day, and I had one of my perennial cases of very bad sunburn, sunburn on the tops of my feet. There's not much more to say about the stay in Panama. I did take a train trip over to the Pacific side.

When we left Panama we went to Fort-de-France, Martinique. That was particularly intriguing, because the franc had fallen to about five cents, and the local economy had not really caught up with the devaluation, so French champagne cost something like 60 cents a bottle. There's not too much I can say about Martinique, even if Josephine did come from there, and has a statue there.*

We went to St. Kitts for a day or two. One of the other ships had gone to St. Kitts originally, I think. We had a peculiar squadron that year including, among other things, the

---

*Josephine Bonaparte was the first wife of French Emperor Napoleon; she was born in Martinique.

Olympia.*

Q: She was quite venerable by then.

Captain Dyer: She was. In one sense I always regretted that I didn't make the Olympia, but in others I was very glad I didn't. From St. Kitts we went up to the island of Culebra, which at that time was almost uninhabited. A few years ago, it figured in the news because there were objections to the Navy's use of it as a target range.

We got over to St. Thomas for a weekend. Then we hit one good port. We went to Halifax, and then back to Annapolis, and that was that.

Q: You were pretty well up and down the Eastern seaboard.

Captain Dyer: Yes, we were very well up and down the Eastern seaboard. Most of it we'd just as leave passed up. Panama was interesting, because that was the first time most of us had seen any part of the Canal or anything like it.

The first class cruise in some ways corresponded to the youngster cruise. We went first to Copenhagen and found that

---

*The cruiser Olympia, commissioned in 1895, was Commodore George Dewey's flagship at the Battle of Manila Bay in 1898.

thoroughly enjoyable, and then to Scotland, Greenock, and a repeat on Lisbon and Gibraltar.

One of those things that sticks in your mind--we were coaling ship in Gibraltar when we got word of the death of President Harding.* And then back to Guantanamo again. That year we did fire a target practice.

Q: What ship were you in then?

Captain Dyer: The Arkansas, or as we called it, the "Jolly Ar-KAN-sas."

Q: She was a newer ship than the others. Did you notice a difference in accommodations?

Captain Dyer: There wasn't all that much difference. There was a little bit. Of course, as first classmen we had a little bit better deal on the thing. I would say there was quite a bit of difference between her, the Minnesota, and the Arkansas. The Delaware was not as striking a difference.

Q: You had added responsibilities, I take it, during your first class cruise over what you had in the previous ones.

---

*U.S. President Warren G. Harding died at San Francisco on 2 August 1923 while on a speaking tour.

Dyer #1 - 40

Captain Dyer: Oh yes, a little bit. In exchange for using the office assigned to the midshipmen's executive officer from the Academy, we acted as yeomen for him. We had a couple of portable typewriters, and we typed all his orders and memos, but it still didn't get me out of being late getting back in Scotland.

Q: At what point during the four years did you decide that you were going to stick with the Navy instead of going into medicine?

Captain Dyer: There isn't any point that I could really say that that's when I decided, but I think that by the end of my plebe year, certainly by the end of my first cruise, I was going to stay if they would have me. I never could understand the whys and the wherefores; I never had any eye trouble before or on entrance. But in February of my plebe year I had a physical examination, and I didn't see as well as I should have. That's when I started wearing glasses. There was a question of whether I would be able to stay in the Navy on account of my eyes. Of course, a person's human nature, I guess--if they wanted to throw me out, I wanted to stay.

Q: It sounds like the smoking.

Captain Dyer: The eye problems plagued me later in my career.

Dyer #1 - 41

It would seem that even though I was prescribed glasses by two or three different people while I was a midshipman, all the prescriptions were wrong.

Q: You must have been pretty rare as a midshipman to be wearing glasses at the Naval Academy.

Captain Dyer: There weren't too many.

Q: Did you get involved in intramural sports while you were at the Naval Academy?

Captain Dyer: No, I'm sorry. I was more what you would call a "Mexican athlete."

Q: What's a Mexican athlete?

Captain Dyer: Throwing the bull. Or a member of the Radiator Club.

Q: I'll be your straight man again. What's the Radiator Club?

Captain Dyer: They are the people who spend their time hugging the radiator and shooting the bull when the others are out on the athletic field. After the _Lucky Bag_ staff started out, there was an awful lot to do.* We spent every afternoon from right after drill to time for the evening meal up in the Lucky Bag office, writing letters, soliciting advertising, this, that and the other thing. There was quite a bit to do.

Q: How much of a social life did you have?

Captain Dyer: Very little. I was what was known as a "Red Mike."** I didn't go to hops except very, very rarely. I did, I guess it was my youngster year, have a date for June Week as an accommodation to a friend of mine who wanted his girl to come down, and she wanted her friend to come with her. That didn't work out too well.

Q: Did you go home on your September leaves?

Captain Dyer: I went home on September leave, and I went home at Christmas my youngster and second class year. Plebe year, Christmas leave was all of four days, which was a bit short to go as far as Kansas City. Youngster Christmas I went home. I don't know how come it worked out quite so late; we should have arrived in Kansas City about 6:00 o'clock in the evening on the 25th.

---
*Lucky Bag is the name of the Naval Academy yearbook.
**"Red Mike" is Naval Academy slang for a midshipman who has few dates with girls.

But the locomotive broke a connecting rod, and we spent most of Christmas Day sitting out in a corn field. When they finally did get an engine to tow us in, it was a freight engine. We arrived in Kansas City about 4:00 o'clock in the morning on the 26th.

There was a first classman going with us. His family had figured on having their Christmas dinner when he got there. By golly, they did. They sat down at the table somewhere around 4:30 in the morning on the 26th.

Q: A memorable meal.

Captain Dyer: By my first class year, my family had moved to Oregon. While I'd have liked to have seen my parents and the brother I had living out there, it seemed an awful long way to go. So I more or less stayed around the Academy. The Lucky Bag manager and I went up to Philadelphia and New York soliciting advertising. Otherwise, I did stay at the Academy. I don't know what I did Christmas; I guess I stayed there. Maybe I visited somebody in Washington; I don't know.

Q: How did your parents view your budding naval career?

Captain Dyer: They were apparently quite proud of me.

Q: Can you say some more about your role on the Lucky Bag? What sorts of places would you approach for advertisements?

Captain Dyer: One of the most unusual experiences was with a man at Standard Oil of New York. I don't know where we got his name. I went down there on lower Broadway or wherever the place was, asked for him, and I got sent up to the 11th floor. It was an office pretty close to the description of Mussolini's office--two big desks, one that he worked at, another one he could turn around to and talk to you over.* I gave him my sales pitch and got absolutely nowhere. I was carrying that year's Lucky Bag in my briefcase, so I asked, "How would you like to look at the medium I'm trying to get you interested in?"

He turned two pages and said, "I think we can do this. Give me the dope." He didn't say that, but that was the gist of what he said. I gave it to him and took my departure. I got back to Annapolis and dated the same day was an order from their advertising agency for a full page. So I got curious as to who he was. He was the secretary of the corporation.

Q: You succeeded on that one.

Captain Dyer: Quite the opposite of Texaco, where I got in to see the advertising manager, but I got absolutely nowhere.

---

*Benito Mussolini, Italian dictator in the 1930s and 1940s.

One of the odder experiences was with Babcock & Wilcox. Their office was down, not on Wall Street, I don't know, maybe Green Street, somewhere down in that area not far from Wall Street. I walked in their office, and I thought I had stumbled into a place out of Dickens. The people were wearing frock coats and gray ties and standing collars. They were polite, but they didn't buy an ad. It was a unique experience, nevertheless. Ultimately, B & W did buy an ad, but I didn't get anywhere that day.

One of my worst experiences was back in Annapolis when I tried to sell one of the insurance agents for John Hancock. To make a long story short, I got out with a $5,000 insurance policy and no ad. He bought one later, but I began to think I was not such a hot salesman.

Q: Did you wind up selling enough to cover your costs?

Captain Dyer: Yes. We had a surplus on our yearbook of about $2,500. I've forgotten the exact amount. Of course, we sold the yearbooks to a captive audience, the regiment, but even so, you needed several thousand dollars worth of advertising to make up the difference.

Q: E.M. Eller was a year behind you, and he was working with the literary magazine, the Trident.* Did you get involved in that?

Captain Dyer: No. To back up a little bit, there is something I think should get in somewhere. Back when I was in high school, in 1919, I began to hear about an organization that started in Kansas City called the Order of DeMolay. The more I heard about it, the more intrigued I was. I applied for membership and was accepted and initiated in December of 1919. At that time there were a little fewer than 200 members. I was very enthusiastic about it when I got in. Next spring when they went to Omaha to establish a second chapter, though I was not an officer, I was taken along. I can claim the distinction of being the first member of DeMolay to go to any of the service academies or to be a commissioned officer in any of the services. No particular credit except being in the right place at the right time.

Q: But you did it.

Captain Dyer: But I did it. As a consequence, as soon as I was 21, I wanted to join the Masons. My first class year I did devote quite a bit of time, after I got in, to coaching other

---

*Midshipman Ernest M. Eller, USN, who later became a rear admiral and director of naval history, is the subject of a Naval Institute oral history.

midshipmen who were going into Annapolis Lodge. I joined Annapolis Lodge for the sole reason that I figured that if I stayed in the Navy I would be in Annapolis more than I would be anywhere else. I never had a single day of duty in Annapolis. But I'm still a member of Annapolis Lodge. This is my 60th year.

Q: The Superintendent during those years, Admiral Wilson, was very popular.* What do you recall of him?

Captain Dyer: I had very little direct contact with him. Among other things, though, that he did was to introduce the new uniform. Up to that time, we had had the cadet-type uniform with the standing collar. When I was at the Academy on September leave my first class year, it was suggested or asked that I go down to Jake Reed's and get measured for a new uniform.** I was one of the 12 or 14 guinea pigs who got the new uniform. When they were delivered, we put them on. Admiral Wilson came over to the commandant's office, and we displayed them. He made a couple of suggestions, slight alterations or something. He gave us permission right then and there to wear them on liberty and things of that kind, not for drill or parade or anything.

There was a classmate of mine, not a close friend, in there,

---
*Rear Admiral Henry B. Wilson, USN.
**Jacob Reed's Sons, which had a branch on Maryland Avenue in Annapolis, up the street from the Naval Academy.

there, too. This was probably on a Tuesday. The next day was the Superintendent's usual Wednesday afternoon at home for midshipmen. We agreed we would put on the new uniform and meet over there. There wasn't any point in our meeting somewhere else and going together. The son of a gun never did show up. I got over there, and our battalion officer, a lieutenant commander, cornered me. He was giving me a pretty hard time about my collar and my tie and this, that, and the other thing. They hadn't gotten any of those things at the midshipmen's store yet. You had to go out in town and buy them. And just then Admiral Wilson came along. "Well, Richardson, what do you think of this wonderful new uniform? Isn't it great?"*

Q: That ended the criticism.

Captain Dyer: That ended the criticism.

Q: Did you ever run afoul of the notorious Red Magruder?**

Captain Dyer: Not really. My bête noire was a man by the name of Dyer.***

---
*Lieutenant Commander William N. Richardson, USN.
**Lieutenant Commander Cary W. Magruder, USN.
***Lieutenant Robert A. Dyer III, USN.

Q: Oh?

Captain Dyer: He was around there, I don't know, I guess my first three years. He was my company officer my plebe year, I know that. I came back from class or somewhere to find a note to report to the battalion office. I went down, knocked on the door, and said, "Midshipman Dyer, fourth class, sir."

"What's your name?"

"Midshipman Dyer, sir."

"How do you spell it?"

"D-Y-E-R, sir."

"Oh yes, Mr. Dyer, you're on report for room in gross disorder." It was my introduction to him. I couldn't recount all of the encounters.

My second class year, somebody conceived the bright idea that at the end of youngster year if you were in the first battalion you'd switch to the third battalion and so on. I don't know whether they do any silly thing like that now or not.

Anyway, I was coming back from class. As usual, there was a certain amount of conversation going on in the section. And Dyer stopped us and told his mate, "Put the section leader down for neglect of duty, section in disorder." And he said, "Put Mr. Dyer down for talking in ranks." He turned to me and said, "You weren't the only one, but you're the only one I recognized." That was my last encounter with him.

Q: Unfortunate coincidence of names.

Captain Dyer: I thought that ought to give me a little bit of consideration. He oughtn't to dislike anybody with the name of Dyer. I guess he wanted to bring me up in the way he thought I should go.

Q: As your years in Annapolis drew toward a close, were you sorry to leave the place or eager to get out to the fleet?

Captain Dyer: I was eager for the next thing on the way to the rainbow.

Q: What do you remember about the graduation ceremony?

Captain Dyer: Not too much. The speaker was Teddy Roosevelt, Jr. He was Assistant SecNav, I guess.

Q: Yes.

Captain Dyer: At that time everybody got to go up and get his own diploma. In a way, it was kind of a blur. After all, it has been 58 years.

Q: Was Prohibition violated in your celebration of graduation?

Dyer #1 - 51

Captain Dyer: Not too directly. I mean, I went out. I don't think I can remember his name now, but I called on a math prof and his wife whom I knew fairly well, kind of a farewell call. They gave me a drink, but that was about the extent of it. I went to Kansas City. One brother was still living there. I stopped there for a couple of days and then went on out to Portland, Oregon.

Q: Your first ship as an officer was the New Mexico. How did that assignment come about?

Captain Dyer: Some of us on the Lucky Bag staff decided we wanted to try to stick together. I don't know what they do now, but at that time we drew numbers for our choice of assignments. We talked it all over amongst ourselves. We wanted a West Coast ship, but we didn't want to ask for the real late ships, the California, the West Virginia, the Maryland, because we thought they'd be more popular. We thought there was a better chance of most of us getting the New Mexico, so we chose the New Mexico. There wasn't any particularly reasoned idea, but she was modern to the extent of being the first electric drive.

Q: She still had the cage masts at that time, didn't she?

Captain Dyer: Yes.

Q: What were your impressions of the ship as you reported aboard?

Captain Dyer: She seemed like a nice ship. That's about all you can say. At the moment, she was still the flagship of Admiral Wiley, who was Commander Battleships.*

She was a little crowded. Four of us--Bill Cochran, who got out, he was the editor of the Lucky Bag; and Bull Towner, he's vice admiral; and I'm not sure who the fourth one was--Chestly Baldwin, I think--and I were given a room which was really clear out in the crew's country.** I mean, you left the JO mess, passed an office, and went about 40 feet, and then there was a room with four bunks in it.*** That's where we were. I'm not sure how the bottom part of the class were fitted into places at all. They didn't have a bunk room like some of the ships did, but they got them in somehow, I guess.

When Admiral Wiley left in the fall and went to the West Virginia, the housing situation eased up. I mean, a staff of five instead of a staff of 12 or 13 made quite a difference.

Q: Was there still a division commander on board?

---
*Vice Admiral Henry A. Wiley, USN, Commander Battleship Divisions, Battle Fleet.
**Ensign William P. Cochran, Jr., USN; Ensign George C. Towner, USN; Ensign John A. Baldwin, USN.
***JO--junior officer.

Captain Dyer: Yes, Admiral Pratt came on as Commander Battleship Division Four.* I was assigned as assistant radio officer. Joe Redman was the communication officer on Wiley's staff.** He had been radio officer of the New Mexico at one point, and he still seemed to think he was. There was a lieutenant by the name of Murphy who was the radio officer, and he was sent away to school.*** There were four assistant radio officers. Since I was senior, I was acting radio officer for a couple of months. Incidentally, there was a man in '23 by the name of Batterton who came around and did some very ardent recruiting for the radio department.**** I sort of naturally assumed I would go into gunnery, but he persuaded me to go into radio. I got in there I think partly because I never had quite understood vacuum tubes. I thought maybe I could find out something; I still don't know anything about it. Nevertheless, that assignment had a great effect on my career.

At that time, Laurance Safford was in charge of the research desk in the Navy Department, OP-20GX.***** He had conceived the idea of putting a cryptogram in the monthly Communication Division bulletin. This was about the time that crossword puzzles were really getting popular. I thought I was good; I

---
*Rear Admiral William V. Pratt, USN.
**Lieutenant Joseph R. Redman, USN.
***Lieutenant John V. Murphy, USN.
****Ensign Henry D. Batterton, USN.
*****Lieutenant Laurance F. Safford, USN.

knew I was pretty good. He'd enciphered a crossword puzzle and put it in there as a problem. So that was a challenge. It seemed to be right down my alley. I solved it. There was a little squib that said, "If you solve this, send in your solution to the Chief of Naval Operations, OP-20G." So I did. In due time I got back a letter from the Chief of Naval Operations signed by some commander by direction, congratulating me and so on and so on, and encouraging me.*

I said, "Here I am getting right up there amongst the top brass somehow." So the next month I had to work hard and solve this darn thing and send it in. I think I sent in, maybe not every one, but 90% for the next couple of years or so. That led to my being ordered in 1927 to the Navy Department for a three-month course. And that is the beginning of what turned out, I guess, to be my career. Just the smallest chances. I happened to join the Navy to begin with, just by pure chance, fluke, call it what you will. Not any great thinking on my part. Getting into cryptography or cryptanalysis was just something to do as a pastime. So it goes.

Q: What were the duties of an assistant radio officer in the battleship?

---
*"By direction" means that various officers were authorized to sign correspondence on behalf of the Chief of Naval Operations--that is, by his direction.

Captain Dyer: Well, among other things you were supposed to learn how to be a radio operator, which I never did very successfully. In our division we had one circuit that was supposed to be manned for certain periods of the day on each shift by an assistant radio officer. We helped with the administration. Just general division officer duties.

As I look back on it, I don't think there was any specific duty, except for learning how to be an operator, which I never did, then or later. When I was communication officer of a destroyer, part of the competition involved demonstrating proficiency as an operator, but I still couldn't do it. I never could learn to be an operator. I tried. I was conscientious about it, too.

Q: Did the ship have its own communication organization, or were you temporarily assigned to the flag?

Captain Dyer: The ship had its own communication organization. We were supposed to become familiar with codes and ciphers and things of that kind for the ship. There was an ensign, I guess out of '23, who had come aboard with the staff, a nephew of "Red" Ruble.* He decided he had been playing with the staff long enough. I don't know why, but they decided that they wanted me for assistant communication officer on the staff. The flag

---
*Ensign Richard W. Ruble, USN, was an officer on the staff of Commander Battleship Division Four.

secretary, it turned out, had been my company officer my first class year. The rest of the staff I did not know.

Q: Was that Russell Berkey?

Captain Dyer: No, Russell Berkey was radio officer on that staff. Jimmy Campbell was flag lieutenant, Clarke was flag secretary, and Berkey was radio officer.* I was assistant communication officer. And Admiral Pratt was Commander Battleship Division Four. I thoroughly enjoyed that.

Q: What was enjoyable about it?

Captain Dyer: Hard work and a feeling of a sort of authority. I was the guy who was willing to take the staff duty 90% of the time so that they could go home.

Q: I bet they loved that.

Captain Dyer: They did. I don't know whether it was then or later that we were anchoring in at San Pedro, and the Arizona came in and anchored a bit too close to us, close enough that if the two ships happened to swing in opposite directions, they

---

*Lieutenant Charles W.A. Campbell, USN; Lieutenant Horace D. Clarke, Jr., USN; Lieutenant Russell S. Berkey, USN.

would sure as hell have bumped.

The ship had a senior officer on board, kind of a nervous Nellie. He complained to me, and I sent a dispatch to the ComBatDiv 3 and asked him to have his flagship moved.* After an exchange of two or three dispatches, they did move. I felt pretty big exercising my authority telling the admiral to have his ship moved. I was very careful to use the staff duty officer's number and not my own number on the dispatch.

Q: What personal contact did you have with Admiral Pratt in that role?

Captain Dyer: Quite a bit, although it didn't last too long. We had a fleet problem in the Pacific, including Honolulu. I was on the flag bridge all day, and Admiral Pratt was up there. For a while it scared the life out of me, because his flag lieutenant was a mustang whom he had picked up on the New York when he was captain of the New York in the Grand Fleet, and who had been with him ever since and who, as a matter of fact, stayed with him until he retired as Chief of Naval Operations.**

Q: Jimmy Campbell.

---
*ComBatDiv 3--Commander Battleship Division Three.
**"Mustang" is a Navy term for an officer who was previously an enlisted man.

Captain Dyer: Jimmy Campbell. I finally figured out that the admiral kept Campbell, as much as anything else, because Campbell would disagree with him and pull no bones about it. They would be up there and something would come up about maneuvers or something, and Campbell would say, "I think so-and-so."

The admiral would say, "You're crazy." And they'd argue a little bit. Then Campbell would go over to the port side of the bridge. The admiral would go padding over after him and renew the argument. When it came to the showdown, sometimes Campbell won, and sometimes the admiral won. But here was a lieutenant and a two-star admiral arguing, and I mean arguing violently, and here was a poor, raw, redneck ensign looking for a hole to crawl into, because he didn't want to be a witness at the court-martial. But I got used to it.

When we got out to Honolulu along in June, all of a sudden out of the clear sky, Admiral Pratt got dispatch orders to go back to be president again of the War College and to leave almost immediately.

Q: This is 1925?

Captain Dyer: 1925. He had already invited Admiral Hugh Rodman to go with us.* We were just before going to Australia. Admiral

---
*Rear Admiral Hugh Rodman, USN, (Ret.), who had retired from active duty in January 1923.

MacDougall, William Dugald MacDougall, who was commander of the East Coast Train, and was already on his way back to the West Coast, was ordered to return to Honolulu and take over BatDiv 4. Admiral Pratt stewed a little bit and finally he sent MacDougall a dispatch telling him that Admiral Rodman was on his way and would MacDougall be courteous enough to extend the invitation to Rodman. In due course, MacDougall arrived. He was about as different from Admiral Pratt as you can imagine. I did not like the gentleman. I suppose I shouldn't speak evil of the dead.

Q: In what ways was he different?

Captain Dyer: He was a prissy old son of a bitch. Here's an example. When he was captain of a battleship, he required each of his officers to submit a detailed schedule for every day. I mean, not a day at a time, but a schedule that would hold. He would look at that schedule, call his Marine orderly, and say, "Go up to the wardroom head and tell Lieutenant Jones that I want to see him right away. If he isn't there, come back and tell me."

Chances were Lieutenant Jones was not there. Maybe he'd been a little early, or maybe he'd been a little late, or maybe he didn't feel like he had to go up that day. And the orderly would come back, and MacDougall would say, "Now you go find Lieutenant Jones and tell him I want to see him." And when Lieutenant Jones would come in, the admiral would say, "Your schedule says that at 10:17 you're supposed to be in the wardroom head. You weren't there."

Another incident. If somebody happened to refer to one of the officers as "Commander Smith," MacDougall would say, "He isn't Commander Smith; he's Lieutenant Commander Smith." The next morning, that particular individual said, "Good morning, rear admiral."

Admiral Pratt was that type. He usually wore brown shoes. I didn't usually wear a cap. In fact, no one ever wore a cap on the flag bridge. He would say, "Doesn't the hair get in your eyes without a cap on?" or something like that. He didn't say, "Blankety-blank Dyer, put your hat on." He always--well, that's enough on that.

Except I've got to tell this. Just before Rodman arrived, I don't know whether it was Clarke or Berkey who was in the admiral's cabin, but Admiral MacDougall said to him, "You know, all the time Rodman was on the selection board I didn't get selected. Now he's coming here as my guest. Ha,ha,ha."

Maybe it wasn't exactly the right thing to do, but whichever one it was knew Rodman very well and had served with him in the war. He told Rodman about it. And Rodman said, "Yeah, and if I'd stayed one more year, the son of a bitch never would have

Dyer #1 - 61

been selected." So much for him.

Q: How well do you remember the great cruise to Australia?

Captain Dyer: That was one of the high points. We stopped at Samoa on the way down. The fleet divided--half went to Melbourne and half to Sydney. We went to Sydney. They gave us a wonderful time. I think it is best illustrated by the fact that a couple of us JOs decided one afternoon that to go to a demonstration given by schoolchildren out at the cricket grounds.* Every time we went around anywhere on shore, people would talk about coming out to the ship, and we'd say, "Come ahead." They would come ahead, and they'd ask for you. If you were aboard ship, you had to entertain them.

So we said, "Let's go out there. That ought to be a nice, quiet, peaceful afternoon." We got out there, and a gentleman came up and welcomed us enthusiastically.

He said, "Do you think you can keep one down?" We allowed as how we might be able to. He took us down in the stands, and there was one of the longest bars I've ever seen in my life. He had a roll of tickets that would choke a horse, so that he could tear off and buy drinks for the visiting firemen. We had a drink. That was all right.

We went back up and watched one number of whatever the
_____
*JOs--junior officers.

exhibition was. Here he was back again. "How about another one?" Well, that quiet afternoon was about the roughest afternoon any of us had had. The culmination was all 10,000 schoolchildren out in the middle of the cricket grounds with colored cards. They made alternately a U.S. shield and a New South Wales shield. It was kind of whirling around by that time.

We went from Sydney to Auckland, which was equally enjoyable, but about as different as day and night.

Q: In what ways was it different?

Captain Dyer: Australians are comparable to Canadians. New Zealanders are straight English, almost phlegmatic in their initial approach. Wherever you went in Sydney, somebody would come up and greet you like you were a long-lost brother. The New Zealanders were entirely different. They'd warm up after they got to know you a little bit.

We were invited to make an excursion to Rotorua, which is their Yellowstone Park, and to where the Maoris live. It was an overnight affair, and we had to catch a train real early. I think we missed breakfast aboard ship, and we weren't feeling very chipper anyway after the night before. We got about halfway there, and the train stopped. We were informed that they were stopping so that the train crew could have their tea and that they had a little tea prepared for visiting firemen in the station, so we should get off. We got off. They had mountains of healthy sandwiches, tea, and what have you. I thought that was a wonderful idea to stop for morning tea. I never heard of stopping a train so the crew could have tea, but . . .

Q: Especially after you hadn't had any breakfast. Did you get to go to any of the parties or receptions where Admiral Coontz was?*

Captain Dyer: Let's see. Admiral Coontz was with the Melbourne detachment.

Q: I see.

Captain Dyer: I'm trying to think. I guess Hank Wiley or S.S. Robison was the senior officer with our outfit. I'm not really sure. Maybe not.

In Sydney Admiral MacDougall had been over to dinner or something at the governor's, Sir Rawson de Chair.** Young Rodney had asked the admiral if he could bring some of his schoolmates out to the flagship. The admiral sent for me.

---

*Admiral Robert E. Coontz, USN, Commander in Chief U.S. Fleet. He was the overall commander of the expedition to Australia and New Zealand.
**The Governor of New South Wales, the state which included Sydney and Melbourne, was His Excellency Admiral Sir Dudley Rawson Stratford de Chair, K.C.B., M.V.O.

"Dyer, take the barge and go into the landing and pick up young Rodney de Chair and his schoolmates and bring them out to the ship." I got in there and there were I don't know how many, but every barge that was available from the ships present was there and a whole flock of kids from King School. Young Rodney was like a generalissimo, saying, "You go to this one, you go to this one, you go to this one." He, of course, didn't come with me; he went with the senior ship. I guess that was Admiral Robison then on the California.*

I thought for an 11-year-old, 12-year-old kid, that was pretty smart. He asked each of these admirals if he could bring a few of his classmates out to see his flagship, and then he brought the whole school and parcelled them out.

Q: That was one of the few times between the World Wars that the fleet really operated together and made a long journey. Was that beneficial?

Captain Dyer: I think so. Of course, I was too wet behind the ears to know too much what was going on, even if I did think that as a flunky on the admiral's staff I was pretty important.

---
*Admiral Samuel S. Robison, USN, Commander in Chief Battle Fleet.

Dyer #1 - 65

Q: Had you already gotten diverted away from the idea of being a regular deck watch officer by that point?

Captain Dyer: Oh, no. I was going to spend a reasonable amount of time in that job and go back to being a naval officer. I did go back after we got back from Australia. Not too terrifically long after we returned, MacDougall was relieved by Louie de Steiguer.*

Q: What kind of a personality did he have?

Captain Dyer: On the whole, pretty good. Kind of gruff. He had an asthmatic condition that was a little unpleasant--made him bark. MacDougall had essentially inherited his staff, but de Steiguer assembled a new staff. Mick Carney was the flag secretary.** A man by the name of James was flag lieutenant.*** C.W. Brewington was the radio officer.**** There are no particular highlights, I guess, of my tour with de Steiguer.

Along about February or March, just a little over a year total, I went back to the New Mexico and was assigned to the antiaircraft division. About that time the ship had orders to

---
*Rear Admiral Louis R. de Steiguer, USN.
**Lieutenant Robert B. Carney, USN, who later became Chief of Naval Operations.
***Lieutenant Commander Charles M. James, USN.
****Lieutenant Carl W. Brewington, USN.

nominate two officers for submarine school. I was one of the lucky or unlucky ones, I don't know which. That was in the days when people in submarines were drafted. They had done away with submarine pay and special privileges. So Admiral Chase's son and I were the two who were so honored.*

I was detached in June and reported to New London the first of July. And then the doctors didn't like me. They said I couldn't see well enough to be a submarine officer. I argued a little bit. What's there to look at in a submarine, anyway? But they seemed to think there was, so I lasted for only three weeks.

There's an amusing sidelight to that. I don't mean to be critical of these things, but the Navy register at that time had one number that was put after your name for completion of the course in Submarine School, New London, Connecticut, and another number for qualified for command of submarines. Along about '36 or '37, my class put out a periodic bulletin. Somebody had figured out there were, say, 92 naval aviators and that there were so many in this or that category. And there were 42 people who had completed the course at submarine school, all but one of whom were qualified for command. And to quote verbatim, I said, "I wonder who that dumb son of a bitch is?" Then it dawned on me. By some clerical miscue, the Bureau [of Navigation] had been putting that "30" after my name, and I had never earned even

---
*The father was Rear Admiral Jehu V. Chase, USN. His son was Ensign Harry T. Chase, USN.

that.* Anyway, I left there. I went to the good ship _Antares_.

---

*The code number 30 after an officer's name in the annual Navy Register indicated that he had "Completed course in submarine instruction."

Interview Number 2 with Captain Thomas H. Dyer, U.S. Navy (Retired)

Place: Captain Dyer's cottage, Sykesville, Maryland

Date: Monday, 22 August 1983

Subject: Biography

Interviewer: Paul Stillwell

Q: Captain, when we left off last time, you said you were just about to report to the good ship _Antares_. Could you pick it up at that point, please?

Captain Dyer: I have a little question as to whether it was the good ship _Antares_ or not. The _Antares_ was at that time the flagship of Train Squadron One, which was the logistical supply unit of the Atlantic Fleet. I would say that in all my naval career, that year was about as unproductive as any that I spent. It did not further my professional qualifications in any manner that I can see. All I did was mark time.

We spent a good deal of time at Guantanamo. Practically every afternoon when we didn't have watch, we went outside on the Cuban soil and drank beer. I suppose it increased my beer-drinking capacity somewhat. Otherwise, it did very little.

One of the highlights of the year was when one of the cruisers challenged the wardrooms of all ships present to a series of athletic events--tennis, swimming, whaleboat racing, bridge, acey-deucy, and right and left-hand drinking. This last was unsuccessful because they could not keep the referees from imbibing also. But it did help to pass the time. I was very thankful to receive orders at the end of the year to go to Washington for duty under instruction in naval communications.

Q: You say it wasn't too good as far as professional development. Had you already decided then that you wanted to specialize in communications?

Captain Dyer: No. I did not know that. While most of my service had been in communications, I was still desirous of getting back and being a naval officer. But a ship that spent most of its time circling around what was called Soupbone Reef (so called because the ship stayed anchored in one place and filled up a reef with discarded bones) was not a way to professional advancement.

Q: Where was the ship's official home port?

Captain Dyer: Norfolk.

Q: How much time did you spend there?

Captain Dyer: I joined the ship in Newport, and that was a

unique experience. We started to leave, but we couldn't make the engines work, but we traveled from Newport to Portsmouth Navy Yard on the end of a towline. My first watch as an officer of the deck on the Antares was on a towed ship. We went into the navy yard and stayed for probably two months and then went off to Guantanamo, returning in late November, remaining over Christmas, going back to Guantanamo in January and remaining until May with a little time out visiting Kingston, Jamaica, and one or two other Caribbean ports.

Q: Nominally the ship's mission was target repair and towing. How much time did you spend at that?

Captain Dyer: We didn't do any towing. Our mission was merely to be the place where the admirals in command of the training squadrons lived. We did a small amount of supply function. We had a photo lab on board that didn't do much. We had two saluting guns on the bow and a gunner's mate to look after them. That was one of the great worries when you had the deck, the fear that somebody would come in and fire a salute to the admiral's flag and that would entail a return.

Q: Was the purpose of the photo lab to support the fleet camera party and to photograph gunnery exercises?

Dyer #2 - 71

Captain Dyer: I never knew for sure. In spite of the fact that some of the people in the lab were in my division, their work effort was semi-classified. I wasn't privileged to know what they were doing.

Q: It makes it rather difficult. What were your specific duties?

Captain Dyer: Just watch and division officer. I had the division that consisted mostly of all the spare parts.

Q: Do you remember the captain? Do you have any impressions of him as a leader, helping to further your career and so forth?

Captain Dyer: My impressions of him are largely negative. I wouldn't say he was a disciplinarian, but he was rather a nervous, picayune type. His name was H.E. Cook.[*]

Q: Recognizing the limitations of the ship for officer development, did he try to give you other avenues for training?

Captain Dyer: I had very few relations with the captain during the first half of my year on the Antares. The executive officer was a chronic alcoholic. He was relieved by a very fine officer, Willis Lee, who made a sincere effort to do something for and

---
[*]Captain Harold E. Cook, USN.

with his officers.* He did succeed in teaching most of us how to really handle a .45. For a month or two, every day after noon meal, we got on the quarterdeck and had snapping drill with a .45. He finally took us to the range, and I would say over half of us qualified as something or other.

Q: He won several Gold Medals for his shooting at the Olympics in 1920, so you had an expert teacher.

Captain Dyer: He was a wonderful marksman with both rifle and pistol, and a very fine individual personally.

Q: What do you remember of his personality?

Captain Dyer: It was excellent. Ensigns do not get to know commanders too well, but years later when I was ordered to the Pennsylvania and learned that he was executive officer, I was very happy. Then I got there and found he was leaving in about three days.

Q: He was probably a good deal more approachable in an ensign-commander relationship than many commanders were.

Captain Dyer: Yes, he was, a great deal.

---
*Commander Willis A. Lee, Jr., USN, later vice admiral.

Q: He's been described as having a perpetual twinkle in his eye and a good sense of humor. Did you observe that?

Captain Dyer: Yes, I think that's true. It was almost 60 years ago.

Q: He's also been described as not having much of an interest in administration. Do you remember that side of it? He tended to let other people handle the paperwork; he was more interested in operational and tactical type things.

Captain Dyer: There were very few operational or tactical things to do on the Antares. I guess I had only four or five months with Willis Lee, but I formed a very high opinion of him in that time.

Q: The fleet train at that point was relatively limited in size and scope, wasn't it?

Captain Dyer: I can't remember just what all we had. We had a repair ship. I guess the Vestal was our repair ship. We had some tankers that were under our administrative command. There were various other miscellaneous craft, but I don't remember just what. It wasn't a huge organization. There was a supply ship of some kind.

Q: This was at the time when the fleet was converting from coal to oil. Did you observe that transition?

Captain Dyer: By that time the transition was pretty nearly complete. I made all my missions and cruises on coal-burning battleships. But I never had contact with another coal-burner of any kind after I graduated. There were some, but I can't remember any colliers being attached to Train Squadron One.

Q: Were there any attempts at underway replenishment during that period?

Captain Dyer: No, not to my knowledge.

Q: So was the standard method then for two ships to go alongside each other in port and pass things from side to side?

Captain Dyer: Yes, unless it was something that could be handled by boat. A good deal of it was handled by boat, unloaded from a ship into a boat and then carried across to the other ship.

Q: In later years people in the service force acquired something of a reputation as second class citizens. Was that true in that time also?

Dyer #2 - 75

Captain Dyer: Pretty much so. They weren't in the fighting Navy. It didn't matter if there was any fighting to be done or not; it didn't win you much respect.

Q: So you weren't at all disappointed when it came time to go to Washington for the communications course?

Captain Dyer: I was very happy. In fact, I so desired to get off the ship that I put in a request for Asiatic duty, which Captain Cook disapproved. I never did get Asiatic duty until I went to Japan several years after the war ended.

Q: Would you describe the events then when you reported for the communications course?

Captain Dyer: When I arrived in Washington, I reported according to my orders, and was sent down to the section which was headed by Lieutenant Rochefort.* He was the officer in charge of what was known at that time as OP-20GX. "20G" embraced all of the things having to do with secret communications, registered publications, code compilation, and the signal book. "X" was the so-called research desk. There were two other officers, Tommy

---

*Lieutenant Joseph J. Rochefort, USN, is the subject of a Naval Institute oral history.

Birtley and Frank Bond.*

Q: Were they also students?

Captain Dyer: They were. They were both from one class senior to me at the Naval Academy. I'd known Bond somewhat, but not Birtley.

Q: Was there a formal course of instruction?

Captain Dyer: We were turned over to a man by the name of Klaus Bogel. I am somewhat vague as to what his official capacity was. He was carried as a cryptanalyst, but he really wasn't much of a cryptanalyst. He had been an actor, he had worked at the Library of Congress, and I don't know what else.

They had a pamphlet, for want of a better name, which contained a series of cryptograms of progressive difficulty. We were given the pamphlet, a copy of Friedman's book The Elements of Cryptanalysis, an Army training pamphlet, a supply of paper and pencils and told to go to work.** There was not much in the way of instruction. That probably is a good thing. In my

---
*Lieutenant (junior grade) Thomas B. Birtley, Jr., USN; Lieutenant (junior grade) Frank H. Bond, USN.
**William Friedman, who has been referred to as the father of cryptanalysis in the United States. For his biography, see Ronald Clark's The Man Who Broke Purple: The Life of Colonel William Friedman, Who Deciphered the Japanese Code in World War II (Boston: Little, Brown and Company, 1977).

opinion, you cannot develop an original cryptanalyst by telling him how to do everything and then put him up against a completely unknown problem, something new and different, and expect him to solve it.

Q: So Bogel was just mainly somebody to hand you the book and the pencil and the paper.

Captain Dyer: He'd answer a few questions. He was a nice old duck. We were supposed to be there for about three months. They had some actual material, a code of some kind that we worked on as we became more proficient. The very last part of our stay, Birtley and I--I'm not sure, I don't believe Bond was involved-- were sent to work to decode some of the Japanese Navy traffic. We admitted it was a complete mystery because we didn't understand enough about the language. We could look up a code group and write down the Japanese word after it, but we couldn't make any sense out of it. But it was our first introduction to Japanese. Birtley, while he was there, was selected for transfer to Tokyo as a language student.

Q: Were you interested in getting into that also?

Captain Dyer: No, not at that time, I was not.

Q: Why not?

Captain Dyer: I don't know. I didn't think I wanted to go to Japan for three years.

Q: Did you have much contact with Lieutenant Rochefort at that point?

Captain Dyer: Limited. I had some contact with him, some with Mrs. Driscoll.*

Q: What were their respective roles in the school?

Captain Dyer: Rochefort was in essence the officer in charge. He had a lot of other duties besides looking out for the students. It was not until we started decoding some of this material that we really got to know Mrs. Driscoll. There were two or three rooms in the part of the sixth wing which we occupied. Initially we were in the outer room and were moved into the inner sanctum when we started decoding. It was an interesting experience, and we learned quite a bit, I think.

Q: I take it this was in the Navy Department building on Constitution Avenue?

---

*Mrs. Agnes Meyer Driscoll, who was considered to be a first-rate cryptanalyst, instructed the Navy's young codebreakers.

Captain Dyer: Back of the sixth wing of the Main Navy on Constitution Avenue.*

Q: Was there an increased degree of security protection for your activities, in the rest of the building, or in the rest of naval communications?

Captain Dyer: The whole section was under security. We were compiling codes for Navy use. Of course, the main registered publication issuing office was secure. That whole part of the wing was to a degree under security. I think it was a lax sort of security, but it was under security.

Q: Were there Marine guards or passwords?

Captain Dyer: No passwords or combinations. I can't remember whether there were Marine guards in 1927. I know we had them later when I returned there in '31-'32.

Q: Were you able to pick up the codebreaking techniques with a good deal of facility?

---

*Main Navy was the common name for the complex of buildings along Constitution Avenue in Washington, D.C., not far from the Lincoln Memorial. They were built as World War I temporaries but continued in use by the Navy until torn down during the Nixon Administration in the early 1970s.

Captain Dyer: The Japanese experience was not codebreaking. Rochefort's oral history is a little vague on this subject. I suppose there are those who would think I am talking out of turn. But The Broken Seal and the Zacharias book contain this, and I think it's important to put it in.*

Somewhere in the early Twenties, the Office of Naval Intelligence reports vary a little bit as to where it was--New York or somewhere else--and who he was, an inspector of material or consul general. In any case, a Japanese "someone" had a copy of the Japanese Navy fleet code. Certain individuals went in at night and borrowed it and photographed it. It was a very large code in kata-kana syllabary characters. The size of the code was on the order of 100,000, three characters to a group.

When ONI got this code, they decided they ought to do something about translating it.** I know this was in The Broken Seal. They hired a retired missionary to translate it, and he worked on it for years and years. It was a big job. Then there was some collaboration between ONI and naval communications. Naval communications had begun to receive some Japanese intercepts from people in the Asiatic station who were self-taught. Mrs. Driscoll entered the picture, I guess Rochefort entered it, and so forth. Without going into technical details,

---
*Ladislas Farago, The Broken Seal: The Story of "Operation Magic" and the Pearl Harbor Disaster (New York: Random House, 1967); Rear Admiral Ellis M. Zacharias, USN, Secret Missions: The Story of an Intelligence Officer (New York: G.P. Putnam's. 1946).
**ONI--Office of Naval Intelligence.

this code was always used with a cipher. As far as I know, all the ciphers are of the transposition type. Not important.

In what we were doing, the cipher had been removed. We would look up, for example, code group "ro-hi-ka" in the book and see what the translator said the Japanese for it was, and also the English meaning. We'd write that down. It was purely a clerical, mechanical action. It was not anything. I know now one of the things that confused us to no end was not understanding much about Japanese proper names. Many times they give characters for a proper noun going in to make up a name. So we would write in "in-the-paddyfield" and wonder what a paddyfield had to do with naval affairs. And it was probably "Mr. Tanaka" whom they were talking about or something. We couldn't understand that.

That came to an end. I had so enjoyed my earlier stay with Admiral Pratt that I wrote to Flag Secretary Berkey.* They were going to go to the West Coast to command battleships. I indicated that if they thought they needed an errand boy on the staff, I would not be averse to getting the job. They accepted my offer, and I received orders. That was in the days, though, when there was economy in the Navy and economy in the government. When I finally concluded my duty in Washington along in

---

*Vice Admiral William V. Pratt, USN, Commander Battleship Divisions Battle Fleet; Lieutenant Commander Russell S. Berkey, USN.

Dyer #2 - 82

September, I had two days leave. Then I reported to Hampton Roads and sat around for about three weeks waiting for a ship to go to the West Coast. They didn't feel like spending the money to buy me a train ticket; they'd rather pay my salary for two or three months to do nothing. I arrived out there somewhere around the end of November 1927. In the meantime, I had been promoted to junior lieutenant. I made the trip around on the ammunition ship Nitro. That in itself was somewhat of an experience.

Q: What do you remember about that experience?

Captain Dyer: Not a great deal, except that I did stand deck watches on the way around. The captain was a bridge enthusiast, and I played bridge with the captain. One night a fire alarm sounded. I one-eyed the deck, and I had difficulty finding out where the fire was. I didn't want to sound general quarters or anything until I found out. But on a ship carrying ammunition, I didn't like to take chances, either. It turned out to be in the tailor shop or someplace like that.

Q: I'd say if you were standing watches, the Navy wasn't exactly wasting your salary by putting you on board this ship.

Captain Dyer: They had a full crew of officers on the ship. They didn't need me. It just gave the regular ship's officers less to do. However, that's neither here nor there.

Q: You mentioned bridge. Is there any connection between skill at bridge and codebreaking?

Captain Dyer: I don't know. A great many competent cryptanalysts are good bridge players. During the war, Oswald Jacoby was assigned to the outfit and worked for me in Pearl Harbor.* But that's getting ahead of the story. At one time after the war we had some matches between the Army and Navy before we unified. They were pretty tough, pretty good duplicate matches. Whether there is any connection, I couldn't say.

I reported to the West Virginia and was made assistant staff communication officer.

Q: Who was the communication officer?

Captain Dyer: A lieutenant commander by the name of Causey. Isaiah, I think, was his name.** I had four ensigns as watch officers under me. There's not a great deal one can say about it. It was a very enjoyable duty. When the fleet problem came along in the spring, I made a real effort all by myself to try to

---
*Lieutenant Oswald Jacoby, U.S. Naval Reserve, noted author of books on contract bridge, poker, backgammon, and other card games.
**Lieutenant Commander William Isaiah Causey, Jr., USN.

do something with the enemy's communications and had no luck at all. But along in mid-1928, Admiral Pratt was moved up to Commander Battle Fleet--it was Battle Fleet at that time.* And we moved to the California.

Q: Can you draw any comparisons between the two ships as far as how well run they were, smartness of handling and so forth?

Captain Dyer: No, they were both very good. I can't remember even who the captain of the West Virginia was. It may come to me later. Claude Bloch had the California.** It was a more or less routine operation. I inherited the management of a little shore radio station that was available to people on board ship to send personal messages, emergency or otherwise, to their wives and sweethearts.

Q: Would the shore station pass them to Western Union?

Captain Dyer: Mostly delivered by telephone. You'd send a message for Mrs. So-and-so, give her telephone number, and they'd call. I think it was possible to send telegrams, but in general not. There was only a small fee charged, and it went through me.

---
*In 1927-1928, as a vice admiral, Pratt was Commander Battleship Divisions Battle Fleet. In 1928-1929, as a full admiral, he was Commander Battle Fleet.
**Captain Claude C. Bloch, USN, later admiral.

I did the bookkeeping.

When it came time for the fleet problem in early 1929, we got a letter from the Navy Department informing us that there were officers available for forming a communications intelligence or coding unit or cryptanalytic unit or whatever they wanted to call it. They gave us the names of Laurance Safford, Joseph Rochefort, and Thomas Dyer. The other two were ordered to the California for the duration of the fleet problem. Safford chose to devote himself to traffic analysis and call identification, things of that kind. Rochefort and I worked together on the enemy code.

Q: When you say the enemy, are you talking about the U.S. fleet that was portraying the enemy?

Captain Dyer: Really the Scouting Fleet--the Atlantic Fleet, in other words. That was the enemy.

Q: How good were U.S. Navy codes at that point?

Captain Dyer: They were fairly good, not outstanding. For the purpose of the fleet problem, we were using the cylindrical cipher device. At that time it was thought that maybe they ought to use something that had some potential for vulnerability. It would be unrealistic in a two-week fleet problem to give them the most difficult thing that you knew how to concoct and also to make it too easy. So whoever decided it, decided that year that both sides would use the cylindrical cipher device. Rochefort and I were quite successful. We solved every key change that they had and read every message that we were able to intercept.

Q: That was much better than you had done the year before.

Captain Dyer: Much better than the year before.

Q: Do you attribute that to Rochefort's presence?

Captain Dyer: Not entirely. I attribute it mostly to the device I invented for the solution of that particular system. I might as well say this. I yield to no one in my admiration for Rochefort as an intelligence officer and analyst. He was inspired; there's no other word for it. But anyone who really knows about it, knows that he was not the world's greatest cryptanalyst as he's been painted.

Q: Why not? Why has he gotten overrated in that regard?

Captain Dyer: In his own oral history he forgot about this fleet problem. According to Kahn, he mentioned something about Safford and Dyer being in on the fleet problem.* He didn't even mention the fact that he was there. He went to Japan, he studied the language, he came back to a straight intelligence billet. Until he reported to Pearl Harbor, I guess in June of 1941, he had virtually not been in touch with or doing anything in cryptanalysis for a period of 14 years.

Q: Except for this fleet problem.

Captain Dyer: Well, 12 years counting that fleet problem, yes. I would hate to have anyone think that I'm denigrating his abilities in any way, but they lay in a different direction. Even in the Japanese field, he did not do any real original cryptanalysis.

Q: Would it be fair to say that his forte was in leadership?

Captain Dyer: No, analysis. That's where he shone. He could take a message that was only half there and mentally fill in the blanks to the extent of getting the sense out of it. But when it came to the nuts and bolts of saying that "this code group means this," and "this code group means that," I won't say he never did it, but I mean he just did not--you can't do everything.

---

*David Kahn, author of The Codebreakers (New York: The Macmillan Co., 1967).

Q: He seemed to think that he had an advantage in that he had a good deal of operational experience and experience on fleet staffs that would give him a better background for analysis than a pure cryptanalyst technician would have. Is that a fair statement?

Captain Dyer: I am inclined to agree that fleet operational experience is invaluable to a cryptanalyst. After all the time I spent with Admiral Pratt and the other staffs I served with, I think it gave me a pretty good background.

Q: What sort of device was this that you invented for the fleet problem?

Captain Dyer: I can't describe it without going into an awful lot of technical detail. It was almost pure Rube Goldberg, but it worked.* It was a series of rollers with plastic belts. We set it up for the first ten letters of the message and then sort of made wild guesses as to what the first word was and cranked that in. It would give us a setting of the device, if it were correct. And if it weren't correct, it wouldn't yield a setting. Actually it just obviated an awful lot of writing, because we'd write it all down in advance and then just crank it in.

---
*Reuben L. Goldberg was a newspaper cartoonist of the era. He is best known for drawings of absurdly complicated devices designed to perform relatively simple functions.

Q: Was there any kind of a critique or comparison after the fleet problem on how each side had done on codebreaking?

Captain Dyer: There was a critique done on codebreaking. I always felt a little guilty about this, but there's nothing I could do about it since I was on the staff and available. When they were planning the major critique of the fleet problem, the chief of staff, Admiral Hepburn, called me in and gave me eight minutes to talk about what we had done, what we had accomplished.* Safford is the one who should have made this speech as the senior officer, but he had gone back to his destroyer. Besides, Safford couldn't speak very well. Well, there was no reason to designate Rochefort, if he was in the same division with Safford and also executive of a destroyer. Why take the middle man? So the junior man got the plum.

The critique came along, and I went over there. The speakers were mostly admirals with a sprinkling of captains and one very junior, junior lieutenant. It's probably an exaggeration, but a number of people were kind enough to say that my talk was the best one of the two hours.

Q: Did the other side seem surprised that you had penetrated their codes?

---

*Captain Arthur J. Hepburn, USN, later admiral.

Captain Dyer: I don't know. I think it kind of leaked out before the critique and they weren't surprised. I tried to stress the fact that our success was due largely to a lack of proper security considerations on the part of the people who sent the messages. But it was my moment of glory, anyway.

When we got back to the West Coast, this added problem was in the Panama area.

Q: This was really the ground-breaking in the use of aircraft carriers as part of the battle fleet, wasn't it?

Captain Dyer: It was one of the earliest things. Admiral Pratt was promoted to Commander in Chief U.S. Fleet and his flag was in the Texas.

Q: Before that, he'd been working for Admiral Wiley. What can you say about the relationship between Admiral Pratt and Admiral Wiley?*

Captain Dyer: Admiral Pratt did not exactly confide in me, but it was a rather open secret that he did not have a great deal of admiration for Admiral Wiley.

---

*Admiral Henry A. Wiley, USN, Commander in Chief U.S. Fleet, 1927-1929.

Q: So he wasn't exactly displaying complete loyalty to the boss?

Captain Dyer: I think he was loyal, but you can be loyal to somebody and still think he's stupid. In California, Royal Ingersoll joined the staff as operations officer or something.* He began the compilation of a magnificent set of battle plans to meet just about any conceivable situation. The idea was that if we had this set of plans, we could send out a signal, and maybe a caveat or two in the signal with some modification, and we would be ahead of the game that much by having a plan already.

Q: Were the plans also for use against our allies at the time?

Captain Dyer: They were just tactical situations regardless of who the opposition was. It wasn't a war plan. It was, "If you are faced with this particular tactical situation, here's what you do."

I do remember that someone on Wiley's staff--it might have been Wiley himself--objected to these things. He said, "To use something like that, you'd have to be a tactical expert."

And the remark was made by someone--not Admiral Pratt--that, "It is to be presumed that the Commander in Chief United States Fleet is a tactical expert."

---

*Captain Royal E. Ingersoll, USN, later admiral.

Q: Hence his consideration that the admiral might have been a bit stupid.

Captain Dyer: If Admiral Pratt voiced any real criticism, he would usually direct it toward some member of Admiral Wiley's staff rather than the commander in chief. But to me, at least, it seemed rather implicit that the commander in chief, after all, had that guy on his staff and therefore had to take responsibility for him.

Q: You mentioned Captain Ingersoll. Rochefort said that he was a great flag officer but he had one flaw: he was overly modest. How would you describe him?

Captain Dyer: I think that's a perfect description. When he was on either the California or the Texas, I would go into his cabin with something. Remember, I was still fairly junior--a junior lieutenant--and he was a captain. But whatever he happened to be working on, he used to stop and go over it with me and ask me what I thought. I'm sure that he really didn't care a whole lot for my opinion, but he had the--well, sometimes I could make some comment. "Maybe that's so; try it." The thing I'm trying to stress is that he was never too busy to stop and to treat you as more or less an equal.

Q: A fellow human being.

Captain Dyer: A fellow human being. This is way off sequence, but after the war, we were scheduled to leave Hawaii the day after Christmas for San Francisco. We knew it was almost impossible to get out by train or to get hotel accommodations, either one. I could without any hesitation write to Royal Ingersoll, who was a four-star admiral in command of the Western Sea Frontier and ask him if he would be kind enough to have one of his bright young men arrange things, and he did.

Q: A nice gesture. How much contact did you have with Admiral Pratt?

Captain Dyer: I think this would best be told from the standpoint of the Texas.* On the West Virginia and the California I had relatively little contact with Admiral Pratt. I'd see him quite a bit on the bridge when we were at sea, but not otherwise. But when we were in the California, Jimmy Thach-- now, this is the older brother--had reported as assistant flag secretary.** Russell Berkey was flag secretary.*** And I was still assistant communication officer. While we were on the

---
*USS Texas (BB-35) was flagship of the U.S. Fleet.
**Lieutenant James H. Thach, Jr., USN. His younger brother, John S. Thach, was also known as "Jimmy."
***Lieutenant Commander Russell S. Berkey, USN.

California, since we were not members of the staff, but staff flunkies, as it were, we ate in the wardroom. All of the actual staff ate in the cabin with the admiral. He had done this when he was a rear admiral. It was just his habit and way of doing things. When we got to the Texas, I think the first day we were aboard he called Campbell, his flag lieutenant, and said, "Campbell, do you know how many people we've got in this mess?"*

And Campbell said, "No, sir."

"Thirteen." He said, "What are young Thach and Dyer doing?"

"They're eating in the wardroom."

"Bring them up here."

That set up the scene for the most rewarding year I had in my whole life in the Navy, really, sitting at one table with a four-star admiral and a two-star admiral.

Q: The two-star, was that Hepburn?

Captain Dyer: That was Hepburn. And, of course, Royal Ingersoll, a senior civil engineer, a couple of very senior commanders, and so on. Sitting down at the foot of the table on one side was Thach and on the other side was Dyer. The most lowly thing near us was the fleet radio officer, Ajax Spriggs, out of class of '20.** We got to hear all of the conversation,

---
*Lieutenant Charles W.A. Campbell, USN.
**Lieutenant Alva J. Spriggs, USN.

and a good deal of shop talk, and a good deal of idle chatter. The admiral had a pretty good sense of humor and so did some of the others.

Q: Do you remember any examples of the admiral's humor? Did he tell stories or jokes? Was he quick-witted?

Captain Dyer: This is a little elaborate. The fleet engineer officer was Hollis Cooley.* His stateroom had a peculiar little alcove in it, and he conceived the idea of installing some sanitary facilities in this alcove, sort of a steamer wash basin that folded up and a commode. And so they all concocted this scheme. They wrote a letter addressed to the captain of the <u>Texas</u>. It was from the Bureau of Construction and Repair, saying that an unauthorized alteration had been made on the ship.

Q: Who signed the letter? Somebody at the Construction and Repair Bureau?

Captain Dyer: Ostensibly the chief, I think.

Q: But he had been tipped off by somebody?

Captain Dyer: He was in on the thing. But the original, of

---
*Commander Hollis M. Cooley, USN.

course, was never sent. It was addressed to Andrews, the captain, with a copy to the commander in chief.* So they brought the copy back and gave it to the admiral, and he sent for Commander Cooley. He says, "Now, I got this letter here. It's addressed to the captain of the flagship, but if there's a member of my staff concerned, I think we'll have to be the one to answer it. You go draft a letter explaining just why . . ."

Cooley sweat for at least two days over the thing, but finally he caught on that it was all a scam and Pratt was in on it.

Q: The younger Thach brother was on board the California also.

Captain Dyer: He was the watch officer in the communications office.

Q: Did he work for you?

Captain Dyer: Yes.

Q: What do you remember about him?

Captain Dyer: Not very much. He was a nice kid.

---
*Captain Adolphus Andrews, USN, later a vice admiral.

During the year while I was in the Texas, the country was preparing for the London Conference.* The Texas used to go up to Annapolis Roads and anchor every time it was feasible, so that the admiral could go over to Washington for conferences. And, of course, he went to London and left us under Hepburn. The flagship went to New Orleans for Mardi Gras, which was quite an experience, but hardly worth a lot of paper to report any details about it.

Then we went down to Panama and joined up. We had two fleet problems that year. I went to the California, I guess, for the first fleet problem. That was the first time that I worked with Ham Wright.** We were quite unsuccessful in that problem. They had prescribed a system that was just a little too much for the amount of time and traffic available.

Q: What was Wright's capacity at that point?

Captain Dyer: He had been to Washington after me, as a student. He was a graduate of the Navy Department's "university of cryptanalysis." He was in a destroyer at the time, but he was ordered to the California for the problem. There was probably

---
*The London naval disarmament conference, January to April 1930, established the battleship tonnage ratio for the United States, Great Britain, and Japan at 10:10:7.
**Ensign Wesley A. Wright, USN, who was later one of the codebreakers at Pearl Harbor in World War II.

somebody else who didn't make enough of an impression for me to remember.

Nothing happened on that problem, except for a personal note. While we were in New Orleans, I went to the burlesque show and felt a pain in my side, which later turned out to be appendicitis. When we got back to Guantanamo, I went over to the hospital ship Relief, supposedly for an examination and diagnosis. Two hours after I got there, I was on the operating table.

Q: It's good that she was nearby.

Captain Dyer: It probably wasn't that urgent, but the white blood count had shot up. The surgeon said he'd better get on with it. That was St. Patrick's Day, 1930. This is just human interest and has no particular merit. I'd been writing to her every day.* We still weren't married; we were engaged.

Q: We should say that the "her" at that point was Edith B. Miller.

Captain Dyer: Yes. I waited until I figured that she would stop receiving my letters in Kansas, and then I sent her a message and

---
*He said this while gesturing to Mrs. Dyer, who was in the room during the interview.

told her I had been operated on and was doing fine. I recovered sufficiently to participate in the second fleet problem. That time, I went to the other side, the Scouting Force on the *Wyoming*. The Battle Force was again using the cylindrical cipher device, and again we had a great deal of luck. Members of the Battle Force staff were referees for the second problem. John McClaran was on that staff.* Thinking about my earlier speech, he offered me 12 minutes for the critique, if I wanted to stay down in Guantanamo until then. Foolishly, I guess, I decided to go on back to New York. I wrote the speech, and Commander McClaran delivered it and got credit.

I went back to New York, and the admiral came back from London. I got orders detaching me from the staff. I had requested it, because I wanted to go to the West Coast and get married out there.

Q: Was New York the home port for the *Texas*?

Captain Dyer: As the U.S. Fleet flagship, it didn't specifically have a home port, but yes, New York was more or less it, although the staff was back on the West Coast not too much later. I was detached and went to the *Pruitt* (DD-347). I hadn't much more than gotten aboard when the *Pruitt* got a dispatch from somewhere

---

*Lieutenant Commander John W. McClaran, USN.

telling them to nominate one officer to leave the ship in Panama and go to Nicaragua for "X" number of months to supervise the election. When the dispatch was received, all the available officers on the destroyer, other than the exec and the engineering officer, were called in to draw cards. That's how I came to be chosen. No one had it in for me or anything. But I thought this would really put my plans in limbo. Although I could probably go back to the Texas and pull some strings, I couldn't figure any honorable way I could get out of it. Just about the time that I had sweat all I could, a volunteer came from somewhere and I didn't have to go. One hurdle crossed.

I had just begun to breathe easy when they got another dispatch to nominate an officer for transfer to the Badger on arrival on the West Coast.

Q: The Badger was then in mothballs, wasn't she?

Captain Dyer: She had been recommissioned. The captain said he wasn't going to go through the business of trying to select anyone again; I was it. But he would help me. I could put in a request for leave and send it on. So I requested 30 days leave to get married.

I had to go to the Commander in Chief Battle Fleet. He was down in Panama. He came back and said, "Leave in excess of 15 days can be granted only for urgent personal or business reasons." I allowed that I didn't know if my getting married was urgent, but it was damn personal. But it kind of put me on a limb a little bit. When when I got back and reported over to the Badger, I found out that at the expiration of my leave, they would be halfway between Prince Rupert and Juneau, Alaska, on a reserve cruise. The captain of the Badger told me to go over to the Commander Destroyers and see what I could find out. So I went over there. The chief of staff was Betty Stark, who later was a little bit better known.* He thought a minute and said, "I'll tell you what you do. You go on leave, and you report at the expiration of your leave by dispatch to the ship and join it when it gets back to Seattle."

I went back and told Captain Best that, and he said, "That's fine, but you don't need to bother sending a dispatch.** You be waiting on the dock when we get in."

I was. But I got, I guess, 28 of my 30 days leave and was charged for only 15 of them, so I won.

Q: Could you describe that leave period?

Captain Dyer: My honeymoon?

Q: Just the when and the where; you don't have to go into all the details.

---
*Captain Harold R. Stark, USN, later admiral, Chief of Naval Operations from 1939 to 1942.
**Commander Charles L. Best, USN.

Captain Dyer: For what seemed to us good and sufficient reasons, we were married at the home of the groom.* I had a car of sorts which, while I was meandering around the East Coast, I had left in Oregon with my parents. By going there to get married, we could pick up the car. If I went all the way back to Kansas City, we'd just have to get on a train and come back out to the West Coast. It didn't make too much sense. For a few days, we went over to a lovely little inn at a place called Nesquan, on the Oregon coast. But it was too cold. It was late June, but it was still too cold to be around there. So we came back, and we stayed near Forest Grove for a few days and took a trip up around Mount Hood and back. That's about all.

Q: Where had your wife been in the meantime?

Captain Dyer: She had been teaching school in Hutchinson, Kansas. Her home was really Kansas City, Missouri. When school was out, I guess she went back to Kansas City until time to leave for Oregon, just a few weeks.

It didn't seem logical for her to drive down from Seattle to San Diego by herself, so she boarded the coastal steamer with the car. While we were somewhere, she passed us or we passed them. She told somebody on the ship that her husband was over on that

---

*The wedding took place on 25 June 1930 in Forest Grove, Oregon.

destroyer, and they asked what she was doing, and she said, "Well, we're on our honeymoon."

We lived in San Diego from July to the following January. Then it came time for fleet problem again, and I was going back to the California. The Badger was being transferred from the West Coast to Charleston on the East Coast. So Edith took a ship around through the canal to the East Coast, stopping in Panama when I was there. Then she went on up to New York and back out to Kansas City.

The Badger came into Charleston, I guess, around the end of May. I was detached practically on arrival in Charleston and ordered to Washington.

Q: Let me go back before we get into that and cover a little more on your days with Admiral Pratt. You talked about Captain Ingersoll. What do you remember about Admiral Hepburn?

Captain Dyer: I had a great deal of respect for Admiral Hepburn, but he was not as approachable as either Admiral Pratt or Captain Ingersoll. He was not as cold and methodical as Raymond Spruance by any means, but he was what you might call a military man.* Probably that's one reason Admiral Pratt had him, because Admiral Pratt was inclined to be a bit easygoing in many respects. And

---
*Admiral Raymond A. Spruance, USN.

therefore he felt that the chief of staff should instill some discipline.

Q: What about Commander Berkey?

Captain Dyer: He was one of the boys. I think when he got stars he got a little bit stuffy. I didn't see much of him after the war. He was very pleasant. Jimmy Campbell was extremely pleasant.

Q: He was almost a personal servant type, wasn't he, because he had a long relationship with the admiral?

Captain Dyer: He had a continuous relationship with Admiral Pratt from the time that Admiral Pratt had the New York in the Sixth Battle Squadron during World War I until Admiral Pratt retired in 1933.

Q: Was there any sense that he was the admiral's spy in the midst of the rest of the staff?

Captain Dyer: No. If there was any sense of anything at all, it was that he was a sort of buffer who protected the rest of the staff from the admiral. I think one of the reasons the admiral kept him all those years was because when he thought it was called for, Campbell could be very outspoken in disagreeing with the admiral.

Q: I think you mentioned that the last time.

Captain Dyer: It took some getting used to the first time I was with them. The whole staff was really very congenial. There was one slightly odd note, and I can't even remember his name. That was the Marine colonel we had on the Texas. Somehow he didn't seem to fit in. When the junior officers on the Texas, I believe it was, saw him for the first time, they rather callously said, "My god, Dracula!"

Q: Admiral Pratt had in mind to reorganize the fleet more along ship type lines, ship type commands and tactical organization. Was Captain Ingersoll the sparkplug on that?

Captain Dyer: I think to a great extent, yes.

Q: How much were you involved at your level in that type of a change?

Captain Dyer: Practically none. If I could keep the communications going, that's all they expected of me. I could hear things and hear discussions. Maybe I shouldn't tell this either, tales out of school, but Admiral Pratt came back from Washington one day, after spending an hour or two with the Chief of Naval Operations, and sat down and wrote a letter to the Secretary of the Navy. He said, "You recently were kind enough to ask me what I would like to do upon completion of my tour of duty, and I indicated at the time that I would be very happy to return to the War College. Now I would like to apply for the job of Chief of Naval Operations."

Q: What kind of response did he get?

Captain Dyer: He got the job.*

Q: I think Pratt had caught the eye of President Hoover earlier, which helped him, didn't it?

Captain Dyer: I don't know. Probably. Of course, I'm sure he had caught the eye of the Secretary of the Navy, Charles Francis Adams.** And there was another ordinary individual, as it were. Many was the time I stood in the cafeteria line either in front of or behind Charles Francis Adams when he was Secretary of the Navy. He came over to the cafeteria, and he got in line with the

---
*Admiral V. Pratt, USN, was Chief of Naval Operations from 17 September 1930 to 30 June 1933.
**Charles Francis Adams was Secretary of the Navy from March 1929 to March 1933.

trade just like anybody else, like a GS-1 messenger or something.

Q: He came from quite a blue-blood heritage, I think.

Captain Dyer: Oh, yes. I can't think who his assistant secretary was now.* Mr. Adams used to answer his own phone. When the phone on his desk rang, he'd pick up the receiver and say, "Adams." And the Assistant Secretary of the Navy would give all three of his names and, "The Assistant Secretary of the United States Navy speaking." Just a contrast of individuals.

Q: The Texas was an older ship compared with the West Virginia and the California.

Captain Dyer: Considerably.

Q: Why was that the fleet flagship?

Captain Dyer: I never asked that question, but I think it was because they didn't want to take one of the really first-line battleships out of the battle line. The Texas was a little more free to be here or there, go to the West Coast, go to the East Coast. And she did have space enough for the staff.

---
*Ernest Lee Jahncke was Assistant Secretary of the Navy.

Dyer #2 - 108

Q: How did the communications facilities compare with the other two flagships you'd been in?

Captain Dyer: They were fully comparable. No essential difference.

Q: So the commander in chief didn't really rate anything special in that regard?

Captain Dyer: He didn't need it.

Q: Was there a difference in what key lists and codes they had access to? Was there any hierarchy in that regard?

Captain Dyer: No, we didn't have anything on the Texas that we would not have had on the California.

Q: Was it Admiral Pratt's practice to confer with his immediate subordinates?

Captain Dyer: I would say yes. He kept his finger on the pulse of what was going on pretty well.

Q: How much were you aware of aviation becoming a factor during this time on these staffs with Admiral Pratt?

Captain Dyer: Very much, because he was very much sold on the necessity of air cover for fleet operations, the need for carriers and so on.

Q: What about the idea of the aircraft as an offensive striking force?

Captain Dyer: I would say that "human missile" exploits did not carry the conviction with any of the senior officers I knew that it did with some people. The protection for "sitting ducks" is air cover. And that is what we didn't have on the seventh of December.* We had a sitting duck situation, but, in my opinion, I don't think there is anything approaching a categorical answer of air against surface, really. You always have to make your answer somewhat conditional. Certainly from where I sit, nothing that happened during the war really gives you an answer in black and white.

Q: On the Badger, what were your duties?

Captain Dyer: I was communication officer, commissary officer, ship service officer, watch officer. That's about all.

---

*This is a reference to the Japanese attack on the U.S. battle line at Pearl Harbor on 7 December 1941.

Dyer #2 - 110

Q: That's enough.

Captain Dyer: I thought it was at the time.

Q: Did you seek out the communications job in that case?

Captain Dyer: No. Once you get tarred with the brush, you're apt to--of course, if they had had somebody in the slot, they might not have relieved him, but they had a vacancy when I reported aboard, so, "You're it." That was, in a sense, a mistake. There was a competition in communication, and the communication officer was supposed to send and receive Morse as part of the competition. That is an achievement I was never able to accomplish in my life. I sweat blood over it at times, trying to become reasonably proficient as a radio operator, but I was never able to do so.

Q: How would you explain that? I would think that would be an easier skill to master than codebreaking.

Captain Dyer: There's just no similarity. I think it's akin to the fact that languages are difficult for me. In high school I had as much difficulty with Latin as I did with any other subject. At the Naval Academy I certainly had more difficulty with Spanish than I did with any other subject. And we haven't come to that part yet, but when I went to Berlitz and took Russian, I didn't make the progress I should have.*

Q: Is that perhaps the reason that you didn't take the Japanese language training?

Captain Dyer: It may have been, but it was not a rational decision. I did not sit down and say, "Well, I can't learn language, so I won't go out there." I think it was more that it never particularly occurred to me. I never had it pointed out that there was such a thing as a language course, until I inadvertently was ordered out there. Going back to a staff with people I very much admired and wanted to be with, it didn't occur to me that I might want to go to Japan. I don't think I ever really seriously approached the idea. If I'd been footloose and fancy free, I think I might have wanted to go to Russia.

Q: Except for your year in the <u>Antares</u>, this tour in the <u>Badger</u> was about the only time you didn't spend in battleships. Did you enjoy the service in a small ship?

Captain Dyer: I liked the destroyers pretty much, except when the sea got too rough. In my humble opinion, anyone that says

---

*Berlitz was the name of a commercial school teaching foreign languages.

that he could ride one of the old World War I destroyers in really rough weather and not feel at least somewhat under the weather, is a liar.

Q: Were you fairly proficient as a shiphandler and a watch officer?

Captain Dyer: I thought so.

Q: Did you enjoy steaming with the other destroyers?

Captain Dyer: Yes. We were out one night. My wife was just a bride. Steaming in the fog, we were following the Jacob Jones. She suddenly swerved off to the right, and I chose not to follow her. A little later there was a crash. She'd gone over and run into a ship in the adjacent column. We eventually got over there and took off a couple of injured people and went into San Diego. The radio blared forth that the Badger had been in a collision. She [Mrs. Dyer] was up in Los Angeles visiting relatives with no way to find out any information and too new to the Navy anyway to try to find out anything. That was one of the more exciting moments in life in the Badger.

Q: What kind of material condition was the ship in after having been in the lay-up fleet for a while?

Captain Dyer: In much better material condition than the ships that were being replaced. That's all you could say for it. It may be apocryphal, I don't know, but it was said of one of the destroyers in service that somebody was chipping paint in the bottom somewhere and the chipping hammer went right through. That's one of the things that inspired the sudden call for replacing them and decommissioning.

Q: It was a much less formal system, I think, then than it got to be later when they used specific preservation techniques after World War II, wasn't it?

Captain Dyer: I think better now, yes. But, of course, the Badger was completely out of mothballs when I joined her, so I don't know just what shape she was in when they first started putting her back in service.

Q: The skipper sounded like a reasonable sort in granting your leave extension. How was he as a leader during operations?

Captain Dyer: He was one of the best shiphandlers I have ever seen. He had only one severe defect. He was very hard of hearing and like so many people who are deaf, he spoke in a very low tone of voice. When he was on the bridge conning the ship, somebody had to stand at the foot of him to hear what he said and repeat it to the engines or the wheel. To sit next to him in the wardroom was torture, because he would say something and you had no idea what it was.

Q: Did he give the junior officers plenty of chance to handle the ship and grow?

Captain Dyer: Yes and no. He gave them some opportunity, but probably not as much as he should have. But, of course, in those days when they had so little oil, we didn't have as many opportunities. When he had the ship, and I was officer of the deck, I don't know that he ever told me anything. He was relieved before we went on that cruise to the East Coast. His relief was not a really good experienced destroyer man. He would sit up there on the bridge and say, "I think you're getting a little too close. Don't you think you're a little too far away?" "Don't you think this," and "Don't you think that?" It was just a constant stream, not of helpful hints, but of criticism.

Q: Back seat driver.

Captain Dyer: Back seat driving. And, "How far are you away now?" If your eye is any good, you should develop a feeling that you don't have to measure with a stadimeter every ten seconds to know whether you're along or not. "I think you'd better take off a couple of turns," and, "I think you'd better put on a couple of turns." You'd leave the bridge after four hours feeling completely exhausted and frustrated. Charlie Best was never that way.* In fact, one time we were anchoring out at the island, and I didn't back down soon enough. I had to back down more than full. He didn't give me hell, but he did sort of indicate that he didn't think that was a first class maneuver.

Q: You already knew.

Captain Dyer: I already knew.

Q: Who was the second captain?

Captain Dyer: Maloney.** And we lost a good executive officer and got a foul ball as exec. Henry Nielson was the original executive officer, and he was relieved by Asel Baylis Kerr.***

Q: That must have been a real problem when you had a bad CO and a bad XO.

Captain Dyer: It was. I was fully thankful to get off as soon

---
*Commander Charles L. Best, USN.
**Commander James D. Maloney, USN.
***Lieutenant Henry S. Nielson, USN; Lieutenant Asel B. Kerr, USN.

as possible after arrival in Charleston.

Q: What was the role of destroyers in those years?

Captain Dyer: They were an attack force with torpedoes. They were screening vessels, antisubmarine screening vessels.

Q: Was antiaircraft emphasized very much?

Captain Dyer: No. With the ordnance we had at that time, the destroyer was not a good gun platform from which to shoot at an airplane, not if you wanted to hit anything, that is.

Q: Did the antisubmarine listening devices come under you as the communication officer?

Captain Dyer: I'm trying to think. We didn't have any sonar. That was later.

Q: There were sort of hydrophones at that time, weren't they?

Captain Dyer: I can't remember having anything to do with any underwater listening at that time.

Q: You said you were a commissary officer. Did you have any

supply training?

Captain Dyer: No. But I had to take monthly inventory of all the commissary supplies. We were on some kind of balanced ration deal at that time and had--it still amuses me--two items on the sheet--tomatoes as tomatoes and tomatoes as a vegetable. Same tomatoes.

Q: I wonder what they were when they weren't a vegetable?

Captain Dyer: They were tomatoes. We were supposed to get a certain amount of tomatoes in the standard ration over a certain period as an antiscorbutic.* So that was tomatoes as tomatoes. We were supposed to have a certain proportion of overall food as a vegetable. So after we had served our tomatoes as tomatoes, if you wanted to open a couple of cans of tomatoes instead of a couple of cans of beans, then it became tomatoes as a vegetable. But it still kind of startles me when I think of it.

Q: How did you go about getting released from this unpleasant duty and going back to naval communications?

Captain Dyer: I didn't. I had had seven years at sea, barring three months at the Navy Department.

---
*An antiscorbutic is something to prevent scurvy.

Q: So you were due to go ashore then.

Captain Dyer: If you went to postgraduate school, you got to go ashore at five years. If you chose to be uneducated, you had seven years on your first sea cruise. I was just due for shore duty, and they ordered me back to the Navy Department.

Q: Had you expressed a preference for that duty?

Captain Dyer: I think it was the other way around. By that time Safford was back in control of OP-20GX. He went there just a few months after the first fleet problem I told you about. I think he expressed a preference for me. I may have indicated, but there wasn't much of a way you could indicate what you wanted to do.

Q: You probably had a good reputation from the various fleet problems you had been in.

Captain Dyer: Yes, I did. Commander McClaran, whom I had known during the second set of fleet problems, had gone to the Navy Department. He was head of the whole OP-20G layout. We were acquainted. I saw it more or less as a matter of course that I would go there.

However, I was a little bit put out when I got there.

Originally, my orders had given me 30 days leave before I had to report to the Navy Department. Shortly before I was detached, I got dispatch modifications detaching me to proceed to the Navy Department. When I got there, and I found out that they had ordered three of us to OP-20GX early so that the people regularly assigned to the Navy Department code room could go on leave. We had to give up our leave so they could have theirs. That made me a bit provoked, to say the least.

Q: Did you raise a protest?

Captain Dyer: I grumbled, but it didn't do any good. I can't think of his name, but I did not go to the director of naval communications or anybody like that. I think I may have told Safford I didn't think it was quite fair. He agreed, and that was the end of that.

Q: So were you then a watch officer for a while?

Captain Dyer: I was the watch officer in the code room. Night watches, what have you. It had to be manned around the clock.

Q: Were things routinely encoded in the operational traffic? What was the practice?

Captain Dyer: No, there wasn't too much. There wasn't too much and probably more than there should have been. They were sending things in codes that didn't need to be. I don't suppose an eight-hour watch would have more than half a dozen on the average.

Q: That's not too taxing.

Captain Dyer: It's not too taxing.

Q: But it wasn't leave, either.

Captain Dyer: It wasn't leave, and it wasn't what I'd been led to believe I was coming to the Navy Department for. Or what I wanted to do.

Q: Were machine cipher systems used for codes at this point?

Captain Dyer: No. There weren't any machines yet. If it was confidential, it was probably a straight "E" code. In a rare case where it was secret, it was "A" code enciphered with the Navy cipher box, for which Russell Willson got $15,000.* There

---
*As a lieutenant, Russell Willson designed a cylinder coding device which was used by the Navy, and for which Congress awarded him $15,000 in 1935.

were a couple of other systems--minor things, nothing very sophisticated.

Q: How long did this assignment as a watch officer last?

Captain Dyer: We got there in early June; it was all of June and, I guess, through July.

Q: Did you enjoy Washington as a place to live and be stationed?

Captain Dyer: Pretty well. We succeeded in finding a furnished apartment. It was only about four or five blocks from Main Navy up on 23rd Street--easy walking distance. We enjoyed the cultural opportunities of Washington at the time, to whatever extent a junior lieutenant could afford them, which wasn't too much. We could go to the National Theater occasionally and things of that kind. We thought it was a pleasant place to live.

The first winter we were there (I'm getting a little ahead of things), we were invited to the White House for the annual reception of Army and Navy. I think that is a comment of some kind. We were invited the first year. The second year, Calvin Coolidge ungraciously decided to die at the wrong time and the White House social season was curtailed.* The first year I was

---

*Former President Calvin Coolidge died on 5 January 1933.

there, I was senior enough to be invited to the White House. I never was senior enough after that.

Q: The level moved up much higher.

Captain Dyer: I went back to Washington as a captain, and when I retired, I was something like the second ranking line captain in the Navy, but I never again was high enough to be invited to the White House.

Q: Did you meet the Hoovers personally?

Captain Dyer: Oh, yes. They were in the receiving line. I was at the White House when the Trumans were there but not officially. And I met Harry several other times.

Q: Your work with Safford--do you want to start with that now or cover that the next time?

Captain Dyer: Whatever you like. Maybe it would be as well to wait. It's kind of involved.

Q: Okay. We'll wrap it up with this one unless you've got any more on what we've talked about so far.

Captain Dyer: I think that does it. I can say that in due course, I was permitted to go to the job for which I was intended in OP-20GX.

Dyer #3 - 124

Interview Number 3 with Captain Thomas H. Dyer, U.S. Navy (Retired)

Place: Captain Dyer's cottage, Sykesville, Maryland

Date: Monday, 29 August 1983

Subject: Biography

Interviewer: Paul Stillwell

Q: Captain, when we broke off the last time, you were discussing the time when you reported to Washington and experienced some frustration in not being able to get into your regular assignment right away.

Captain Dyer: Like all good or bad things, that came to an end eventually, and some two to three months later than I should have I did report to OP-20G for duty. At that time Commander McClaran was OP-20G, and Laurance Safford was OP-20GX.* Initially I was at loose ends for a brief period. Then I was asked to work on the Japanese naval system. As I mentioned previously, we had acquired a Japanese naval code published in 1919 and quite a bit of work had been done on it. It was always an enciphered code, and periodically the cipher was changed. With the limited facilities, it was not always possible to keep up to date. My assignment was to recover the new ciphers for the code.

---
*Commander John W. McClaran, USN; Lieutenant Commander Laurance F. Safford, USN.

Q: Did the code itself remain unchanged?

Captain Dyer: Presumably it had, but nothing had been done on it from about 1929.

Q: Why not?

Captain Dyer: Lack of people. There were only Mrs. Driscoll and Safford.* Safford had a great many other things to do.

Q: Why was that not considered important enough to put people on it full time?

Captain Dyer: In the first place, very few people knew anything about it. And some who knew, took a rather dim view of the activity. While we had some supporters here and there throughout the Navy Department, for the most part the people who might have been able to make personnel available thought we were a bunch of blue-sky merchants, indulging in a pipe dream.

Q: Would it also be a factor that very few people had the training by this point to work on it?

---

*Mrs. Agnes Driscoll was a civilian cryptanalyst in OP-20G.

Captain Dyer: That also entered into it. In any event, I was put to work to recover the ciphers. I struggled for a while at a desk adjacent to Mrs. Driscoll's. One day she looked over my shoulder to see what I was doing and took a paper from my hand. After a few minutes she said, "This is a new code." It turned out she was correct. Whereas the original code had been composed of three kata-kana groups, the new code was composed of four. It was enciphered in two forms, a relatively simple cipher for confidential purposes and a much more sophisticated cipher for secret purposes. But with the help I received from Mrs. Driscoll, I was soon able to get into both types of ciphers, and we could reduce the messages as received to pure code.

Somewhere during the late fall, early winter of 1931-32, Safford went to sea, and I became officer in charge of the research desk. We were faced with a very serious and severe problem--the problem of analytically recovering a code which in round numbers consisted of about 100,000 code groups. It required a terrific amount of compilation of data. We would have had to have a force of 30 or 40 clerks at least, even to begin to do the work that was required.

Q: Was this because there was no machine or computer or something that could perform these calculations?

Captain Dyer: There was none at the moment that we knew of, but we constantly searched for some aid to the solution of the problem. One must keep in mind that this was in 1931 at the depth of the Depression, when money for essentials was very tight. But we scouted around, discussed various possibilities and finally discovered that Remington Rand Corporation had developed a punch card system that would handle alphabetic information. We investigated that and then discovered that IBM had also developed alphabetic machinery.* Because of the difference in underlying principles--Remington Rand was a purely mechanical device and IBM was electrical--IBM had a greater flexibility and would obviously be superior for our purposes. Somehow Commander McClaran succeeded in getting from some source $5,000 for the first year's rental of IBM machines. We installed two key punches, a sorter and a printing tabulator. Normally when you install an IBM accounting system, you turn to the company and they give you all kinds of help. We could not do that.

Q: Because you didn't want outsiders to know what you were using it for.

Captain Dyer: We didn't want them to know what we were going to do. If I wanted to know how to do something, I had to try to couch the question in business terms or accounting terms or
_____
*IBM--International Business Machines.

something—how do you do this? Admittedly, once you're committed to a line of behavior, you're rather stuck with the first setup of procedures for some time. They were far from perfect; they were rather crude. But I did have to design all the operating procedures, the method of punching the cards and so on. For a brief time I operated the sorter myself.

At that time we had, in addition to Mrs. Driscoll and myself, two GS-3 clerk typists. They were trained to operate the key punches. We needed a fifth person to operate the other machinery. At that time, believe it or not, to add one live body to a complement anywhere in the the Federal Government required the signature of one Herbert Hoover, as President of the United States. So that was out.

Q: That would also explain why you couldn't hire somebody from IBM and get them cleared, wouldn't it?

Captain Dyer: Yes, but we never even considered that as a possibility. We finally succeeded in borrowing a woman from the code preparation section—the nicest person I've ever known, with probably the least mechanical sense of any person I've ever known. But she did learn to operate the machines. She could put the cards in the sorter, take them out, put them in boxes, and then call on me. I would reassemble them ready for the next run. She could run the cards through the tabulator and print whatever

Dyer #3 - 129

was necessary. The original had what was known as a fixed plug board. If you wanted to change it, you had to pull out about 75 or 100 electric wires and put them back in a new arrangement. I had to do that. In addition to that, I was keeping up with the keys in that system. We had about four diplomatic systems which we were trying to keep up with. And I had sort of administrative charge over the worldwide intercept operators organization. I had charge of the intercept operators school, which was on the roof of the Navy Department. All in all, I had quite a bit to do.

Q: Could you describe this intercept network, how it was set up, where you had the people?

Captain Dyer: Primarily we had stations at Cavite.* I'm a little vague whether we had anything in Shanghai or Peking at that time. At one time we had. And we had a station in Guam and one in Manawahua in the Hawaiian Islands.

Q: I think the Asiatic Fleet flagship had some sort of organization, didn't it?

Captain Dyer: They had an officer assigned and possibly a couple

---
*Philippine Islands, headquarters for the U.S. Navy's Sixteenth Naval District.

of radio operators, but the principal reliance of the Asiatic station was on the Cavite station. Actually, the whole intercept operation was at that time a relatively new proposition. If I'm not mistaken, the first class for training of intercept operators was either in '28 or '29. So it was a small organization.

Q: You oversaw that effort, too?

Captain Dyer: I oversaw that effort, too.

Q: How many instructors did you have?

Captain Dyer: One. One chief.

Q: What form did they take the intercepts in? Did they type them in the Japanese kata-kana?

Captain Dyer: Earlier--I don't know whether it was in the late administration of Safford or during Rochefort's time--the Underwood Typewriter Company had done the work of developing a typewriter that would print the kata-kana characters.[*] Then somebody got the bright idea that that was a little bit stupid when they could just as well print the Romagi form, Roman letter

---
[*]Lieutenant Joseph J. Rochefort, USN.

form, of the kata-kana characters. By the time I got in the act, they were doing that.

Q: This was still just a typewriter, though, not an electromechanical device.

Captain Dyer: Just a typewriter. And in order to accommodate the whole 48 characters, some of them had to be reached with the shift key. I never knew too much about operating the typewriter. Actually, all the operator had to learn was, with a certain Morse combination, you press this key.

Q: What was the crossover between Morse and the 48 characters, since there's only 26 characters in Morse?

Captain Dyer: The Japanese developed their own Morse equivalent, which may or may not have resembled any of ours. Some of them did, some of them didn't. I had very little occasion to deal with the Japanese Morse. But the operators, of course, had to learn it in place of the American Morse.

Q: Did you try to take people who didn't already know the American Morse?

Captain Dyer: No, we tried to get people who had shown

Dyer #3 - 132

outstanding proficiency as radio operators. For for the most part, we did get the cream of the crop.

Q: This involved a few Marines also, did it not?

Captain Dyer: There were a few Marines. There were no Marines, I believe, during my time there, but I think 159 was the total number of operators trained before the war. They're perpetuated now in the organization known as the "On the Roof Gang." Just this past summer a tablet was erected at Naval Station Nebraska Avenue commemorating the "On the Roof Gang."

Q: Why on the roof? Was the classroom physically on the roof?

Captain Dyer: The classroom was, I suppose, technically a penthouse, but actually a little shack on the roof of the sixth wing of the Navy Department.

Q: So it was there, rather than at Nebraska Avenue?

Captain Dyer: Nebraska Avenue did not come into the picture until well into World War II.*

---

*The Naval Security Station is on Nebraska Avenue in Washington, D.C.

Dyer #3 - 133

Q: I see. I've heard a reference to Bellevue. Was that tied in with this?*

Captain Dyer: Later, but not during my time. I think it's interesting to note that about half of the "On the Roof Gang" were commissioned during the war, and about another quarter to a third achieved warrant rank. So they were a rather select group.

Q: Did many of the people whom you had trained wind up in Hawaii during World War II?

Captain Dyer: I'm not sure.

Q: Did they have to undergo any additional security clearances to get into this program?

Captain Dyer: The idea of formal security clearances was a rather late development. When we sent out a call for nominations we stipulated that they be of the highest character. In that regard, I was never cleared until about one year after the war ended.

---

*During World War II a Special Projects School had been set up in the Naval Research Laboratory, Bellevue, District of Columbia, which operated advanced training components for radio technicians in radio materiel and radio countermeasures.

Dyer #3 - 134

Q: There were occasional cases of dealings with the Japanese during the Thirties. Was this just so exceptional as to be nonexistent?

Captain Dyer: I don't know of any cases of any dealings with the Japanese.

Q: I've heard of one case of a Naval Academy graduate from around a class in the mid-teens who was dismissed as a result of his activities.*

Captain Dyer: I never heard of it. It's possible. Anything's possible.

Q: But that was not seen as a major problem, I take it.

Captain Dyer: No.

Q: What portion of your activity in this period was devoted to the school?

Captain Dyer: Practically none. I had a chief petty officer in

---

*John S. Farnsworth, Naval Academy class of 1915, was convicted in 1936 for selling confidential naval documents to the Japanese. As a lieutenant commander in 1925, he had been court-martialed and dismissed from the Navy.

whom I put absolute trust. He ran the school. If he had a problem, he came to me and asked me. Otherwise, I left him alone, he left me alone.

Q: Were there simultaneous efforts to protect our own codes and determine if there was a possibility of them being penetrated?

Captain Dyer: That was an assigned function of the research section. A good bit had been done in working to try to develop a satisfactory cipher machine, particularly under Safford. Later the development of the electrical cipher machine by the Navy was largely under the research desk. During my time, there was only a little incidental input in that direction. Somebody would have a bright idea and maybe I would have to shoot it down. One must remember that I was only a junior lieutenant during most of my stay and did not carry much weight anywhere.

Q: Under these circuits that you were copying, could you give an estimate of how much of the traffic you were able to break?

Captain Dyer: As far as the cipher was concerned, I think at least 90-95% was recovered in the form of code. But up to the time I left Washington, we had not made enough progress on the code solution to consider anything but the absolutely most routine messages readable. I mean, we might be able to read a message saying, "Departed Shanghai at 0800," but who cares about that three months later?

Q: Were you working primarily on naval codes rather than diplomatic at that point?

Captain Dyer: We were trying to get the main fleet Navy code in some sort of shape. From the standpoint of war readiness, that was our biggest thing, to get as far along as we could. Most of the diplomatic traffic was of no interest to anyone. We did not supply the front office with translations, except very rarely.

At the time of the Lytton Commission, in investigating the Manchukuo affair, we were able to read a copy of the Lytton Commission's report, which the Japanese had acquired before it was released.* I did send a copy of that up to the Chief of Naval Operations. That's about the only thing specifically that I can remember.

Q: Admiral Pratt was CNO by then and a great friend of the Japanese Admiral Nomura.** Despite this personal relationship, do you think it would be fair to say that each assumed the other

---
*The Lytton Report was prepared in 1932 by the League of Nations' Lytton Commission, headed by British diplomat Victor Alexander Bulwer-Lytton, which investigated the Japanese military occupation in 1930 of Manchukuo, or Manchuria, China.
**Rear Admiral Nomura, IJN, who later became Japanese ambassador to the United States in 1941.

was trying to break the other one's codes and ciphers?

Captain Dyer: I would say that certainly Pratt would assume that and Nomura might very well assume the same.

Q: In your efforts did war with Japan seem a likely eventuality?

Captain Dyer: From the time I entered active service, Orange was always the enemy in any war exercise, war game.* I say always; it wasn't really. It was in the war plans, but in a Navy problem you might call them "black" and "blue." But I think everybody considered that if we did have a war, it would be with Japan. Japan was very belligerent from the time of the '22 arms conference on up. And the Oriental Exclusion Act did not help matters any.** It was one of the things that you just took for granted.

I may have already mentioned this, but in my estimation, after Japan, Russia posed the greatest threat to this country. I persuaded the Navy Department to send me to Berlitz School for a course in Russian, but before I finished the course, I was so

---
*Colors were assigned to various players in prewar exercises. Players representing Japan were typically given orange. War plans covering Japan were also associated with the color orange.
**In an act passed by the U.S. Congress in 1924, Orientals were prevented from immigrating to the United States. It was viewed as an insult by the Japanese because they had voluntarily agreed in 1907 not to immigrate to the United States.

deeply involved in the Japanese problem that I had to forget about Russia. I don't claim to have a crystal ball or to be any kind of a seer, but I think that I perceived Russia as a great threat to this country long before many people in public life did.

Q: In his oral history, Admiral Kemp Tolley talked about his own efforts to learn Russian during that period.* There was almost no support from the Navy Department. It was almost as if there would be no value in this sort of thing.

Captain Dyer: That's right. There was an interesting sidelight on security. Admiral Brooks Upham was ordered as Commander in Chief Asiatic Fleet, and so he was brought down for a tour of the section.** He was so impressed with the potential importance and value of the thing--he was at that time chief of the Bureau of Navigation, which was the personnel bureau at that time--that when he returned, he decided to improve our security by taking my name out of the Navy Directory.*** It wasn't exactly a

---

*Rear Admiral Kemp Tolley, USN(Ret.), subject of a Naval Institute oral history.
**Admiral Frank Brooks Upham, USN, Commander in Chief U.S. Asiatic Fleet from 1933 to 1936.
***The Navy Directory was a quarterly publication of nearly 300 pages. It listed U.S. Navy officers alphabetically and, in another section, grouped by duty stations. The directory was published by the Bureau of Navigation.

satisfactory way of achieving security, but his motives were honorable and right.

Q: If he saw the value of your work, I wonder why a sideline of his visit wouldn't have been to provide you more in the way of personnel.

Captain Dyer: Where was he going to get them? This was the Depression.

Q: Even one or two more would have helped, I think.

Captain Dyer: He couldn't provide them. He'd have to go to the White House to get an okay.

Q: Captain Rochefort said that people in this line of work were considered eccentrics or even a little bit crazy. You used the term blue-sky merchants. Do you think that added to the bias against adding personnel?

Captain Dyer: Everything did. By and large, I think the idea was abroad that we were harmless and so they might as well let us play around with our toys, as you might with a half-intelligent moronic child.

Q: Sort of a patronizing attitude.

Captain Dyer: Rather. Remember, this was shortly after Secretary Stimson said, "Gentlemen don't read each other's mail," which never affected us because no one could accuse us of being gentlemen.*

Q: Do you think the fact that the code had changed was the major selling point in getting the IBM installation?

Captain Dyer: I really don't know. That was my sole selling point to Commander McClaran. When he went up to try to get the money, I don't know what arguments he used. I didn't go with him, but I imagine he used something like that. In this day and age, you get $5,000 if you have a couple of screws missing out of something. In those days it took a lot more doing.

Q: How long did it take you to get that system shaken down so you could build some confidence in it?

Captain Dyer: The operation proved its worth almost immediately, but before we'd gone too far with the thing, it came time for me

---

*Henry L. Stimson, U.S. Secretary of State, made the statement in 1929 while objecting to message interception and cryptanalysis as being unethical. Later, as Secretary of War from 1940 to 1945, he accepted and valued such intelligence.

to go to sea.

Q: Before we get to that, maybe you could describe how the machines were used in attacking ciphers and codes.

Captain Dyer: I don't want to say never, but in this context, they did not enter into attacking ciphers. The solution of a code depends on the ability to easily study all previous uses of a given code group, with hopefully the group that immediately precedes it and the group that immediately follows it. So the approach that we used was to adopt an indexing procedure which was punched into the card together with, one at a time, each code group. Initially we were not able to put in the immediately preceding and following group without a great deal of work. We just had to do without it. That did develop later, particularly after IBM invented one additional machine. We would take a message in its deciphered form, set up a card with the indexing elements, punch the group into it, then punch the next card and so on. When we finished a bunch of cards, we could sort them alphabetically and produce lists that showed you where to look for the occurrence of a particular group. From the same cards, before they were sorted, in their original message form, we could print worksheets for working on the code.

During the war, jumping ahead a little bit, we indexed over a million groups in just one Japanese code.

Q: What might have been your number back during this period in the Thirties?

Captain Dyer: Up until the time I left, probably 5,000-6,000.

Q: The atmosphere in the basement in Pearl Harbor in early 1942 has been characterized as almost chaotic, a great deal of pressure, paper piled on the floor, and all that. How would you compare that to the period that we've been discussing?

Captain Dyer: It was calm enough. Part of the time we had a returned language officer assigned to us. If there was anything that could be translated, he translated it. We had one room about this size that housed Mrs. Driscoll and the language officer and me.* Calm enough. And there was a small room with the two typists and a little larger room with the larger machines in it. That was it. Not very hectic, because there weren't enough people to make it hectic.

Q: Were you on eight-hour days during that time?

Captain Dyer: Oh, yes.

---

*Captain Dyer's living room was 14 feet by 21 feet.

Dyer #3 - 143

Q: Captain Rochefort said that even though you didn't have to know the Japanese language, you had to know the characteristics of the language, such as word endings and plurals. Did you find that to be the case?

Captain Dyer: I don't thoroughly agree with him as to what you need to know. I still don't know Japanese. But with all due modesty, I think that I equalled anyone I've ever known in the initial work of breaking into a Japanese code. When it gets to a certain point, I'm more or less lost. When it gets into filling in blanks in a sentence and knowing what Japanese word goes in where, I have no idea. Even the word endings. There's lots of structures that don't depend on language at all. The thing you do is learn as you go along.

For instance, "Ki kimitsu denrai dai nani nani go" is the way a Japanese message is apt to start, which means literally, "Your secret telegram number so-and-so." Sometimes that is given as one group followed by a couple of numbers; sometimes it's all spelled out in kana. It depends on what kind of system you're working on. That may be the first group. The first group isn't always the first thing in a message. It may be twisted around. These are the things you look for. There are things that the trained cryptanalyst will look for that a trained linguist will miss completely and vice versa.

Several times during the war I had bets with Finnegan about

some point.* I don't think I ever lost one of them, and yet he was a highly competent linguist.

Q: In addition to word endings and things of that sort, what about idioms and thought patterns and the way the Japanese would typically express something? Did you get into that?

Captain Dyer: To a certain extent. You learn certain words. For instance, "chaku" means arrive, and "hatsu" means depart. "Chimbotsu" means sunk. You don't need to know what the Japanese is, often, to know that they're saying that they left Shanghai or Singapore. There's always a lot of mechanics to a code. The first time you run into it, you don't know what it means, and you have to figure it out. A knowledge of a language doesn't help you a bit.

Q: Was there any correlation between the old code and the new code that helped you?

Captain Dyer: The overall vocabulary of 100,000 groups was pretty much the same. But there was one great difference, as I remember it. The old code was what was usually known as the "Red Code" merely because the binder was red; it was not a Japanese

---
*Lieutenant Joseph Finnegan, USN.

name. The new one that came in immediately after that was the "Blue Code." The red code was essentially a one-part code. By that, I mean that when you arrange the code groups in alphabetical order, the meanings were pretty much in alphabetical order. You used the same volume for encoding and decoding. The Blue Code was a two-part code. When the code groups were in alphabetical order, the meanings were not, and so on, which is a lot harder problem. However, the one help, so to speak, was that the Red Code was three kana characters, where the total number was 45 or 48, whatever it was they used, cubed. All possible combinations were in there.

The more modern way of doing it is to design a code so that each group varies from every other group by two letters. Nebraska Avenue might object to my saying that, but it's known worldwide, so I don't know why. It's what's known as a garble check. If you have one letter wrong, then that group won't be in the code. You can change one letter at a time to find one that is in there. And that's a terrific help.

Q: Did the Japanese use padding in their messages?

Captain Dyer: They did anything that any civilized country ever did and some things that no one else ever did.

Q: What did they do that no one else ever did?

Captain Dyer: I'd rather not say.

Q: Okay. Who was the Japanese language officer you had with you?

Captain Dyer: A Marine by the name of Pyzick, and one officer whom I mentioned previously--Tommy Birtley, who was a student with me, originally in cryptanalysis.* Whether there was a third one or not, I don't remember. We didn't always have one. It depended on the availability.

Q: It sounds as if you didn't always need one, either.

Captain Dyer: That's true.

Q: Wasn't Thomas Huckins with you part of this time also?**

Captain Dyer: He was not a language officer. He was there, yes. He came towards--I guess he was there most of the last year I was there.

Q: What was his role?

---

*First Lieutenant Frank P. Pyzick, USMC; Lieutenant Thomas B. Birtley, Jr., USN.
**Lieutenant Thomas A. Huckins, USN.

Dyer #3 - 147

Captain Dyer: He eventually relieved me, but he would just help out, whatever I wanted him to do. I don't remember just when he did come.

Q: Was he something of an understudy, then, that you were preparing to take over?

Captain Dyer: Yes, that seemed to be the intention.

Q: You mentioned you went back to sea in '33. What was your career pattern and plan at this point?

Captain Dyer: I didn't have any plan. I expected to have the regular rotation of sea and shore duty that a naval officer had.

Q: Had you been in touch with the Bureau of Navigation about what your next assignment would be?

Captain Dyer: Mildly. I wanted to go to the West Coast, and they said I could go to the Pennsylvania. I wanted ship's duty, definitely. Having spent most of my life on battleships, I really preferred to return to a battleship, although I'd have been quite happy to go to a destroyer.

Q: Did you specifically ask for a billet other than

communications for this tour?

Captain Dyer: You don't do that. In those days you were sent to a ship and the ship used you as they saw fit. It's true I did not want to be in communications. But I mean, since I was not a postgraduate student in radio or anything, there was no particular reason why they should put me there. I hoped to go to the gunnery department, which I eventually did. For reasons which were perfectly clear to them, but left me a little bit confused, I was initially assigned ship's service officer.

Q: What duties came under that heading?

Captain Dyer: You had a ship's service store, you had the tailor shop, you had the ice cream factory, you had the barber shop, the laundry.

Q: Why was that not a supply officer's function?

Captain Dyer: Because it operates largely with unappropriated funds. That may not seem like a reason, but the members of the Supply Corps deal only with appropriated funds.

Q: Did this mean then that the individuals on board the ship had to pay for their laundry and haircuts and that sort of thing?

Captain Dyer: Right. They may have gotten laundry free, but the officers, I think, paid. I don't know. That's a long time ago. Mostly I was running the ship's service store and things of that kind.

Q: But they were Navy men performing these functions, weren't they?

Captain Dyer: Oh, yes.

Q: But they were paid from nonappropriated funds.

Captain Dyer: Yes. Paid extra or something.

Q: So that was a sideline duty for them?

Captain Dyer: The things we sold in the store we collected for, and in the tailor shop we paid for that, for cleaning and pressing. And I guess we paid for laundry. I just don't remember.

Q: What were the profits used for, welfare and recreation?

Dyer #3 - 150

Captain Dyer: Welfare and recreation.

Q: Did you have that duty also or was that someone else's?

Captain Dyer: The executive officer had the final control over expenditures. I didn't stay in the job too long. I reported to the ship in June, and I guess at the end of August I turned it over to somebody else.

Q: Was that something you were glad to get away from?

Captain Dyer: Yes, because I didn't see any future in it. It wasn't particularly calculated to further my naval career.

Q: Was it generally the practice to rotate line officers among various departments in the ship to give them a well-rounded background?

Captain Dyer: Not within the ship. They might, when you went to a new ship, give you a different job. But if you went to a battleship, for instance, and were assigned as a turret officer, and if by rank and so forth you were not promoted out of the eligibility, you would keep that assignment during your entire stay. A very junior officer, a fresh-caught ensign, might be shifted some. But there was not a great deal of shifting at that

Dyer #3 - 151

time. If you went to engineering, you stayed in engineering.

Q: Why were you then changed from ship's service to gunnery?

Captain Dyer: They didn't tell me. And as a very junior lieutenant--I was a senior lieutenant, but very junior--I did what I was told.* But I was glad to get the change. I thought there was a certain odd element to it. The officer who relieved me reported to the ship at the same time I did. They had some kind of summer gunnery school on one of the other ships. He went to that, while I was being ship's service officer, and then he came back from that and became ship's service officer and I got the turret. I felt I was sort of gypped a little bit, because I was denied some training that should have been useful to me.

Q: Wasn't it also during this period that you were having some problems with myopia?

Captain Dyer: I had that primarily when I was still at the Navy Department. I became due for promotion to lieutenant, and I was found not physically qualified for promotion. And that requires a little bit of an explanatory note.

---
*This means he had only recently been promoted to full lieutenant from lieutenant (junior grade).

There was an order signed by the Secretary of the Navy which said that you were not qualified for promotion unless you could see 15/20 without glasses. If the defect was myopic astigmatism, you were not qualified. And since, when I appeared for the examination, I saw 8 feet with my good eye and 6 feet with my not-so-good eye, they found me not qualified. I found out that the order had been drafted, not by anyone in the Bureau of Medicine and Surgery, but by somebody in the Bureau of Navigation. However, that didn't help me any. Commander McClaran interceded somewhere with the front office and got me a stay of execution for six months to be reexamined at the end of that time. Before I came up again, another officer was found disqualified by the examining board. In due course, his papers were forwarded hither and yon and got to the Bureau of Medicine and Surgery. They refused to approve them, because the order under which he was being retired was not their order, nor had it ever been referred to them. To make a long story short, the order was cancelled.

I appeared before them, and I saw no more, or essentially no more, than I did originally. They found me qualified because I could see 20/20 with glasses. But it did give me concern a little later about going back to Washington because it was, I figured, pretty hard on my eyes.

Q: In your job in the *Pennsylvania*, did you routinely stand deck watches?

Captain Dyer: I routinely stood deck watches, and I was at one point senior watch officer. Then in the fall of '34, I guess, we had a short-range battle practice and had an unfortunate incident in my turret. In one sense I have to accept responsibility for it, because I had not foreseen clearly enough the possibility and had not drilled the crew sufficiently on handling a broken powder bag. On investigation I was not found culpable; I was not censured nor reprimanded or anything of that kind. But I was relieved of my turret and assigned as ship's secretary.

Q: What had been the incident?

Captain Dyer: Broken powder bag.

Q: Why would this reflect negatively on you?

Captain Dyer: It wasn't handled properly.

Q: How was it handled?

Captain Dyer: This gets kind of involved. When a powder bag is broken, somebody in the gun chamber yells, "Silence," and everybody's supposed to freeze until they carefully get the powder picked up. They didn't do that. They had a pillow slip available, and they gathered up the powder and stuck it in the pillow slip, and along with the broken bag, stuck it in the gun and we fired. It was a fairly common way of handling it, but it's wrong. It's contrary to regulations. As I say, I had not anticipated the probability sufficiently and so I have to take the responsibility.

Q: Where were you when it was happening? Were you in the turret?

Captain Dyer: I was in the booth of the turret. The booth of the turret is completely back of the turret, separated by a bulkhead from the compartment where the guns are. You have no view nor communication except by voice tube.

Q: If there was no ill effect, why was it raised as a problem?

Captain Dyer: It might have had. In the first place, you're not supposed to put a pillow slip in the gun chamber and fire it. It's cotton. There might be an ember in there. Because your powder bags are silk, they're consumed immediately. There may be a 1000 to 1 chance, maybe more or less chance, that 60 people could be blown up because of the failure to carry out the regulations. It's serious.

Dyer #3 - 155

Q: How was it revealed? Did the gun captain report it afterward?

Captain Dyer: At the target practice, you have a number of observers from another ship watching you--watching everything. They are not necessarily going to keep quiet about something like that.

Q: Did this go into the ship's overall score for competition purposes?

Captain Dyer: I don't know that they got any penalty, but we didn't distinguish ourselves on the practice.

Q: Could you discuss your duties as a turret officer up to that point?

Captain Dyer: You drill your crew repeatedly in handling the projectiles and powder. You use dummy loads for drill purposes-- canvas bags, not silk bags. You drill for time. You have to train your pointer and trainer in handling the gun. There isn't too much you can say. Just drill, repetitive drill, practically daily.

Q: How many men did you have in your division?

Captain Dyer: We should have had about 80; we had about 55 or 60. We did not really have enough. As I stressed before, this was the Depression. The Navy had a total of 80,000 enlisted men. You did not have enough personnel to fully man all four turrets. In other words, you had to borrow for practice. We had to borrow men from the adjacent turret to work in the lower handling room during target practice. We loaned some of our men to them.

Q: Which turret did you have?

Captain Dyer: Three.

Q: So that's the higher one aft?

Captain Dyer: Higher aft, yes.

Q: What can you say about the caliber of the men that you were able to get during that Depression time when jobs were scarce?

Captain Dyer: On the whole they were good. There was one other factor that entered into the casualty, as it were. I had two petty officers--I had more than that--but in particular in the division, a gunner's mate in whom I had a great deal of confidence and a turret captain in whom I had very little confidence. I was using the gunner's mate in the turret and less than a week before the practice he was transferred. I had to move the turret captain up to the turret, much against my better judgment, but there wasn't anyone I could go to. I protested the transfer, but that was that. I think probably had the gunner's mate been there, everything would have been all right.

Q: What was the difference between those two ratings?

Captain Dyer: They were the same grade, both first class. A turret captain is theoretically more specialized in turrets. A gunner's mate normally is associated with the possibly smaller caliber. But it's in essence a distinction without any difference.

Q: And it was sort of a quirk in this case that the gunner's mate was better at the turret than the turret captain.

Captain Dyer: Yes. He was just a better man all around.

Q: Was it the turret captain who had done this pillow slip thing with the powder bags?

Captain Dyer: I assume so.

Q: As far as administrative duties, did you have an assistant division officer?

Captain Dyer: I had an ensign who has since become an admiral.

Q: Who is he?

Captain Dyer: Red Baumberger.* So I didn't ruin his career completely, at least.

Q: How was he in carrying out his duties?

Captain Dyer: He was a good JO.

Q: Did he take care of the routine things like inspections of the men in the departments and cleaning?

Captain Dyer: No, it was pretty much a shared responsibility. I did not pull the old gag of telling him that we'd take turns, "I've had it for the last six months, you take it for the next."

Q: When you were standing the deck watches can you describe how the ship handled in formation steaming with other battleships?

---

*Ensign Walter H. Baumberger, USN, later vice admiral.

Captain Dyer: By and large that was fairly simple because, as fleet flagship for the most part, we were the guide. We just plowed along and let them worry about keeping station on us.

Q: Did you have occasion to take her into anchorages or piers?

Captain Dyer: No, sir. That's something that the captain did.

Q: What do you recall about the captain as a shiphandler?

Captain Dyer: Most of the first two years I was there the captain was Frank Sadler.* He was a very good shiphandler. I say very good, he was certainly acceptable. I don't think he had any outstanding flair. I think I indicated one destroyer skipper I had was an outstanding shiphandler. He could make a ship roll over and play dead. But Captain Sadler was certainly competent.

Q: Were battleship skippers in that era typically cautious in handling their ships?

Captain Dyer: When you're handling something of that size and power, it pays to be cautious. I wouldn't want to be running around with anyone who wasn't.

---

*Captain Frank H. Sadler, USN.

Q: What can you say about the skipper's leadership qualities?

Captain Dyer: I guess they were adequate. I don't think that he was the type that inspires unswerving loyalty and obedience from all of his officers. But on the other hand, I don't think that anyone had any particular bones to pick with him. He was a good captain.

Q: How much leeway did he give the officers of the deck in running the ship?

Captain Dyer: I would say considerable. If you had the deck and he was on the bridge, he did not interfere one way or the other. I suppose he would have, if he thought it was necessary, but in minor matters he left you alone.

Q: What sorts of burdens were imposed on the Pennsylvania that other battleships didn't have by virtue of being the fleet flagship?

Captain Dyer: Spit and polish.

Q: How much was that carried out?

Captain Dyer: Considerable. I had, along with number three

turret, the starboard side of the quarterdeck. That was my space, my next space to take care of. The bitts on the deck had brass sheets on top of them. I finally succeeded in getting those replaced with stainless steel. And that saved an infinity of labor in keeping them shined where you could see your face in them. I class it as one of my major achievements

Q: Especially since they were exposed to salt water.

Captain Dyer: Yes.

Q: What about holystoning?* Was that a regular practice?

Captain Dyer: Oh, yes. Fridays.

Q: Followed by inspection on Saturday, probably.

Captain Dyer: Followed by inspection on Saturday.

Q: What do you remember about the fleet commander in chief?

Captain Dyer: Which one?

---

*The wooden decks of naval ships were "holystoned," or scoured clean with a flat piece of sandstone.

Q: The first one was Admiral Reeves, wasn't he?*

Captain Dyer: No, the first one was Admiral Sellers.** Frankly, after having been closely associated with Admiral Pratt, I wondered how Sellers ever got the four stars.

Q: Why?

Captain Dyer: I just didn't think he had what it takes. I don't suppose a lieutenant has much business passing judgment on a four-star admiral, but he did not impress me. He seemed to be picayunish about a lot of things. I can't give a for-instance. Anyway, I was very happy to see him leave.

Q: Would it be fair to say he tended to concentrate on the details rather than on the big picture that should be the fleet commander's job?

Captain Dyer: That was my impression. I might be doing him an injustice. They thought highly enough of him to send him to the Naval Academy. I didn't think highly of him. I didn't think

---

*Admiral Joseph M. Reeves, USN, Commander in Chief U.S. Fleet, 1934-1936.
**Admiral David F. Sellers, USN, Commander in Chief U.S. Fleet, 1933-1934.

very highly of his chief of staff. I didn't think very highly of various other members of his staff. There's very little concrete that I could put my finger on. It was just my impression after being with people whom I considered highly competent. Maybe I was overly critical.

Q: Was there any unpleasantness between the staff and the ship's wardroom officers?

Captain Dyer: No, I don't think there was any specific unpleasantness.

Q: Did line officers generally prefer to serve in the fleet flagship or would they rather have been somewhere else?

Captain Dyer: That's a generalization you cannot make. Some one, some the other. Some think it's an opportunity, some think that it's a sure way to damnation.

Q: How about yourself? What was your view?

Captain Dyer: Having spent most of my life on flagships, I had no objection to returning. I think I might have been better off if I had gone to one at the tail end of the line or something, but I don't know.

Q: When you went to the New Mexico, you engineered that so you could be with a number of your classmates. This time it came about that you were with several others.

Captain Dyer: Yes. Ed Layton was there; we had adjacent rooms. Lew Coley.*

Q: Sam Latimer.**

Captain Dyer: Sam Latimer was there.

Q: Bill Bailey and Harrel Hall.***

Captain Dyer: Bill Bailey and Harrel Hall were all there.

Q: Was there a bond amongst you as contemporaries?

Captain Dyer: To a certain extent, yes.

Q: At the same time was there competition?

---
*Lieutenant Edwin T. Layton, USN, later rear admiral and subject of a Naval Institute oral history; Lieutenant (junior grade) Lewis E. Coley, USN, later rear admiral.
**Lieutenant Samuel E. Latimer, USN, later rear admiral.
***Lieutenant William B. Bailey, USN, later rear admiral; Lieutenant (junior grade) Harrell W. Hall, USN.

Captain Dyer: No, I don't think there was any real competition. Of course, Lew Coley was in engineering. I guess there was a little competition between Ed Layton and me, because he had number four turret and I had number three. They were all very friendly.

Q: What do you remember about Layton from that period?

Captain Dyer: He got married, for the second time, if that's important. We had very friendly relationships. That's about all I can say. At that point in life I was the senior one in the class. That didn't make any difference, except that I got a little bit better room. There wasn't that much difference in them, but Eddie's was farther aft than mine. And Lew Coley's was farther aft than his.

Q: Was there a disadvantage to being farther aft?

Captain Dyer: There's more motion when the ship is pitching.

Q: Did you have individual staterooms as lieutenants?

Captain Dyer: Oh, yes.

Q: Was it a relatively comfortable ship to live and work in?

Captain Dyer: It was quite comfortable.

Q: What do you remember then about Admiral Reeves when he took over?

Captain Dyer: I liked him and I liked his staff very much. Right at the moment I can't think who his chief of staff was, but I thought highly of him. And Reeves seemed to be more in the mold that I had taken from Admiral Pratt. He could enter into the spirit of things. We invited him to dinner in the wardroom and prevailed on him to present the chaplain with a white shotgun, the chaplain having been very good about marrying off some of the bluejackets who had gotten girls in trouble. Admiral Reeves could enter into the spirit of that with a bunch of juniors all in the spirit of good, clean fun.

Q: He's been portrayed as having a good sense of humor. This would bear that out.

Captain Dyer: But there, of course, is never too much contact between the ship and the flag, really. They're two separate worlds.

Q: By serving in a flagship, do you get a better picture of what's happening throughout the fleet as a whole?

Dyer #3 - 167

Captain Dyer: I doubt it. Occasionally yes. If some of the senior staff members are friendly and talkative, they will discuss things with you. That's rather the exception than the rule.

Q: Could you talk to staff members that were about your same seniority?

Captain Dyer: I don't remember that there were any.

Q: You knew Rochefort from before.

Captain Dyer: Yes.

Q: Was he a good contact for you?

Captain Dyer: We didn't have very many dealings with each other, really. I guess Ham Wright was on there for a while. But I'm not really sure about Ham. Something sticks in the back of my mind that . . .

Q: Was there anything particularly memorable about fleet problems during your years in the Pennsylvania?

Captain Dyer: Not for a young lieutenant. One fleet problem I did go somewhere to do something--I don't know what--and we didn't succeed in doing anything. But the others were just so much drudgery as far as I was concerned.

Q: Was this sort of a letdown after the very important roles you had had previously in the fleet problems?

Captain Dyer: I suppose so. But I was perfectly well satisfied. I suppose there's one unpleasant thing on the Pennsylvania I have to bring up. In the spring of '35, late spring, Captain Sadler was relieved by Russell Willson, who, as luck would have it, was connected in some manner with the cryptanalytic and cryptographic activities in World War I.* He had designed an improvement to a device called the Navy code box. In the early Thirties, he endeavored to persuade Congress that he should be given $15,000 for the invention. Something had come down to my desk a while back, and I'm afraid that I took a somewhat dim view of the proposal.

Q: This is back during the time when you were in OP-20GX?

Captain Dyer: Yes. Now whether he ever knew that or not, I do not know. I was the ship's secretary by the time he came aboard.

---

*Captain Russell Willson served as commanding officer of the Pennsylvania (BB-38) from April 1935 to October 1936.

I do know that he made a great point of showing me the check from the Treasurer of the United States for $15,000. But that's neither here nor there.

One day when I was not present, they had an election in the wardroom to elect a new treasurer for the wardroom cigar mess or wine mess, whatever you want to call it, which is an informal association of officers, which provides cigarettes and cigars and other sundries for the officers. Non-members are charged 10% more for the things. They have a treasurer. The guy who had been treasurer for almost two years was being detached. I was elected in absentia to replace him. That was all right. You accept those things.

Q: But generally this is a position that is not sought after.

Captain Dyer: It's not particularly sought after. So I took over the books. I don't want to make a long story out of it, but I soon found out that there was some $2,000 missing. I first became aware of the problem when I got a dunning bill from a San Francisco wholesaler for three or four cases of cigarettes. The books didn't show they had ever been received. Then I was faced with the problem.

I went to the captain and told him what I had found. I am still, after 40-odd years, or whatever it is, at a loss to understand his attitude. He acted as though I had done something reprehensible in uncovering embezzlement which reflected adversely on his ship, and he didn't like it. And he kept that attitude throughout the whole incident. The officer concerned was ordered back and tried in court-martial and dismissed from the Navy.

When an officer reported aboard, the net worth of the cigar mess was figured, and the officer bought a share. When he left, the net worth was figured again, and he was paid off for his share. A number of people had been paid off on a nonexistent net worth. So we wrote to everybody who had been detached, and, as a sort of moral obligation, if they so considered it, asked that they return at least what they had received as profits since the value of shares had been going up in the previous administration. We had to assess all the members a sizable sum to get out of debt.

Captain Willson did not join the cigar mess. And he made a great point of telling me that we were charging 10% more for this, that, and the other thing, say, golf balls, than he had to pay somewhere else.

I thought Captain Willson was greatly overrated as a shiphandler. I thought he was open to question as a leader. Not so much for his treatment of me, but we had a chief engineer who had won the engineering "E" for the year and was coming up for selection for promotion to commander. On his fitness report where you were supposed to write out in words your evaluation, there was one sort of standard sentence. I've served on selection boards and I considered it damning. It was, "An excellent personal military character and qualified for promotion when due." That is all Willson put on the fitness report of this chief engineer. A chief engineer who had just won the red "E" for battleships was not selected.* To me, that was a definite failure of leadership. So aside from any way that I might have been affected, I think that it should be obvious that I have at least a modicum of reason to not think in the highest terms of one Russell Willson.

Q: Was there a general discontent among wardroom officers about him, specifically as a result of the chief engineer getting that fitness report?

Captain Dyer: Most of the officers did not know what the fitness report was. It was not posted, not published. And I'm sure the chief engineer did not tell other people. He told me because three times while I was ship's secretary, selection lists came out. While we were in the navy yard, I called up the individuals at home and told them they were not on the list. It's a hard thing to do, but I thought that was kinder than having them come in and somebody say, "The list's out," and they go look at it and

---
*The ship's engineer officer was Lieutenant Commander Preston Marshall, USN. He retired in that rank but was later recalled to active duty for World War II and eventually promoted to captain.

don't find their names. I know what that is too, although there was no one there when I didn't find my name.

Q: You say he was overrated as a shiphandler. Did he generally have a good reputation?

Captain Dyer: He was supposed to be a genius. He designed something called a course angle card that was supposed to be the answer to all our problems. I never knew but one person that ever used the thing.

Q: Was this like the "is-was" for finding a course to station?*

Captain Dyer: Sort of. It was a plastic template that you used. I suppose I do feel more or less as I do, that I judged him a little bit unjustly, but I think I think he judged some other people unjustly too.

My failure of selection to lieutenant commander initially was not due to anything Frank Sadler said, which he very well might have about the turret affair, but, I felt, was due largely to one thing that Willson wrote on one fitness report. There was a question considering the requirements of the service in peace and war, would you particularly desire to have him and be satisfied

---

*The "is-was" was essentially a circular slide rule.

to have him, and so on? He indicated that in my unnamed speciality, he might particularly desire to have me, but as a seagoing officer he would be satisfied--damning with faint praise. And he said down at the bottom, "The officer is better in an office than on a bridge or in a turret."

I'd never stood a watch for him, because as ship's secretary and later as communication officer, I was not a watch stander. I had never been in a turret for him, and even if it were true, I thought it was unjust for him to say so on the basis of hearsay.

Q: Was there any mechanism in that period for submitting a rebuttal to a fitness report?

Captain Dyer: Not really, not as there is now. If the fitness report really classed you as unsatisfactory, then it supposedly had to be referred to you and you could make a statement. But otherwise, there wasn't any mechanism in existence.

Q: Did you routinely get to see a fitness report when it was written? Did the captain call you in and talk about it?

Captain Dyer: He didn't. I think Sadler always let his be seen. He didn't call you in, but you could see them. Willson did a few times, and then he lost his nerve.

Dyer #3 - 174

Q: Do you think this lukewarm fitness report was a residual from the cigar mess incident?

Captain Dyer: I don't know. It might even have been a residual from my letter of disapproval for his $15,000.

Q: That almost sounds like a classic case of slaying the messenger who brings you the bad news.

Captain Dyer: It really was a very uncomfortable time for me. Here I was sitting up half the night trying to get the books straightened out. I was getting no sympathy at all from the powers that be.

Q: Had there not been an audit at the time that you relieved the previous man?

Captain Dyer: There had been an audit every month. But the auditors were never called on the carpet.

Q: It sounds as if you were a scapegoat.

Captain Dyer: It was unbelievable that this individual ever thought he could get by with this thing. When he was returned to the ship for trial, he tried to greet everybody as though he'd just been on a week's leave and was glad to be back. If I didn't learn anything else in that case, I learned that if you are going to be crooked, you'd better keep the most accurate set of double books that anybody ever heard of--because he had no idea where he stood.

Q: Did you have to then reconstruct where he had stood?

Captain Dyer: Not where he had stood, but I had to reconstruct where we stood. I had to go to such extremes as to write Ralph Williamson and say, "Do we owe you any money?"*

Q: So all you had was the doctored books.

Captain Dyer: Yes. And Ralph Williamson came back and said, "Yes, you owe us for a case of cigarettes."

Q: That was like a blank check.

Captain Dyer: I knew the San Francisco wholesaler's first bill. I knew that he would give me straight information. He told me exactly when they were delivered and everything else. No question about it.

---
*The wholesaler.

Q: So they had been sort of sold on the black market rather than being entered into the system?

Captain Dyer: Yes. They were never taken up on the books, but they weren't sold on the black market. He just sold them in the mess, and he put the receipts from them in his pocket.

Q: How did you get the job of ship's secretary? Wasn't that normally a warrant officer's job?

Captain Dyer: No, it was usually a commissioned officer's job. I don't know. I wasn't asking any questions about it at the time.

Q: What did the duties entail in that position?

Captain Dyer: You open all the incoming mail, decide what should be disposed of, all routine reports, things of that kind. It's just more or less the job of a secretary in any fairly large organization as distinguished from a clerk stenographer.

Q: Did the personnel records come under you also?

Captain Dyer: No. Enlisted personnel were in a different office.

Q: What about control of classified material?

Captain Dyer: I can't remember whether I had the classified material. I've had it so many times in my life, it's hard to remember whether I did on that job or not.

Q: Did you say you eventually got shifted from that to the ship communication department?

Captain Dyer: It was part of communications, anyway. The radio officer and the ship's secretary were under the communication officer. The communication officer on the ship was by profession a meteorologist. He was transferred to Admiral Reeves's staff as fleet meteorologist, leaving a vacancy. Then I was made communication officer, and I kept, I guess for the remainder of the stay, my job as ship's secretary. I had both.

Q: How long a period did you do both?

Captain Dyer: About six months.

Q: Did you feel comfortable moving into that billet?

Captain Dyer: Yes, because I'd done my training on staff communications. It was fairly simple and easy.

Q: Did you have any sense that you were under a cloud and you needed to redeem yourself?

Captain Dyer: I suppose some feeling of that kind. In fact, somewhere along the line I submitted an application to go to Harvard to the supply course school, and then withdrew it. I figured that paymasters didn't have to see very well, and that was the thing that concerned me. I didn't wind up a paymaster. I told my classmates that when they got to be admirals, so maybe I should have gone up. I'm glad I didn't get to be an admiral in my own racket, though.

Q: Why not?

Captain Dyer: Because I'd be dead today if I had. The human body will take just so much and it's going to collapse. The frustrations of--I'll get to that in due course--of such outfits as NSA are beyond reason.*

Q: When you were the ship's communication officer, did this bring you in pretty close contact with the admiral's staff?

Captain Dyer: No.

---

*NSA--National Security Agency.

Q: Did he have a separate communication organization?

Captain Dyer: Oh, yes. He had a communication officer, he had a radio officer. I don't remember who they were.

Q: In some cases it's a practice to send the ship's communication organization TAD and have an interchange with the flag staff, but evidently that wasn't the case.*

Captain Dyer: That's sometimes done with small staffs, but not a fleet staff, I don't believe.

Q: Did they have their own separate transmitters and machinery and so forth?

Captain Dyer: No, no. We handled their radio traffic. Just like you can go send a message by Western Union without running Western Union.

Q: Would theirs be encrypted and decrypted separately?

Captain Dyer: Probably. There was very little classified

---

*"TAD" stands for "temporary additional duty," a short-term duty assignment away from permanent duty assignment, to which one returned after temporary duty was completed.

Dyer #3 - 180

traffic handled when you come right down to it. If there was any, that was handled by their own watch officers.

Q: So there was not then a concern that the ship's radio people would know what the fleet traffic was in general?

Captain Dyer: No. No concern of that kind.

Q: Did you enjoy that tour as communication officer?

Captain Dyer: It was a job. When we were at sea, I spent practically all the daylight hours on the bridge, and maybe some of the night hours too, which is something I always enjoyed. But it can get a little bit tiresome.

Q: Why on the bridge rather than in radio?

Captain Dyer: Because you are not maneuvering by radio. Essentially, your maneuvering is going to be done by visual.

Q: Did you have a separate signal officer working for you?

Captain Dyer: No, I didn't have a separate signal officer, no.

Q: What part did the Club Trouville play in the life on the

Pennsylvania? I got that name out of one of your class reunion update books.

Captain Dyer: Unless you're talking about the speakeasy in San Francisco, I don't know what they're talking about.

Q: I think that must be it.

Captain Dyer: It did not play too great a part. It seems to me there was a Club Deauville, which was one of the most elegant speakeasies that I've ever been in. That thing you're sitting on would not have been anywhere near nice enough to furnish it with. It was all overstuffed furniture and cocktail tables and coffee tables. Just a few months before the Deauville, the same people opened Trouville, which was probably a little more elegant. I think I was there only a couple of times. We didn't spend too much time in San Francisco, really.

Q: Could you as a lieutenant afford to spend much time at a club like that?

Captain Dyer: Oh, yes. In San Francisco prices weren't high. You couldn't spend all your time in there, but you could go out for an evening and have probably all you wanted to drink for $5.00.

Q: Did naval officers frequent speakeasies during the Prohibition period?

Captain Dyer: Some did and some didn't, but more did than didn't, particularly in San Francisco.

Q: Generally did they observe the prohibition against drinking on board ship?

Captain Dyer: Some did and some didn't. You cannot generalize. Did they bring illegal liquor back from foreign climes? Some did and some didn't.

Q: How much time did the Pennsylvania spend in home port?

Captain Dyer: It was home-ported in the Long Beach-San Pedro area. I suppose it operated in that area for some 60 to 70% of the time. It would usually be a fleet problem cruise. The summer of '34, we went through the Panama Canal and up to New York and came back to the navy yard for two or three months.

Q: By the navy yard, do you mean Mare Island?

Captain Dyer: Bremerton. Home yard. The following year I think we had a fleet problem in Hawaii. And in '36 we were in Panama.

Dyer #3 - 183

That was usual--fleet problem--unless you had an extended cruise to the East Coast. It would be about two months. You could figure, putting it on an annual basis, a month and a half, two months, in the navy yard, although you didn't go. It was about a year and a half between times in the navy yard. So I would figure being in the San Pedro-Long Beach area for about 60 or 70% of the time.

Q: Do you have any particular memories of that visit to New York in 1934?

Captain Dyer: It's difficult to straighten that one out from other visits. Nothing outstanding, no.

Q: Were the city and the citizens generally hospitable?

Captain Dyer: Oh, yes. I don't know whether we had a big banquet that year or not. We did one year. I think that was '27. It must have been when Jimmy Walker was mayor. A huge banquet at the Astor Hotel. No, I don't remember anything particular on that '34 visit. I know we went back. We went back and prepped for the navy yard.

Q: Was it the practice for married officers, say, in your rank to generally live in homes that were close to each other?

Captain Dyer: No, no. You lived wherever you could find accommodations that were reasonably satisfactory and affordable.

Q: Did naval officers usually rent homes?

Captain Dyer: Oh, yes. Particularly when they went on sea duty. That just about finishes up the Pennsylvania, I think.

Q: We need to mention one more thing. Your son was born during that period.

Captain Dyer: Yes, he was born October 26, 1935. While my wife was in labor, I had to go back to the ship for admiral's inspection. Without going into a lot of details, we'd gone 65 miles from San Pedro up to Oxnard to the hospital. That was a rather hectic commute, running back and forth.

Q: He wound up with the same first name as yours but a different middle one. How did that come about?

Captain Dyer: Sort of family tradition. My great-grandfather was Thomas Wilbur. Then it skips a generation. And then my father was Thomas Henry. They didn't want sort of "Big Tom" and "Little Tom;" they didn't want a junior. They decided in my case to keep the initials, so they named me Thomas Harold, and called me Harold until I left home for the Naval Academy. And we decided we wanted to keep the name Thomas but there was nothing important about the middle name, and I didn't particularly like the name Harold or Wilbur or Henry, as far as that goes. My wife figured if we named him Thomas Edward, then we could use his initials and call him Ted. So he was Ted up until the time he died.*

---

*Commander Thomas E. Dyer, USN, was commissioned from the United States Naval Academy, class of 1957. He died 10 June 1981 and was buried in Arlington National Cemetery on 16 June 1981.

Dyer #4 - 186

Interview Number 4 with Captain Thomas H. Dyer, U.S. Navy (Retired)

Place: Captain Dyer's cottage, Sykesville, Maryland

Date: Tuesday, 6 September 1983

Subject: Biography

Interviewer: Paul Stillwell

Q: Captain, today we begin discussing the long tour of duty you began in the Hawaiian Islands in 1936. At the outset, I'd be interested in your recollections of the condition of the base there, which grew much later, but then had not yet advanced too much.

Captain Dyer: I want to back up just a little bit. When it became apparent that I would be going ashore in the summer of 1936, I corresponded with Laurance Safford.* I was looking for a billet other than Washington. He finally suggested that there had been an arrangement between the Chief of Naval Operations and the Commandant to set up a unit in Pearl Harbor, and that they would like to have me go out and do that.**

The fleet went to Panama on a fleet problem cruise, and I, expecting to be detached in June, failed to receive any orders. Finally, in desperation, I communicated with Safford again and

---
*Lieutenant Laurance F. Safford, USN, one of the pioneers in U.S. Navy codebreaking.
**This refers to the Commandant of the 14th Naval District.

got dispatch orders. I came back, and after a brief leave, we embarked on the Lurline, arriving in Honolulu in early July.

It seems to be my fate to get a job relieving somebody else temporarily while something else happens. A yard communication officer was being detached. When I reported for duty, I was told to go up and relieve him until his regular relief arrived a month or so later.

Q: Your orders were to the Fourteenth Naval District, weren't they?

Captain Dyer: To Commandant Fourteenth Naval District for duty. He was also, of course, Commander Navy Yard. The communication officer was also the issuing officer for the district, so I spent the Fourth of July inventorying and taking over the publication issuing library. That duty was relatively uneventful.

The navy yard was not what one would think of in the same terms as the major yards in Bremerton or Norfolk. It was quite competent to handle the submarines and the other craft that were based there, but it just wasn't as going a concern as it later became.

Q: Would you say it was about on par with the yard at Cavite in the Philippines?

Dyer #4 - 188

Captain Dyer: I never was in the Cavite yard so I don't know. But I imagine, because the Cavite yard did have a few larger ships regularly, that it was a little bit better. I don't know. When the officer who had been ordered to the job of communication officer arrived, he turned out to be one of my Naval Academy roommates. I was only too glad to turn over all the duties to him.

Q: Who was he?

Captain Dyer: Arthur Griese.* I then reported to the chief of staff. He was rather unsympathetic to the idea that had been broached and worked out someway in correspondence between the Chief of Naval Operations and the commandant.

Q: Was Admiral Murfin then the commandant?**

Captain Dyer: No, Admiral Yarnell was the commandant.*** I don't have any criticism of him, but the chief of staff was a bit unsympathetic and said, "Well, you won't have anything to do in that regard, so I am going to make you assistant war plans officer." I was left to inform the chief clerk of the district of that assignment. Quite on my own, I added on the job of

---
*Lieutenant Arthur A. Griese, USN.
**Rear Admiral Orin G. Murfin, USN.
***Rear Admiral Harry E. Yarnell, USN.

assistant communication officer, because I thought I was going to need to make fairly frequent trips out to the intercept station on the other side of the island, which would hardly fit in with the role of war plans officer. However, I was assigned a desk at war plans, an essentially open office. There was very little I could do at that time. I just tried to keep things going.

Sometime during the following winter or early spring, there was a fleet problem. Orders were issued from the Navy Department that the intercept station at Heeia and I should adopt the role of the Japanese intercept station and determine what we could learn about the fleet problem from intercepting the traffic. There was no real question of reading it.

We had some minor successes. We were able to sort out the two opposing forces and things of that kind and to follow some of the operations. And I wrote a report which was turned over to one Jack Redman.* That was one of my few personal contacts with him.

A little later, the district communication officer--his name was Poindexter--was hospitalized with stomach ulcers, so I became acting district communication officer.** Along about June, Ken Ringle, who was the assistant district intelligence officer, received orders, and I wound up with an assignment as assistant

---
*Lieutenant Commander John R. Redman, USN, later vice admiral.
**Lieutenant Commander Gale A. Poindexter, USN.

district intelligence officer.*

Q: Was this combination more to your liking?

Captain Dyer: A little bit. It gave me a chance to work at four offices, each about ten miles from the other. I could always leave word that I'd gone to the next one on the list. It gave me considerable freedom of movement.

Q: I'm surprised the chief of staff wasn't more sympathetic to your pursuits since that assignment had grown out of the discussions between the commandant and the CNO.

Captain Dyer: So was I, but I didn't argue with him.

Q: There must have been a communications gap. Who was the chief of staff?

Captain Dyer: I cannot honestly tell you what his name was now. I should know, but I can't put my finger on it.

Q: Did you get some support when it came to playing the side of the Japanese during that fleet problem?

---

*Lieutenant Kenneth D. Ringle, USN, later rear admiral.

Captain Dyer: No, we were entirely on our own. I mean, we weren't bothered. We were not supported, but we were not handicapped in any way.

Q: Do you think that this unsympathetic attitude was an outgrowth of what you discussed earlier--that there was not an appreciation throughout the fleet of the blue-sky merchants?

Captain Dyer: There was no knowledge of them, really. Sometime along in there--these events get a little twisted up--this intelligence officer, Captain Kilpatrick, became acting chief of staff. He was acting chief of staff at the time I was assigned as assistant intelligence officer.*

Somewhere in the picture, I was a member of a court of inquiry to inquire into some irregularities in the commissary store involving one enlisted man who--well, to make it simple, when his friends would come through the check-out line, he rang up five cents for a dollar item and so forth. I became, for some reason, judge advocate of the ensuing court-martial. That took quite a bit of time.

In the meantime, early in the year, Admiral Murfin had relieved Admiral Yarnell. On orders from the Navy Department practically, an internal vault was built, primarily for the

---

*Captain Walter K. Kilpatrick, USN, later rear admiral.

purpose of housing a Multilith machine to be on standby status for producing publications in case of emergency. The vault was fairly large--about 30 feet by 20 feet, I would say. I had gotten an indication that they were going to send some IBM machines out there. So I, sort of as a moonlight requisition, decided that I would move into the vault, too.

Q: What building was the vault in?

Captain Dyer: It was right off the communication office.

Q: In the district headquarters?

Captain Dyer: In the district headquarters, second floor. I am a little hazy on the exact circumstances, but Admiral Murfin asked me something about what the room was going to be used for, and I said I was going to use it mostly. And not always thinking things through carefully before I opened my mouth, I said something to the effect that I'd come out there a year before at a request of the commandant, and sent out by the Chief of Naval Operations to perform a certain job, and up to that point I had been unable to do it. Admiral Murfin somewhat misinterpreted my intentions and thought that I was complaining because I'd been assigned the assistant district communication officer and assistant intelligence officer and court-martial and this, that, and the other thing. It was very undiplomatic, but the result was good. He relieved me of all extraneous duties.

Q: Which ones were the extraneous ones?

Captain Dyer: The court-marital duty, assistant war plans officer, assistant intelligence officer. While that one has a certain fundamental tie-in, it was still extraneous. I couldn't be down in the post office building and as the intelligence officer do the thing I was sent out there to do. I couldn't be out at the radio station, the main radio station at Wailupe, and do what I was sent out there to do.

Q: Did Admiral Murfin have an understanding at that point of what your role was?

Captain Dyer: I'm not sure that he did really. I'm not sure how cognizant he was of the correspondence that had taken place between Admiral Yarnell and CNO. Nevertheless, I was left alone. I managed to set up not only the vault space with machines, but also another room, which was in back of the legal office and entered only through the legal office. Somewhere about that time, I got my first yeoman assistant.

I mention in passing that while I was acting district

communication officer, Amelia Earhart chose to get lost.* I spent the Fourth of July out at the radio station trying to find some trace of her.

Q: That would be the Fourth of July 1937, wouldn't it?

Captain Dyer: I hope so. That's the date I would put it at. At that time I made the acquaintance of a chief radio electrician in the Coast Guard, Henry M. Anthony, about whom I will have occasion to talk at length later.**

Sometime in the period--probably in '37 or early '38--the first language officer was ordered there, Gill Richardson, who had just completed a language course in Tokyo.*** Somewhere around the same time, the Japanese made another major change in codes. The so-called blue book went out, and a somewhat similar code, which became known as the black book, was put into effect.

Q: Was this the first major change since about '31, '32, when you had first . . .

---

*Amelia Earhart, pioneer woman aviator, was lost about 2 July 1937 near Howland Island in the Pacific while attempting an around-the-world flight in a twin-engine aircraft.
**Henry M. Anthony, chief radio electrician, USCG, was an expert in merchant ship communications and worked on the "maru" codes. He later was commissioned in the Coast Guard.
***Lieutenant Gill M. Richardson, USN, later rear admiral.

Captain Dyer: Actually, that one, although we didn't discover it until late '31, was made in late '29.

Q: Then this was the first major one since.

Captain Dyer: Yes, this was the first major one. And in the intervening years, the code that had come in in '29 had been pretty well recovered, in spite of limited personnel.

Q: Was blue book a U.S. designation for the system?

Captain Dyer: Oh, yes. That's just the color of the binder that it was put in. So was black. Red was the original binder. The ciphers that went into effect with this book were somewhat more sophisticated than the early blue book ciphers. There was a period there when we did not make any entry at all. We were working on it, and Ham Wright was working on it in Washington.* He made the first entry, as it were, but his solution contained a trifling error which I succeeded in straightening out, so at something like 5,000 miles we were able to collaborate and really get firm entry into the basic code.

Q: What means did you use in that collaboration? Couriers?

---

*Lieutenant Wesley A. Wright, USN, who had been on the U.S. Fleet staff in the Pennsylvania while Dyer was a member of ship's company.

Captain Dyer: Message. We had our own crypto system, and which one we were using at the time, I'm not sure.

Q: But it wouldn't be readable by the normal fleet?

Captain Dyer: No, no. Once we had gotten into the structure of the basic code, the solution of the ciphers proceeded fairly rapidly. We fairly rapidly developed a volume of straight code material and were able to work on code solutions.

Q: Were these being key punched both in Washington and Hawaii?

Captain Dyer: Yes. By that time we had set up our IBM machines, and Washington was doing the same thing.

Q: Were there any other libraries of these message files besides those two locations at that point?

Captain Dyer: I can't remember about Cavite. I don't believe they were involved at that point, but they may have been. However, sometime around '39 the Japanese introduced the entirely new and different system, the one that was known as JN-25. And that's what we called it. That was assigned to Cavite and Washington. They kept a hand in it. Our assignment was to continue with the black book, which as long as it was in use, we felt contained probably more of the secret traffic than did the JN-25. I suppose it was about 1940 that they replaced that with a new code, for very limited use. It is usually called the flag officers' code, about which to this day very little is known. The amount of traffic in it was wholly inadequate, but we were assigned that code as a primary mission. I batted my head against a stone wall with very little to work on, I suppose, for about a year; I don't know.

To back up a little bit, there had been a gradual increase in enlisted personnel in the unit, and by that time we had four or five first class and chief petty officers.

Q: Did this unit have a specific name at that point?

Captain Dyer: Not yet. Well, it was Hypo, but then, that merely was the international code for letter H. There were two or three officers ordered there for various lengths of time. About '39, I guess, Gill Richardson, the language officer, was relieved by Tommy Birtley. Sometime during 1940 or '41, Huckins was ordered there.* And sometime in '41, I'm pretty sure, Marine Captain Lasswell.** After the fleet came out, and more or less stayed in Pearl Harbor--I think it was after they arrived there--Ham Wright

---
*Lieutenant Commander Thomas A. Huckins, USN.
**Captain Alva B. Lasswell, USMC.

and Jack Williams were ordered to the fleet staff.*

Q: Which was then under Admiral Richardson.

Captain Dyer: Admiral Richardson, or it might have been after Kimmel relieved.** I don't know. In any event, not having any place over in staff headquarters where they could do anything, they just more or less moved into our office. A few reserves were called to active duty in '41--Willis Thomas, who had been commissioned locally, and sometime in late '41, Luke Dilley.***
In the summer of '41, Rochefort came to relieve Birtley.

When Birtley came to relieve [Gill] Richardson, he being one class senior to me, Birtley became the officer in charge. And when Rochefort relieved Birtley, he was even more senior . . .

Q: About five ahead of you, wasn't he?

Captain Dyer: Five years, yes. That change was without any animosity or friction or anything of that kind.

---
*Lieutenant John A. Williams, USN. Though the fleet was based at ports on the U.S. West Coast, it operated out of Pearl Harbor from the spring of 1940 onward.
**Admiral James O. Richardson, USN, Commander in Chief U.S. Fleet, January 1940-February 1941; Admiral Husband E. Kimmel, USN, Commander in Chief U.S. Fleet, February-December 1941.
***Ensign Willis L. Thomas, USNR; Ensign Luther L. L. Dilley, USNR.

Q: Was that because you had known him earlier and had worked with him?

Captain Dyer: Probably. I might have resented some total stranger coming in and upsetting my apple cart. But I was only interested in getting the job done.

Q: You mention people that came in 1941. Jasper Holmes came during that time also, didn't he?*

Captain Dyer: Yes, but let's put Jasper off for just a minute.

Somehow, I don't know yet how I managed to do it, I wangled it mostly. They were building a new wing on the administration building, and I persuaded the public works people to build a large room in the basement with two time-locked vault doors, air conditioned and so forth, as a future home for us. Washington had said to try to do something about it, but they weren't too much help in writing the commandant and telling him to do it. I don't remember just how we did accomplish it, but we did. One entrance to the basement was a stairway leading from the lanai, or porch, and the other was through two offices.

---

*Lieutenant Wilfred J. Holmes, USN(Ret.), later author of Double-Edged Secrets (Annapolis: Naval Institute Press, 1979).

By this time Admiral Bloch had relieved.* I'm sure he consulted other people, but I don't think he consulted me. Just in passing he said, "They've told me I should have a combat intelligence officer. I think that there's a retired officer out at the University of Hawaii who would seem to fit the bill. What do you think?"

I didn't know Jasper at the time, but I did know that under the name Alec Hudson, he wrote short stories for the Saturday Evening Post. It sounded to me as if he'd be a very good choice. It so happened that when they decided to give him an office, it was the office at the head of our stairway. And he was the combat intelligence officer. So what was more logical than to call the unit that was attached physically to his office in some way the Combat Intelligence Unit? It was a perfect name, in my opinion, because you knew that it would have to be secret. It didn't arouse curiosity.

Q: It was a name that was both accurate and misleading at the same time.

Captain Dyer: Right. As it happened, we never really used that entrance. He went back and forth on the stairs some, I think.

---
*Rear Admiral Claude C. Bloch, USN, who had previously served as four-star Commander in Chief U.S. Fleet from 1938 to 1940, reverted to two stars when he was relieved by Admiral Richardson. He was Commandant of the 14th Naval District and Pearl Harbor Navy Yard from 1940 to 1942.

We absorbed Jasper sort of by a process of osmosis.

Q: Initially he was tracking merchant ship positions.

Captain Dyer: Yes. We set up some facilities down in the basement. He only gradually became aware of what was going on around him.

Q: How would the duties of the combat intelligence officer differ from those of the district intelligence officer who was Captain Mayfield?*

Captain Dyer: The district intelligence officer was concerned with the broad field of intelligence. The combat intelligence officer was concerned only with the tactical movements of an enemy that might be in his area.

Q: Captain Mayfield, I think, was interested in subversion and the loyalty of the indigenous population.

Captain Dyer: All those things. Things of that kind.

Q: In that period in the late 1930s and just before the war, how

---
*Captain Irving H. Mayfield, USN, later rear admiral.

much substantive useful material were you getting from the Japanese codes and how much was just training or preparation?

Captain Dyer: We were getting relatively none. As I said, our primary assignment was the flag officers' code which we weren't able to touch. We had no information, no material on JN-25 which concerned the bulk of Navy traffic. There was a little system that showed up which I now know was used to communicate with the Mandate Islands. Merely as a vacation from frustration, I took that, and it was pretty well under control by the seventh.*

Q: Did you read any Japanese traffic on Amelia Earhart?

Captain Dyer: No, there wasn't any. How would they get it?

Q: Some of the legends have it that the Japanese seized her.

Captain Dyer: I don't believe in legends. She wasn't supposed to go up there. All the indications were that she was flying on a straight course for Christmas or Howland, or whatever the island was down there. I can't remember which island it was. She was heard, until she was fairly close to the island, 50 or 75

---

*This refers to the beginning of hostilities on 7 December 1941.

miles, and then nothing. There's just no way you can convince me that she was a spy. I would rather believe that the 007 was on a spy mission.

Q: That's the plane that the Soviets shot down last week, the Korean airliner.*

Captain Dyer: Yes. And I don't believe that either. But I was not in on it particularly. I was aware of it, but just superficially.

A few days before the attack on Pearl Harbor, the people there were persuaded to turn over to us some traffic which had come through the district intelligence officer.

Q: That was from the RCA office?

Captain Dyer: The RCA office. We had a chief in the office at that time, Woodward, who worked on diplomatic systems.** We had been furnished with diplomatic systems, but had never touched them because prior to the first of December we had no traffic. If we had suddenly decided we would jump off and copy commercial

---

*The Soviet Union attacked and shot down a South Korean commercial aircraft 1 September 1983 while the plane was in Soviet airspace over the Sea of Japan. All 240 passengers and 29 crew members were killed.
**Chief Radioman Farnsley C. Woodward, USN.

traffic circuits, that way lies chaos. You do what you're told to do.

Q: Not to mention the fact that it was illegal.

Captain Dyer: The illegality never bothered me particularly, except from the standpoint of publicity. You had to be very careful about handling them. And so these messages were given to Woodward. I didn't pay any attention. I knew he was having difficulty. He didn't ask me for any help. Finally, on the eighth or the ninth, he got it straightened out and decoded. But I don't think that the things would have been of any world-shaking information had he read them on the fifth or sixth. I doubt if Admiral Kimmel would have done things any differently if he had seen them.

The date of their decoding translation is pretty well established. I could not have done this before, but in one of the Pearl Harbor inquiries where I appeared, I had to take our files over and translate these messages. I was asked, "Who did this?"

I said, "I'm not sure." I took it back and was able to beyond any doubt show that the handwritten translation was made by Finnegan.* Finnegan wasn't even attached to our office until

---
*Lieutenant Joseph Finnegan, USN.

after his ship was sunk. He showed up on the ninth. These were translated on the ninth or tenth. No question. I mean, that's crystal clear.

These things are a little out of order. I have distinctive memories of the "winds" warning message.* We had four relatively new men--they were fresh-caught language officers--that we sent out to the radio station to stand a continuous watch on voice circuits from Tokyo because, from all the indications, it was the voice that was being talked about.

Q: Where was the intercept station?

Captain Dyer: At Heeia, which was on the north coast of the island, a little bit west of Kaneohe. They heard nothing. Most of the testimony as to the actual existence of a "winds" execute message make it a Morse, not a voice transmission. With all due respect to the people who are convinced they had the real thing, I think they were just in error.

Q: Even if they had had the real thing, how much difference would it have made?

---

*Prior to the start of the war, the Japanese sent messages identifying countries by wind direction. The United States was "east wind." These messages were to signal to recipients an imminent break in relations with the nations so indicated.

Captain Dyer: It wouldn't have made any difference that I can see, because if you already know that there is a house on fire, and somebody is standing out in front yelling, "Fire!," it's not helping anything. We knew the Japanese were going to do something, probably before mid-December, but what? Our crystal ball was broken.

Q: And especially the where you didn't know.

Captain Dyer: That was what we didn't know.

Q: You spoke about the frustrations in trying to break this flag officers' code with so few messages. How does one keep his physical and mental well-being in that kind of frustrating situation?

Captain Dyer: That's a question. I had a rather severe case of inflammatory colitis as a result of the frustration. Long before it was popular, I was, as prescribed by my doctor, taking both uppers and downers. He first gave me phenobarbital, and I couldn't keep awake while sitting at my desk. I complained about that, so he gave me some Benzedrine sulphate. I would take that in the morning and phenobarbital at night. Incidentally, they were both at that time recommended for the symptoms I had. They worked pretty well.

As a digression, I continued taking Benzedrine as necessary throughout the war. I thought it would ruin my health, but so what? But I was very cautious with it, maybe one pill at night when on a 24-hour schedule.

Q: In his oral history, Captain Rochefort suggested that you had pills on your desk in a candy dish, so you might address that.

Captain Dyer: That is pure unadulterated fiction. I had nothing on my desk for the benefit of anybody else, or even myself. I did not supply anyone else with them. I did tell one other person about them, and that was a mistake, because he was not careful in their use.

Q: How much could you confide in your wife about what the source of your frustration and problems was?

Captain Dyer: None. My wife did not know until--well, essentially until Kahn's book came out--what I'd been doing.*

Q: That was in the late Sixties. What did she think you had been doing?

---

*David Kahn, The Codebreakers (New York: Macmillan, 1967).

Captain Dyer: She knew I had something to do with communications and that's about all. Maybe I was operating a key and sending Morse.

Q: Do you think that the fact that you were in a group that had a mutual understanding of the problem helped, as opposed to if you had been trying to do this all by yourself?

Captain Dyer: I think so. That pretty well brings us up to the beginning of December.

Q: There are a few things I'd like to go back to. You mentioned the last time that you had not been selected for lieutenant commander the first time. How did you then get selected the second time?

Captain Dyer: When I failed of selection the first time, Admiral Murfin called me down to assure me that failure of selection was not due to any differences of opinion that existed between the two of us. He strongly recommended that I apply and go to sea right away. I had already agreed to extend an additional year at Pearl Harbor, so I didn't choose to follow his advice. I just sweated it out.

They had a peculiar kind of selection going in those days. They had numerous categories. The first time at bat, they selected those who were best fitted for promotion. The second time around, they selected any others that, if they had changed their minds, were best fitted. Then they selected another group who were merely fitted, not best fitted. That group was divided into two categories--fitted and retained, and just fitted. I was fitted and retained. They still didn't think I was best fitted. It shouldn't have surprised me a bit, but then I decided that that would see me through 21 years until 1945, and I'd worry about what to do when that came along.

Q: I think it's ironic that the Navy stood the possibility of losing this valuable expertise that you had, because they didn't know what the expertise was.

Captain Dyer: There isn't any way around that. You can't publish secrets on a billboard. I had to do as I could. After I was selected as fitted and retained, it was suggested that I apply for engineering duty only. I think Safford had previously been selected in that category, and maybe somebody else.

Q: This was still in the line, though, as opposed to Construction Corps, wasn't it?

Captain Dyer: Oh, yes. There always has been--well, not always, but once upon a time there was an Engineer Corps, but it was merged with the line. Then they established a group as engineering duty only. There was no requirement of rotation of sea and shore, and they were not eligible to exercise command, so I persuaded them that I could no longer stand duty in the navy yard. I was going to do only another six or seven years. I wanted to do what I was doing. I had no regrets when I submitted my application. In due course, I got notification that I had been chosen to be in engineering duty only. There was one peculiarity about that. The notification was dated the same day that the board met to select people, not even the day that they submitted the report, which wasn't until ten days later. There was some string-pulling there. Of course, to call us engineering duty officers was a little bit irregular, to say the least.

Q: At least in its normal connotation.

Captain Dyer: It wasn't what the category was intended to embrace.

Q: Do you think you had some powerful patron there that was helping you along?

Captain Dyer: I'm pretty sure. I think I did write to Admiral Ingersoll, who was in the CNO's office at the time, and told him I would appreciate any assistance he could give to the cause, because he knew that I had been engaged in this specialty.* He had been on the staff in my earlier moment of glory, and he always continued to be a very good friend. As a matter of fact, I think that possibly McClaran was there again.** I think somebody got to the secretary; and I'm sure the secretary didn't know me.

Q: What were the living conditions like in Hawaii then? Was that a sought-after duty station?

Captain Dyer: As it is today, the cost of living was relatively high. On the other hand, living was very pleasant there. A lot of people liked it very much. We were very happy with it.

Q: Was that a factor at all in your EDO decision?

Captain Dyer: No.

Q: Had you gone back into the fleet at that point, would it have been in a non-communication billet?

Captain Dyer: Yes, undoubtedly.

---
*Rear Admiral Royal E. Ingersoll, USN, who had previously served with Dyer on the Battle Fleet staff.
**Commander John W. McClaran, USN.

Q: Probably exec of a destroyer or something like that?

Captain Dyer: Something of that kind. It was a very pleasant thing. Our daughter was born out there.* Sometime before the war we decided we would probably be there for a number of years, so we got our courage up to buy a house. We bought a house about a year and a half before the war started. When the war came along and we missed the first flurry of the evacuation of dependents, I was able to sit down and write a letter and say, "You can't evacuate us; we live here."

Q: That's what Jasper Holmes was able to pull.

Captain Dyer: Several other people did the same thing.

Q: I'd be interested in your impressions of the various commandants you served under during that prewar period--Yarnell, Murfin, and Bloch.

Captain Dyer: Yarnell I was with a very short time, but he impressed me very favorably. My feelings on Orin Murfin are rather divided. He was not, I didn't think, all that some people thought he was. He had his very good points. He was

---
*Ann Leilani Dyer, born 27 February 1940.

approachable. Of course, I was not close enough to his administration of command, really, in a broad sense, to judge him.

Q: What about his personality? What do you recall in that regard?

Captain Dyer: Rather negative. I did not originate the comment that he was the "littlest S.O.B. in the Navy." As a matter of fact, I didn't think it was deserved. On the other hand, I was not unhappy to see him leave.

Q: Did he have some of the tendencies of a sundowner?*

Captain Dyer: No. A sundowner you can respect because he is so hard-boiled. I may be doing him an injustice, but he seemed to be more niggling.

Claude Bloch I had known when he was captain of the California. I had a great liking for him personally. I think some of the historians have given him just a little bit of a raw deal in that.** While he had responsibilities for defense and so

---

*"Sundowner" is an unreasonably strict officer. The term originated from the requirement that officers be back aboard ship before sundown.
**This is a reference to criticisms in the wake of the 1941 Japanese attack on Pearl Harbor.

forth, it was all laid down very clearly when the commander in chief was there that the commander in chief was boss.* The commandant was just one of his underlings.

Q: It was a very awkward situation in that Bloch had been commander in chief and previously senior to these fellows.

Captain Dyer: That's right. But I don't believe that he stood on prerogatives of seniority, "I was there first, and I know more than you do." I think he would have been a loyal subordinate.

Q: How much interchange was there between the district staff and the fleet staff?

Captain Dyer: That I don't know.

Q: I gather that Rochefort and Layton were pretty close. Did you have that kind of exchange with fleet people?

Captain Dyer: No, that's something that--that kind of thing is done by the top man, not by one of his underlings. I probably talked to Germany Curts, who was the fleet communication officer, twice before the war.** When they moved ashore, they were over

---
*Admiral Husband E. Kimmel, USN, Commander in Chief Pacific Fleet, was senior to the district commandant.
**Commander Maurice E. Curts, USN.

next to the submarine base a couple of miles from where we were. Wright and Williams belonged to them, but I don't know when, if ever, they ceased to belong to one place or the other. I saw Layton very seldom, even though he was someone I had been close to at times. I put in long hours and exhausting hours.

Q: At what point did the pace really begin to pick up in terms of hours?

Captain Dyer: About 1938, '37, whenever the black book went in. The yeomen and I worked out there a great many Saturdays and things like that in overtime.

Q: Was that just your organization or was that the whole base?

Captain Dyer: Just us.

Q: Was there the idea then of the imminence of war?

Captain Dyer: Not that early, no. We just felt it was highly important that we try to get the thing under control. There was indication of tension between the United States and Japan, but I mean, one can't date these things. For instance, when did the

Panay incident happen?*

Q: That was late '37, I think.

Captain Dyer: From then on, anybody was foolish to think that there weren't problems. That just about covers the prewar period, I think, unless you have another question.

Q: Was there any thought, since the Chinese were fighting the Japanese at that point, of giving crypto aid to the Chinese?

Captain Dyer: I wouldn't know that. I doubt it very sincerely. The only one I knew of who was willing to give crypto aid to the Chinese was Herbert Yardley.**

Q: Who was fired by the State Department.

Captain Dyer: He was the Black Chamber. And he was out looking

---

*The U.S. Navy gunboat Panay was attacked and sunk by Japanese aircraft 12 December 1937 while anchored in the Yangtze River about 30 miles from Nanking, China. The Japanese Government claimed the neutral gunboat was mistaken for a Chinese troop carrier and apologized for the incident on 23 December.

**Herbert O. Yardley was a Department of State code clerk who planned and won approval in 1919 for a permanent Department of State organization to study codes and ciphers. The organization was known as "The American Black Chamber." Yardley lost his position in 1929 when the Black Chamber was closed by Secretary of State Stimson. Yardley went on to write The American Black Chamber (Indianapolis: Bobbs-Merrill, 1931).

for a buck.

Q: According to Rochefort, he was not well respected by professional cryptanalysts.

Captain Dyer: That's right. He was not great. Even Friedman, who had worked with him some, didn't have a very good opinion of him.

Q: What do you recall about the events leading right up to the war?

Captain Dyer: Well, I've already mentioned the diplomatic traffic from RCA. But there was very little leading right up to the war. I guess an interesting tale of how I happened to be present at the war's beginning does belong in here.

Our son was taking piano lessons and was having his first recital on the night of the fifth. I couldn't miss that, but I had the duty that night. So I swapped with the officer having the duty on the night of the fourth. Then some friends called us up. They were having a Hawaiian farewell party for their parents who were leaving on the Lurline sometime the fifth or sixth. Could we come? So I made another swap from the night of the fourth to the night of the sixth. And at that time, we had one officer and one enlisted man on duty at night. We were manning the office seven days a week. So Tony Ethier, who was a second class radioman, and I had the duty on the night of the sixth.*

I have previously mentioned the Mandate cipher that I'd been working on for a time. I was doing very well with it, and so I just sat at my desk and kept on working. There were a couple of perfectly good beds there; we could sleep if we chose, just as long as we were there. But I decided it was too late to bother going to bed, so I kept on working.

Somewhere around 6:00 in the morning, we got a message from the communication office, giving us a message from the Ward saying that he'd sunk a submarine off the entrance.** It was none of my business, but I called up the communication office, where I knew there was a rather fresh-caught reserve on duty, and checked to make sure that the message had gone to the commandant. It puzzled me. Along about 7:00 o'clock, I decided to go over to the little Greek restaurant, have some breakfast, and then come back. I had ridden out with the navy yard duty officer, and since he expected to go home shortly after 8:00 o'clock, I expected to go home shortly after 8:00 o'clock.

I got back about 7:30 and sat down at my desk to pile up the

---
*Henry E. "Tony" Ethier later became a commissioned officer.
**The destroyer Ward (DD-139) was patrolling the entrance to Pearl Harbor early on the morning of 7 December. The ship sighted a conning tower of a midget submarine and attacked with gunfire and depth charges, sinking the submarine about 0645.

papers, getting ready to go home. Our office in the basement was relatively soundproof since there were no outer windows, but I heard some explosions. My first thought was that they were antiaircraft guns. I said, "What's the Army shooting for today?" And then there was a louder explosion. I said, "My god, that sounds like the 14-inch guns out at Fort Kamehameha." I never even suspected the real answer.

Just then Chief Woodward came down from the outside and said, "There are planes flying around and they're dropping things." I thought I'd better go see what kind of planes there were dropping what kinds of things. I went up and looked around the corner of the building. About 300 yards away, at an altitude of about 200 feet, was a torpedo plane in a tight bank, a tight turn, and the rising suns were shining right at me. I caught on fast.

I went down and called Rochefort and asked if he'd heard the news. He said, "What news?"

I said, "We're at war."

He said, "What do you mean?"

I said, "We're being bombed out here right now." I never encountered anyone any calmer than he was.

He said, "All right, I'll be right out."

Q: Out from where?

Captain Dyer: He was in town eight miles away. He hadn't

intended to come out since it was Sunday. Exercising the prerogatives of command, he wasn't going to come out that day, but he did.

Q: I take it you're using that term "command" facetiously. That wasn't truly a command, was it?

Captain Dyer: Not really, but he was the officer in charge. There is a difference in being officer in charge and being in command.

Q: He was still the head guy.

Captain Dyer: He was the head guy. And he showed up before long. I didn't know what had happened to the navy yard duty officer. I couldn't locate him. I was getting kind of tired after 26 hours, 28 hours.

Q: You mentioned that you had stayed up all night. Did you often get engrossed in your work and lose track of time?

Captain Dyer: Oh, yes. I was known to do that when I was in destroyers. A cryptogram is just a problem for exercise. During the fleet problem, when we did so well, there was one period when I went about 90 hours straight through.

Q: So despite the colitis, it sounds as if you were blessed with a good deal of stamina.

Captain Dyer: Yes. Anyway, along about 11:00 o'clock, Holtwick decided to go to the radio station on the other side of the island.* Since he had to go through town, I thumbed a ride. He had to go about a mile and a half from where I lived. I got home about 11:30 or 12:00 o'clock.

Q: What was Holtwick's position in the organization?

Captain Dyer: I thought I had gotten him in. He had come out sometime during '41, I guess, just to be one of the troops. I was just one of the troops too, except I was the number two in the seniority. That gave me some little something or other. He was one of the prewar troops. He had been at Cavite, and, before that at the Navy Department.

Q: Did people in the organization tend to develop specialties rather than being interchangeable?

Captain Dyer: Not too much. Well, yes, I'll take that back. There was the broad division into cryptanalysts and traffic

---

*Lieutenant Jack S. Holtwick, Jr., USN.

analysts.

Q: Was there also the division between language officers and non-language officers?

Captain Dyer: Language was definitely a specialty. Of course, to be good, they had to at least develop into cryptanalysts of sorts. But Huckins and Williams were traffic analysts.

Q: It might be helpful if you'd explain what a traffic analyst does.

Captain Dyer: A traffic analyst is a person who tries to derive intelligence from the body of traffic, short of reading it. He may deal with call signs, trying to identify call signs and units. He makes judgments based on the quantity of traffic and the routing of traffic. And he can provide a certain amount of valid intelligence and very valuable intelligence at any time when cryptanalysis is ineffective.

Q: Are there ways that the body of traffic can be masked in the same way that a code can be masked, say, by sending dummy messages to create a false impression of traffic patterns?

Captain Dyer: It can be, but usually it is not very successful.

I think it's fairly well authenticated that the Japanese did attempt to do that by taking radio operators from some of their carriers, putting them at shore stations around the Inland Sea [of Japan] and have them carry on traffic which was supposed to simulate the normal traffic of the attack force, the kido butai or the carrier squadrons. I've heard it disputed that they didn't do it. I think they did. But it was unsuccessful, perhaps because of the frequencies they used. In any case, we never intercepted it.

Q: The reason they used fleet people was because someone's touch on key was supposedly as distinctive as a voice.

Captain Dyer: Some of the operators were. In fact, there was quite a bit of experimental work done right before and in the early part of the war on what was called "radio fingerprinting." But they never were able to get it down to a very scientific basis. But it's true that a really experienced intercept operator could recognize certain operators.

Q: Did you spend any time at all in traffic analysis yourself?

Captain Dyer: For all intents and purposes, none. It didn't interest me.

Q: You hadn't proved particularly adept at it even in your own Navy . . .

Captain Dyer: In the fleet problem, when the three of us worked together, Safford handled the traffic analysis and Rochefort and I worked on the cryptanalysis.

Q: You told me earlier you had not succeeded in becoming a successful Morse sender and receiver.

Captain Dyer: Not successful is pretty good understating it. I was a very poor operator.

Q: Were there any recriminations against your organization for not being able to predict that the Japanese would attack Pearl Harbor when they did?

Captain Dyer: You know that just as well as I do. There was nothing directly against the Pearl Harbor unit. Of course, a lot of ignorant galoots said, "Why didn't they do this?" or "Why didn't they know that?" I cannot agree with Rochefort, who makes quite a case for the fact that he thought, as an officer, he was a failure if he didn't produce a lot of intelligence. I do not think an intelligence officer, or cryptanalyst, or anyone else, is the seventh son of the seventh son or has a crystal ball. If a thing is logically available and you fail to get it, then some blame attaches.

That is one of the minor criticisms I have with Costello's recent article in the Proceedings.* He says that since the change in the JN-25, as moderate as it was, was made the first of December and that knowing as much as we did about it, we should have been back in in time to produce intelligence before the seventh. That was a period of peacetime traffic, not wartime traffic, with a limited volume. Even if we had had a copy of the Japanese codebook itself, it's doubtful if you would have been able, before the seventh of December, to produce anything but the merest fragments, because the cipher stood between us and that. You cannot attack a cipher until you have a reasonably large volume of messages. So that is a very unfair criticism.

Sometime later in the war, on two or three occasions when there was a change, the question came to me from Admiral Nimitz, "When do you think you'll be back in?"**

And I would always have to say, if it was a cipher change, "If nothing goes wrong, we may be back in as soon as three weeks." If there was a code change, I'd have to double that to maybe six weeks.

---

*John E. Costello, "Remember Pearl Harbor," U.S. Naval Institute Proceedings, September 1983, pages 53-62.
**Admiral Chester W. Nimitz, USN, Commander in Chief Pacific Fleet.

Q: It's interesting that at the beginning of your existence as a codebreaker, you were not known to anyone, and later it was taken for granted that you were supposed to perform miracles.

Captain Dyer: Well, President Roosevelt, I believe, is the one who nicknamed the diplomatic traffic "Magic."* That is too much the way that laity--and by laity I include a lot of people who ought to know better--view this. They don't think it's a scientific process of analysis and dealing with cause and effect and all that kind of garbage. They think that it's something that you can--well, if you have a sixth sense, you can do it. A lot of people still think that whatever success I may have had was not due to a lot of hard work, but some kind of intuitive reasoning.

Q: Do you think that there are some people who have an innate gift for this sort of work?

Captain Dyer: Yes. I mentioned Commander Henry Anthony a while ago.** I'll get to him sooner or later, but he worked for me during the war. Along about the latter half of the war, the Coast Guard wanted him back. They kept pressuring us to release

---
*"Magic" was the code word assigned to the project to decode intercepted Japanese diplomatic messages.
**Lieutenant Commander Henry M. Anthony, USCG.

him. Finally the question came through, "How long will it take for you to train a relief for Commander Anthony?"

And I said, "How long would you like to take to train a relief for Jose Iturbi?"*

Q: Fifteen, 20 years.

Captain Dyer: And innate ability.

Q: How much would you assign to ability, to hard work, and to luck? What proportions would you figure?

Captain Dyer: That's almost impossible to do. You're often without any of these elements and to them you have to add one more, extreme patience. You cannot run before you walk. You have to take things one step at a time. The ability to see things--I think that is largely--oh, I don't know what you would call it. Not intuition. But I've tried to tell people that if you observe something long enough, you'll see something peculiar. If you can't see something peculiar, if you stare long enough, then that in itself is peculiar. And then you try to explain why the peculiarity.

---

*Jose Iturbi was an internationally renowned classical pianist and conductor.

Q: Do you go along with Captain Rochefort's contention that codebreakers are peculiar people?

Captain Dyer: For a good part of the war, there was a cartoon tacked up behind my desk with a very weird looking character. And it said, "You don't have to be crazy to work here, but it helps a hell of a lot." Yes, I think all really successful cryptanalysts are a little bit odd, to say the least.

Q: You described the frustration involved in not being able to break a code. How would you describe the exhilaration when you do get a breakthrough?

Captain Dyer: Almost in sexual terms. Physiologically it's not the same, but the emotional feeling is pretty much the same.

Q: I hadn't heard that comparison made before.

Captain Dyer: Maybe it's original. I don't know.

Q: I interviewed John Thach, with whom you served briefly.* As a fighter pilot, he said he could admire a skilled Japanese fighter pilot even though he was on the opposite side. Did you

---

*Admiral John S. Thach, USN (Retired), subject of a two-volume Naval Institute oral history.

have that sense of admiration for the Japanese in being able to pull off a surprise as big as Pearl Harbor, even when we were reading some of their codes?

Captain Dyer: I don't think so, because if you set out to do something like that, the ocean is a hell of a big place. If you can avoid the physical compromise of your plans, I don't think getting the carriers across the Pacific, taking the northern route, is a particularly great feat. The whole concept of the whole plan was rather skillfully put together, but I think that anyone who is willing to ignore the rules of doing things can probably get by with something like that very easily.

Q: What is your opinion of John Toland's claims that the Allied nations were tracking the carrier task force and withholding that information from Pearl Harbor?

Captain Dyer: I think that John Toland has got rocks in his head. I had a fair amount of respect for him for his original, earlier book The Rising Sun.* But I haven't read Infamy, so my critique of it is, to say the least, biased.** But things I have seen cited and quoted--one article says that one of Toland's

---

*John Toland, The Rising Sun: The Decline and Fall of the Japanese Empire: 1936-1945 (New York: Random House, 1970).
**John Toland, Infamy: Pearl Harbor and Its Aftermath (New York: Doubleday and Company, 1982).

claims is being dropped from the paperback edition because apparently even he has decided that it won't stand up.

We had 30 or so very highly trained and skilled operators at Pearl Harbor and another 20 or so at Guam, another bunch in Cavite. It does not seem at all reasonable that all those trained people, who when they were on watch usually used two receivers to cover that much more territory, could miss it and some guy, on a commercial steamer proceeding from San Francisco to Oahu, not only could hear the chatter of a Japanese task force, which according to every Japanese source, was maintaining the strictest kind of radio silence, but also could take bearings on them.

The only way that you can make any sense out of Toland's argument is that all the radio operators in Heeia and all the rest of the people in Pearl Harbor and our direction finder were in on a plot. A conspiracy of that kind just can't work. Not only that, but just where he was on his way from San Francisco to Hawaii, I don't know, but he said it was up in the northwest. Assuming that he heard anything, maybe the people that I spoke about earlier who were doing the dummy traffic around the Inland Sea--maybe he heard some other Japanese radio stations. If you look at a great circle chart or a globe, draw a line from anywhere en route from San Francisco to Hawaii, you will find that the great circle between the two points runs up to the northwest, and probably was about where the task force was advancing. Doesn't prove a thing. And, according to Toland, some guy over on Constitution Avenue pointed to a chart on a wall in naval intelligence, to show a foreign officer where the Japanese were. If he did, he must have had a better crystal ball than we did, because there was no reasonable source of such intelligence.

Q: Would it have been likely that a U.S. officer privy to that information would have shared it with the Dutch?

Captain Dyer: I don't think so. I saw something in there about Singapore being farther along, and the British being farther along. One of Singapore's top officers worked with me at Pearl Harbor for a couple of years and then in Washington afterwards.[*] He never in the slightest way indicated that they could have tipped us off on anything or that they knew anything we didn't know. If they did, I don't know how they did, because there is no indication that there was really anything in JN-25. There were no dispatches sent. So how do you get anything out of it?

Lewin doesn't seem to think that the revisionists have anything to stand on.[**] Prange doesn't seem to think they have anything to stand on.[***] And as far as Costello will go is that

---
[*]Malcolm Burnette.
[**]Ronald Lewin, The American Magic: Codes, Ciphers and the Defeat of Japan (New York: Farrar Straus Giroux, 1982).
[***]Gordon W. Prange, At Dawn We Slept: The Untold Story of Pearl Harbor (New York: McGraw-Hill, 1981).

there might have been some inferences from something. There might have been, but I still don't think that the Monday morning quarterback wins very many football games.

Q: That's right. You mentioned the people in the outlying stations such as Guam and Cavite. Was there any concern that they might be captured by the Japanese and be tortured and reveal what they knew about the system?

Captain Dyer: Yes, and the people on Guam were captured. They spent practically the entire war as prisoners. One of them from Guam--I can't think of his name--was a prisoner of war. I know it perfectly well, but I can't think of it. He attained the rank of captain. I saw him at the dedication of the "On the Roof Gang" memorial.

Q: Had he been an enlisted man before that?

Captain Dyer: Yes. There were two of the "On the Roof Gang" who were enlisted men who became captains. Harold E. Joslin.*

Q: Was the level of knowledge that these people had kept low because they might be captured?

---

*The two were Captain Harold E. Joslin, USN, and Captain Prescott H. Currier, USN.

Captain Dyer: We didn't give them any more than we had to. That's the old doctrine of "need to know." But they managed, all of them, to keep their mouths shut.

Q: So the Japanese must not have known what they had.

Captain Dyer: No, apparently they didn't, or our men probably would have had a much rougher time than they did have, which was bad enough.

Q: What can you say about Captain Rochefort's role as a leader in your group as the war began?*

Captain Dyer: He was outstanding. But his really outstanding quality was as an intelligence analyst. What he was taking was, after all, frequently fragmentary information and arriving at a correct analysis of what it said and what it meant.

Actually, we didn't see too much of each other those first six months of the war. I said I went home on the seventh since the islands had been blacked out. I didn't even attempt to go back until the early morning of the eighth. That started what you might call a watch and watch proposition, theoretically 24 on and 24 off. I would go in in the morning and stay until the next

---

*Commander Joseph J. Rochefort, USN, officer in charge, Combat Intelligence Unit.

morning. Instead of going home when he showed up, we would overlap for four or five hours. But I had my nose buried in what I was doing and he had his buried in what he was doing, and we were at the opposite ends of the basement. We'd occasionally see each other, but only occasionally, casually. That was the watch schedule for the two of us. He may have put in a little more time than I did, because he did sleep down in the basement occasionally. He had a cot. I didn't.

Q: How much did people do as individuals and how much required teamwork?

Captain Dyer: The nature of the problem, without going into any technical details, was such that once you had a start on the solution, it was largely a question of individual effort. There was just no way that two people could work together. On some things Wright and I did work together, but in general the original cipher called for trying to reconstruct 50,000 five-digit numeral groups.* This was the technique you had to use. You got one at a time, whoever you were, whether a brilliant mathematician or a member of the California band.

Q: Why do you think the California band was adept at this kind

---
*Lieutenant Commander Wesley A. Wright, USN.

of work?

Captain Dyer: Well, there seems to be a certain affinity between musical ability and cryptanalytic ability. If there is, I am the great exception that proves the rule.

Q: But that was really just a fortuitous coincidence, wasn't it, discovering that?

Captain Dyer: Yes. All Rochefort was after when he acquired the California band was manpower. Some of the band members had had some typing experience, for instance, or other experience that seemed to qualify them as key punch operators in the machine room. Some of them spent a lot of time in the machine room. Others did other things. When Rochefort came and told me we had just gotten the band, complete with bandmaster, I said, "I figure we can use the band at labor of some kind, but what are we going to do with the bandmaster?" But the bandmaster wound up the war as a commissioned officer. And after the war, he got a pretty good job at IBM out in Gaithersburg, [Maryland].

Q: Did you have to get a substantial amount of new equipment to accommodate the volume of traffic?

Captain Dyer: It was gradual, because there was no source of equipment of that kind in the islands. It was pretty specialized equipment.

Q: You can't get that on a midnight requisition, so how do you explain to the supply system what you need and why you need it?

Captain Dyer: You didn't have to go through them. I don't know now who we did go through. I think Washington placed the order with IBM and it was shipped out. That was true of the original equipment.

Q: How much touch did you keep with the U.S. forces' operational picture, or did you need to know that at all?

Captain Dyer: Only as it might affect you in code solution. By and large, I would say, throughout the war, what I knew about U.S. operations was what I could read in the Honolulu Advertiser. It's not strictly true, but it comes close.

Q: Was that because you didn't have a need to know?

Captain Dyer: There are only 24 hours in a day. You take out a very minimum for eating and sleeping, and it still doesn't leave very much. Trying to do a job that 32 hours a day would not have been enough, you don't have time to waste on unessential things.

Q: I assume you were at least mildly curious as to how things were going.

Captain Dyer: Oh, yes. At Guadalcanal we got some reports of what was going on there, but so did the <u>Advertiser</u>. And sometimes we would get something to remind us of operations. There is a soroban over on that lacquered chest of drawers that belonged to the paymaster on Kwajalein. Somebody in our outfit landing out there was thoughtful enough to bring it to me.

Q: Is soroban the Japanese for abacus?

Captain Dyer: That's right. It's different from the Chinese abacus.

Q: I'm not a connoisseur, so you'll have to explain the difference.

Captain Dyer: The Chinese abacus has five buttons where this has four and two buttons where this has one. This is a much faster thing than the Chinese abacus in the hands of an expert, which I am not.

Q: In his oral history, Admiral Layton described the Wake Island fiasco, the relief expedition coming back, as an even greater

Dyer #4 - 238

tragedy than the Pearl Harbor attack. Was there a feeling in your basement group about that?

Captain Dyer: I don't remember that there was. We hoped that they could be relieved, that they could be saved. If you're completely saturated in a problem, you think that problem is important to the exclusion of all else. Holmes used to put out a daily file of translations. My one indulgence, a little later, was that I used to try to read through it every day, or at least thumb through it. I didn't read them all, just enough to see how we were doing.

Q: When you're concentrating so exclusively on something like that, what becomes of the normal everyday concerns--like whether you've got holes in your shoes or the washing machine is working or things like that?

Captain Dyer: I think the washing machine continued to work. I don't remember having holes in my shoes. I always said my ambition was to get the war over and throw my shoes away, but I'm afraid I haven't ever done it.

Q: So you didn't concern yourself with nonessentials very much?

Captain Dyer: Of course, you have to do something once in a

Dyer #4 - 239

while to relax. We had a Christmas dinner, even in '41.

Q: Are there any other highlights or milestones from that winter of '41-'42 that you want to mention?

Captain Dyer: The second attack on Pearl Harbor. I was home that night. About 2:00 o'clock in the morning, there was a rather loud explosion. It was the fourth of March '42. A single Japanese plane had come over, as near as we could tell, to see if it could. It had dropped its bombs up in a valley about a mile and a half from where we lived. Naturally we both sat bolt upright. My wife said, "That sounds like the real thing."

I said, "Never mind, we'll go on back to sleep."

I had to wait until the next day to find out what had happened. That was the first operation, which has been mentioned elsewhere, in which the Japanese refueled their plane from a submarine at French Frigate Shoal. It was referred to as the AK operation, AK being Pearl Harbor.* That was pretty well established by that time. There was another one planned for later. Some way we managed to have a minesweeper or something at French Frigate Shoal, so the submarine couldn't come up and get in there. We aborted that.

---

*For more on this attack of 4 March 1942, see W.J. Holmes, Double-Edged Secrets (Annapolis: Naval Institute Press, 1979), pages 59-61.

It was about that time that we started hearing some reference to AF.

Q: We're about at the end of the tape, so maybe we can save that story for the next time.

Interview Number 5 with Captain Thomas H. Dyer, U.S. Navy (Retired)

Place: Captain Dyer's cottage, Sykesville, Maryland

Date: Wednesday, 14 September 1983

Subject: Biography

Interviewer: Paul Stillwell

Q: Captain, the last time you had just brought us up to the point where the code letters AF had been discovered in the Japanese communications. Would you pick it up then, please?

Captain Dyer: There has been a lot of misinformation about the Japanese geographical code. Several people were uninformed and claimed that it was a grid type of thing, and it was not. It was more an area type where the letters were assigned rather indiscriminately, sometimes suggested by the geographical location, sometimes not. The A area was the Central Pacific, including the Hawaiian Islands, Midway, and thereabouts.

When the Japanese started talking about AF, the first mention of it, as I remember, was one ship deciding it would need some radio crystals before the AF operation, which, of course, could have meant almost anything. But from various things that had occurred, there was little doubt in the minds of people at FRUPac that AF was Midway.* There was some argument about elsewhere,

---

*FRUPac--Fleet Radio Unit, Pacific.

but as the Japanese talked more and more about AF *sakusen*, AF operation, it became rather clear that the object was Midway. I recall an incident of a Japanese plane reporting a sighting of some kind south of AF. We were able to identify that, but not so conclusively that the doubters were put to rest.

There is in my mind a little bit of uncertainty as to who concocted the stratagem to determine once and for all if AF was Midway. Actually, I did not know about it in advance. The strategy consisted of using the submarine cable to Midway to tell the commander there to send back by radio, in plain language, a message that his evaporators had broken down and they were running short of fresh water. My first knowledge of the matter was when I was decoding something and came across the Japanese message reporting the Midway message. And I said, "Those stupid so-and-sos, why did they send this in plain language?" not knowing that they'd been told to. It was a ruse, but nevertheless, they did send it and it did pinpoint the fact that AF was Midway.

Q: Jasper Holmes claims credit for that strategy in his book.*

Captain Dyer: It's possible that he did. Or Rochefort did. I don't know.

---

*W.J. Holmes, *Double-Edged Secrets* (Annapolis: Naval Institute Press, 1979), page 90.

Q: Rochefort sort of pooh-poohs it in his oral history, so it would probably be unlikely that he came up with it.

Captain Dyer: Well, whoever. It was one time when a little deception did work, which was seldom the case. It was hard at the time to follow the development of the information as to the scope of the operation against Midway. The best that can be said is that it gradually became clear from messages that there was a massive operation involving four carriers and a landing force and that the commander in chief in the Yamato was probably accompanying in some way. There was also talk of an operation of sorts in the Aleutians.

I cannot remember what the code designation was, but apparently at the time there was a very strong feeling in Washington that a major operation was against the Aleutians or against someplace like Seattle, rather than Midway. And there was no doubt in the minds of Rochefort and other people acquainted with it that the operation was aimed primarily at Midway. The information was told to Admiral Nimitz, and he acted on it with determination, getting the Yorktown back from the Battle of the Coral Sea and getting some four months' repairs made in something like three days.

There is one aspect of the thing that I believe Holmes gives me some credit for. And I am entirely innocent. There was an internal time and day code that had appeared only three times in the traffic. One night--I do know this very well--Ham Wright and Joe Finnegan worked all night trying various and sundry things, and finally hit upon the systematic structure of the day code and were able to determine the date.

I'll say in passing that often one of the most difficult things to determine is a future date. Past dates are relatively simple. This was not only a brilliant piece of work on the part of Wright and Finnegan, but also it was of great good fortune that the structure of the code was such that it was possible to reconstruct the entire cable from fragmentary evidence. Had it been an entirely random proposition, there was no way at all you could have done that. And until that was done, the supposition was that the operation was scheduled for a little later than was actually the case.

There was another great piece of good luck. Messages had been intercepted directing the replacement of the JN-25 code and cipher on the first of April. But as the first of April came around, distribution difficulties caused the Japanese to postpone that to the first of May. On the first of May, they were still faced with troubles. What the successive postponements were I don't remember, but the change was made finally on the 25th of May. By that time, the operation orders for the assault, which had been issued, were in our hands. No doubt, the history of the Pacific War would have been entirely different if the Japanese had succeeded in changing their code on either the first of April or the first of May.

There is very little that I can say about the Battle of Midway. We were all on tenterhooks until word had been received that contact had been made. The night after the battle, I came across a message in a tactical code that I was then working on. It said, "Line fleet operation order number so-and-so, the Midway operation is..." And then--blank. I worked for hours trying to fill in the blank, without success. Almost any word you could think of would fit--"cancelled" or "continued" or "suspended" or "postponed." It was not until about a year after the war, when I was reading a report of the strategic bombing survey, that I ran across that particular message. The word was "cancelled."

Q: How much chance did you get to compare things that you had worked on at the time with the actual messages later?

Captain Dyer: There probably could have been a great deal more of that than there was. It involved a terrific amount of work to go back and dig things out of the files and try to dig things out of the bombing survey, that sort of thing. Very little of it was actually done.

Q: Was there any purpose in doing it other than just curiosity?

Captain Dyer: There didn't seem to at the time, and as I look back, I don't see anything to be gained by it now.

Q: Why was it harder to get a future date than a past one?

Captain Dyer: You have nothing to hang it on. If a ship is sunk or attacked or anything of that kind, or some operation takes place on a past date you're able to establish, it's easy to assume that any message concerning that is going to have a date around that time. If something is a month from now, and there is a purely arbitrary code group for the date--oddly enough, the code had a complete table of dates. I think, and this is only a guess, that it was for purposes of internal rather than external security, that they used both place and date code, because they didn't want people in lower echelons in the Japanese Navy to know when or where something was going to happen.

Q: Are you basing that supposition on the idea that they were supremely confident that we were not reading their messages?

Captain Dyer: I see no other real purpose for introducing this additional operation, because they had all the place names that they needed in the code. The coding and decoding would normally be done by lower echelon personnel, possibly in some cases by enlisted personnel or junior officers. These two salient facts could be filled in only by somebody in the higher echelons.

That's a surmise, but it's the only thing that makes sense to me as to why they bothered.

Q: You have praised Captain Rochefort for his analytical abilities. Wasn't this really the high point of it all, his being able to predict in early 1942 essentially the course that the Japanese would take?

Captain Dyer: He did not attempt to predict very much, unless he had something in the way of concrete evidence to base the prediction on. It might be very fragmentary. But that was his ability--to make a silk purse out of a sow's ear. The early messages about Coral Sea, the early messages about Midway, were perfectly capable of being read in a totally different way than the correct way. Knowledge of the character of the Japanese and this, that, and the other, enabled him to get the right meaning.

Q: In his book, Captain Holmes has one particularly descriptive passage about you.* I think it's typical of him that he is able to exemplify something with a particular incident. He describes you coming out of the basement, unshaven, your hair long, your uniform rumpled, looking very tired. And a man from the Yorktown said of you, "There's a chap that needs to get to sea

---

*See Double-Edged Secrets, page 95.

and be straightened out." And Holmes said if he only knew what you had been going through. That was a case where there was not the knowledge, not the understanding on the part of the very people who were being supported. What had you gone through at that point?

Captain Dyer: I am inclined to take Holmes's description as a bit apocryphal. If it happened, I never knew when it happened or anything about it.

Q: Could it have happened?

Captain Dyer: It could have. I believe he ties that with the search for the date group, which I didn't take part in. But that's neither here nor there.

Q: Was your routine essentially as he described it, that you would go for long periods without sleep, without shaving, without haircuts, etc?

Captain Dyer: I think that there's a little poetic license there. From Pearl Harbor to Midway and a little later, Rochefort and I theoretically alternated day on and day off. We were living in Honolulu, and going back and forth at nighttime in the blackout was suicidal, to say the least. Theoretically, it was

24-on and 24-off. But in practice, it was more likely 25-26 on, and 18 to 20 off. During the stretch that I had at Pearl, I never slept a single night. There were cots there. I could have taken a few minutes, but I didn't choose to. I did not work quite the long hours that legend has it, but I did put in about 24-26 hours sitting at my desk pretty substantially the entire time. I carried a lunchbox with me--a couple of sandwiches. Even after Midway, to make things work domestically, at least once a week, if not more often, I would stay out there for 24-28 hours and work right through. Part of the reason for that was so I could go home and my wife could have the car to go grocery shopping. Silly, but you have to eat.

Q: When you'd come to the end of one of those 24-28 hour stretches, could you notice a reduction in your own sharpness and ability to cope with the material?

Captain Dyer: Not particularly, because throughout the war I continued the rather careful and discreet use of uppers, Benzedrine. I figured there were people out there getting shot at. If it should happen that it turned out to inflict some injury on my health in the long run, so what?

Q: Did you make that conscious comparison at the time, that other people were risking their lives and health?

Captain Dyer: I was constantly conscious of it. After all, I was living a rather bombproof existence. What few hazards I was running, so what? But as far as I know in the entire war, the longest period I ever worked continuously was 42 hours.

Q: When was that?

Captain Dyer: It was, I believe, sometime in the spring of 1944. I can't remember why now.

Q: Typically among line officers who were ashore early in the war, there was an itching desire to get to sea. Did you avoid that because you had already mentally adjusted to being ashore?

Captain Dyer: When I became an engineering duty only officer at my own volition, I gave up the idea of going to sea. It was not a particularly happy decision on my part, because I always liked going to sea. But I think, without being overly presumptuous, I realized that in the event of war, my greatest contribution would be in what I was doing. War involves some sacrifice as well as some glory, and that was mine.

Q: In his book, Ronald Lewin describes you as one of the very few top codebreakers in the U.S. Navy at the time.* Without any false modesty, is that a fair assessment?

Captain Dyer: I think without any false modesty that in cryptanalysis only, I was number one.

Q: There's no false modesty in that.

Captain Dyer: In the total combination, in the value to the war effort and to the country, I unhesitatingly step aside for Rochefort. But purely as a cryptanalyst or codebreaker, I think unquestionably I was his superior. The only person that I know of that came close to me was Wright. We developed a number of people that became quite effective in a particular specialized line. But with the exception of the ill-fated flag officers' code we dealt with before the war, I don't remember a single problem that I came up against in actual Japanese that I wasn't able to cope with.

Q: Do you think you would have been even better had you had the Japanese language training?

Captain Dyer: I doubt it.

---

*Ronald Lewin, The American Magic: Codes, Ciphers and the Defeat of Japan (New York: Farrar Straus Giroux, 1982), page 107.

Q: Would it have been a hindrance to you?

Captain Dyer: I don't think it would have made much difference. It would have been useful at times, yes.

I mentioned the message after Midway. Sometime in, I believe, April, Rochefort had asked Washington to attack that particular code, a tactical code entirely different from JN-25, in the fact that it had the name XXXXX. And their reply was that it couldn't be done. It worked out a couple of weeks later I had a few minutes to spare and I started on it, and it could be done.

On the subject of the XXXXX, that brings me to a story that I really want to get into this thing. It was a straight code. There was no cipher involved. And it changed a number of times. Probably about the beginning of '43 there was a change. And I started working on it. It became almost immediately apparent that what looked like a single code was actually two distinctly different codes used for different purposes. By that time, we were assigning letters to the codes, and F was supposed to be the next letter. I sent a message to Washington saying, "It appears to Hypo that there are two codes involved, one of which should be called F and the other we will designate as G." And Washington ignored that message.

I continued sending recoveries, identifying these recoveries as F and these as G. And they just kept bunching them all together. Finally I sent a message and said, "You're causing considerable loss of effort by failure to recognize the fact that there are two codes."

And Washington replied, "Give us an example or tell us something about G." I wrote a message which Bill Goggins would not let me send, saying, "If you'll take a red pencil and fill in the groups that I say are F and a blue pencil and fill in the groups I say are G, it will be very apparent to you which is which.*

Goggins said, "No, just cite them an example." He said to answer their question. I sent, "Such and such a message is in G."

And they came back, "We identify that message as F." A couple of weeks later, they came through with a message saying, "We have discovered that there are two codes involved, and these groups are in G." They reversed the way I had been designating them. We had a newsletter that we periodically sent. Goggins put in something about the fact that they had delayed things by their reluctance to recognize that there could be two codes, and that Commander Dyer was not in the habit of making idle statements.

Q: Was this OP-20G that you tangled with?

---

*Captain William B. Goggins, USN, who was head of the codebreaking group after the departure of Captain Rochefort.

Captain Dyer: Yes. Goggins got back a letter from one Earl Stone.* It was four pages long, quoting about two pages written by Rosie Mason, who said all the confusion was due to Dyer.** And Earl Stone, who knew nothing about the business, really . . .

Q: He was a communications specialist, wasn't he?

Captain Dyer: Yes. He wound up the thing by saying, possibly what Commander Dyer needs is a change of climate or scenery. It was a personal letter to Bill Goggins, but Bill showed it to me.

One more little item. They ordered Ham Wright back to Washington. He was my great support. They sent out a reserve lieutenant commander by the name of Rutherford, who had been assigned the primary responsibility for research on this code, to be my number one assistant. I didn't have energy left to get into arguments and fights. The use of those codes had dwindled to where they were hardly worth any effort, so I let him work on them. From that day on, for some reason, I never had a great deal of love for Earl Stone.

Q: Nor probably for Rosie Mason either.

---

*Captain Earl E. Stone, USN, later rear admiral and first director of the National Security Agency from 1949 to 1951; Commander Redfield Mason, USN, later rear admiral.
**Commander Redfield Mason, USN, later rear admiral.

Captain Dyer: Nor for Rosie Mason either.

Q: He generally has a pretty good reputation as an intelligence officer. Would you separate that from cryptanalytical ability?

Captain Dyer: Yes, he was good. He was a language officer, and he had some cryptanalytic ability. He came out to Pearl later. We were not cordial but very gentlemanly in our relations, except one night when I happened to be there. He came up to the section room where they were doing the basic recovery work and practically told them to drop whatever they were doing and do something else. And I told him, in no uncertain terms, that I didn't want him giving orders to my people when I was in the building.

To start with, he was junior to me. He was class of '25. And he was in my company when he was a plebe. There was an old custom at the Naval Academy at that time that, during June Week, the plebes would be put under the shower at night in their pajamas. He was such a brash guy that he had made friends with all my classmates except me. I made a point of going around and putting him under the shower, because I didn't want him to miss out on that.

Q: When you classify yourself as number one, what is the criterion you're using--that you could break messages that nobody else could?

Captain Dyer: In general you don't break messages; you break systems. I could take a mass of material and make the initial break into a code system or cipher system. I would take something, have no idea what it was, and arrive at the conclusion as to what it was and proceed from there. I might have been a total dud dealing with the German problem. I was so steeped in Japanese. I think there were at least three new Japanese diplomatic systems that went into effect while I was there at the department in '31 to '33. I got into all three of them without too much difficulty.

Q: How were you at speed compared to some of the others?

Captain Dyer: I think in general I could turn out more than they could. At the latter part of the war, to get that new code, I spent practically my entire time in the IBM room operating and using the machines, whereas most people used pencil and paper and let somebody else operate the machines.

Q: Could you describe how you would spend the time during those long stretches, your interactions with various officers and enlisted men, just what you would do?

Captain Dyer: It all depended on what I was working on. In general I gave my subordinates a job and it was theirs to carry out. As the war went on, various systems came into use. There was the so-called maru code, a merchant ship code, which was very similar to the JN-25, except it was four numerals instead of five, indicating a much smaller code. Wright and I worked together on that and got the start on it. But as time went on, without sitting down with organizational charts and drawing pretty rectangles, the Coast Guard officer, Henry M. Anthony, took over the work on the maru code. He had people assisting him. He was highly competent. I didn't bother him, and he didn't bother me. The enlisted man, Tony Ethier, who was on watch with me the night before Pearl Harbor, became our expert in weather systems.* He handled that very effectively. He was later commissioned. I didn't need to stand over his back and tell him what to do.

Sometime in the course of the war the Japanese Navy started using another machine cipher. My old friend Tommy Birtley, a language officer, and a reserve officer by the name of Don Miller, a professor of mathematics, took that over. Of course, Washington was working on it also. Washington outlined a method of procedure. I don't think they really meant what they said, "No other method is to be used in solving this, unless we think

---
*Henry E. Ethier.

of it." Tommy and Don thought of a different method and it worked. All I had to do was put them off by themselves, because for working on a machine, you need quiet. So they took care of that without any problems.

Q: Was the IBM machine your biggest supporter, the thing that you relied on for success?

Captain Dyer: During the latter part of the war, the problem became one that, to me, could be handled directly on machines, and that's what I did. I had two ensigns assisting. We would stay down there actually feeding the cards into the machine and sorter.

Q: How much did you rely on fragments that were floating around in your own memory to put pieces together?

Captain Dyer: You're bound to use your total experience to date.

Q: You have to make guesses sometimes, don't you, that a machine can't make?

Captain Dyer: We didn't use the machine to do the guessing. We used the machine to pick out the thing that we wanted to look at in order to make an intelligent guess. Going into a great many

Dyer #5 - 259

details is not practical, and a lot of the details would make the people on Nebraska Avenue tear their hair about. It's impossible to be more specific.

Q: Did you have any interaction at all with the Army codebreakers?

Captain Dyer: None.

Q: Why not?

Captain Dyer: I don't know that they had any out there. The Army didn't do anything in the Pacific until the very end of the war anyway.

Q: They had some Army planes, for instance, the B-17s at Midway, so I wondered if there was any time they might have had something.

Captain Dyer: I don't know what they had. Originally they set up something called the Intelligence Center Pacific Ocean Area, which was a purely Navy operation. That was later changed into the Joint Intelligence Center Pacific Ocean Area, and that was staffed by Army and Navy. That's where Holmes wound up the latter part of the war. The last half of his book is really more about JICPOA than it is about FRUPac.

Sometime in early '43, we moved from the basement to a building adjacent to Admiral Nimitz's headquarters at Makalapa Crater. Initially we shared the building with JICPOA. Later they built another building the same size alongside; they moved out and we took over all of the first building. When we were in the same building, we had some slight contact with a few of them, although the buildings were so departmentalized that there was no fraternization, really, across the lines.

Q: Why the desire for no fraternization?

Captain Dyer: They didn't need to know anything about what we were doing. Conversely we didn't need to know an awful lot about what they were doing.

Q: So things would come together at Admiral Nimitz's level?

Captain Dyer: We might feed things, product, into them. But they didn't need to know the hows, and wheres, and whys.

Anywhere in the intelligence business, the great guiding light is the need to know. And it operates in direct opposition to human nature. Everyone wants to know, and then when they know, they want to show how great they are by telling everybody else what they know. The only way to maintain anything like security is to tell as few people as possible and hope that you haven't got a blabbermouth amongst them.

Q: Was there a chance to relax for even a moment after the Midway victory had been won?

Captain Dyer: Yes. Rochefort and I quit the around-the-clock business and more or less went on day duty. I don't know, I think his family had left by then. I honestly don't know what he did. He probably lived in the basement as much as he did anywhere else. I went home at night.

Q: Did the pace pick up again after that, such as when the submarine offensive got into high gear?

Captain Dyer: When I say I went home at night, I'm not trying to imply that I put in an eight-hour day, five days a week or anything like that. It was practically from dawn to dusk. Depending on the season of the year, the days were longer or shorter. As long as the blackout continued in Pearl Harbor, any idea of driving at night was strictly for the birds, or at least it wasn't for me.

Sometime in the latter part of the war, I got into a little fight when the OPA, or whoever it was took over the rationing of gasoline, which had been under the military government until they did away with the military government.* They wanted to know why I didn't carry passengers. I said my hours were rather irregular. They demanded that I submit a log for a week or a month or something. At that season of the year, I wasn't leaving home until about 8:00 o'clock in the morning. We were on daylight savings then. And I got home anywhere from 6:00, 7:00, 8:00 in the evening. And at least once a week I didn't go home at all and went home the next day at about noon. It worked out to be an average 85-hour week. They came back and said, well, they could see that my time of leaving Pearl Harbor was rather irregular, but they didn't see why I couldn't carry passengers one-way. Was I supposed to take them out and leave them?

Q: The bureaucracy at work. The circumstances of Captain Rochefort's departure were controversial. I'd like to have your memories of the way you saw it at the time.

Captain Dyer: Sometime after Midway, Jack Redman came out to be communication officer on Nimitz's staff.** He brought with him a message that had come from Rochefort. Previously Washington sent Rochefort a message, "What can we do to help?" It caught him in a bad moment.

---
*OPA--Office of Price Administration.
**Captain John R. Redman, USN, later vice admiral.

He replied, "Send us more men and leave us alone." Redman brought that message back out to show what a terrible person Rochefort was.

Joe Wenger and Jack Redman had a personal cryptographic system with which they exchanged messages, which were seen at the Pearl Harbor end by no one but Jack Redman.* They were delivered to him and he decoded them and showed them to no one. Layton tried to see them but didn't. What those messages contained I don't know. But in my opinion, that is no way to run a railroad--for a couple of subordinates to have a private means of talking behind everybody's back. They used the Navy radio to do it.

I'm sure Redman and Rochefort had served together on a fleet staff at some time. They hadn't gotten along then either. Redman seemed to think that he should have some control over FRUPac. At that time we still belonged to the commandant.** He, I think, tried to sell a bill of goods that there was friction between Rochefort and Layton. I never saw any evidence of it. And Layton denies it. They were both the kind of individuals who are apt to make some derogatory statement like, "You knucklehead," but all in good, clean fun.

In the fall of '42, they set up ICPOA and told Rochefort to act as head of it temporarily, until Roscoe Hillenkoetter got

---
*Commander Joseph N. Wenger, USN, later rear admiral.
**This refers to the Commandant of the 14th Naval District.

there. They indicated that there was supposed to be some connection between it and the Combat Intelligence Unit.* Nothing was spelled out. All of a sudden out of a clear sky, as far as I was concerned, they sent dispatch orders for Rochefort to come to Washington for temporary duty and conferences. At first I took it for a routine sort of thing, but before he left, he said, "I'll never be back." And he wasn't.

He never talked to me beforehand about any difficulties, and even afterwards he never told me an awful lot about it, except that he had discussed the situation with Admiral Reeves, who had been commander in chief. Reeves offered to go to bat for him and go to the White House, if necessary, and Joe said, "No, don't start a fight.** It will just cause more trouble than anything." All I knew was that Joe wound up with command of a dry dock.

Q: Which sounds like quite a waste of talent.

Captain Dyer: Absolutely.

Q: Was the effectiveness of your organization diminished by his departure?

---
*Captain Roscoe H. Hillenkoetter, USN, later vice admiral.
**Admiral Joseph M. Reeves, USN, was Commander in Chief U. S. Fleet from June 1934 to June 1936; Rochefort was a member of his staff at that time.

Captain Dyer: We were missing out on his expertise in analyzing and supporting the intelligence. We were bound to suffer to some extent. No one could step into his shoes. Our two top translators were very good. They balanced each other; Lasswell was very precise and methodical, and Finnegan was given to wild flights of fantasy. I would have hated to have Finnegan producing finished intelligence. I don't know, if you keep your nose to the grindstone, you're not aware of everything that goes on around you. It's impossible.

Q: Did you miss Captain Rochefort's leadership?

Captain Dyer: It wasn't the kind of an organization where leadership played a very large part. As I tried to point out in my own bailiwick, I had people in key positions and I gave them their head.

Q: Doesn't there need to be somebody to draw it all together and act as a spokesman to the fleet intelligence officer?

Captain Dyer: Holmes more or less took over the business of communicating with Layton. It became more a matter of sending the raw translations over to Layton and letting him--of course, not too long after Rochefort left, Bill Goggins arrived on the scene to replace him. Initially I concluded that he was in on the plot, if there was one. I think I treated him with the minimum politeness that a commander could show a captain. But I soon had to reform that opinion. I was forced to the conclusion that he was an innocent bystander who sort of got caught in a little jam.

Q: Wasn't Hillenkoetter sort of out of his element during that short time he was there? He was more of an attache type.*

Captain Dyer: Roscoe had had some experience in intelligence. Just what, I don't know. I never knew him well. I remember he graduated from that to become the first director of the CIA.

Q: I think he was in the attache's office in Paris before he went to Pearl Harbor.

Captain Dyer: An attache at a major embassy is a creature of the intelligence organization.

Q: But not a codebreaker.

Captain Dyer: No. He didn't come into our outfit at all. He came into the intelligence center.

---
*Hillenkoetter was director when the Central Intelligence Agency was formed in 1947.

Q: I see.

Captain Dyer: There was some vague--I don't know if it was ever put down on paper--intimation that we would become a part of, or be subordinate to, the intelligence center. They hadn't anything to do with running it. But it was close enough that Holmes gradually slid from being solely with one outfit to being almost entirely with the other.

Q: Where did Goggins fit into this overall picture?

Captain Dyer: He was the officer in charge of the Combat Intelligence Unit and officer in charge of FRUPac, or whatever our names were at the moment.

Q: Was he a codebreaker himself?

Captain Dyer: Not really. He was a communicator. The communicators thought that they owned codebreaking--an idea that I thought was to a certain extent a mistake--based on the fact that if we didn't have any of them, we wouldn't have any traffic to work on, and therefore there'd be no codebreaking. By the same rather specious logic, I said that the Bureau of Supplies and Accounts ought to run the fleet because they buy the oil. But that again was part of Rochefort's trouble. When Rochefort had been in charge of OP-20GX, he had worked for communications. His language training made him a creature of the Office of Naval Intelligence. I don't like to put it in too crude terms, but there was a certain amount of friction and animosity between the Office of Naval Intelligence and the Office of Naval Communications, a lot of it centering around our activities. And to call a spade a spade, the animosity was due probably to the fact that if there was any honor and glory to be obtained from our activity, each office would claim it for their team.

Q: So professional jealousy reared its ugly head.

Captain Dyer: Very much so. And that's what seemed to happen there. The Redman brothers were also interested, I think, in claiming a little bit of glory and honor personally for something that they had, as far as I'm concerned, not a damn thing to do with.

Q: Maybe they were better politicians than Captain Rochefort was.

Captain Dyer: They were that, all right. The elder brother, Joe, I knew for almost my entire naval career.[*] When I first

---
[*] Rear Admiral Joseph R. Redman, USN.

reported to the New Mexico, he was the radio officer on Admiral Wiley's staff. Shortly before, he had been radio officer of the New Mexico, and still sort of regarded himself as the radio officer of the New Mexico. He was hard to get along with then and he never, as he got older, grew any better. When I was at the Navy Department in the early Thirties, he had a desk in communications. I don't know what it was now. But usually when he spoke to me, it was with that sort of sneering smile on his lips that said, "You poor, ignorant bastard, you think you're doing something useful. You're just wasting your time and the government's money." When it looked as if the activities of that poor dumb bastard were going to pay off, then he wanted to get in on the gravy train.

Q: Fair weather friend.

Captain Dyer: That's about all I can say about the Rochefort case.

Q: Did you get any spinoff from the Chicago Tribune publication of part of the Japanese op order at the time of the Battle of Midway?*

---

*On 7 June 1943, the Chicago Tribune, in a front page story by Stanley Johnston, reported that the Navy had known in advance about the planned attack on Midway. While no mention was made of having broken the Japanese code, that was an obvious inference of the news report. See "Eyewitness," by Robert Mason, U.S. Naval Institute Proceedings, June 1982, pages 41-45.

Captain Dyer: We were rather quickly aware of the article the Tribune published. I think if Colonel McCormick had come within range of the .45 I was still wearing, he would not have survived.* With the passage of time and sober reflection, I still haven't forgiven McCormick or the paper or the reporter or the dumb naval officer who gave out the information. I am relatively convinced that the change in code and cipher that took place shortly after Midway had nothing to do with the leak. I know what it did have to do with.

Q: How did you become convinced that it was not related to the leak?

Captain Dyer: Just a question of timing. To distribute the new material and place it in effect requires a little bit more time. Apparently they started distributing it just about the same time they put the other one into effect. But there were little clues that they apparently planned that change around the time they made it, before the article came out in the Tribune. You can't put your finger on something and say yes, that is so. But that's the impression I got. In other words, the changes followed too closely upon the Tribune story to be occasioned by it.

---

*Colonel Robert R. McCormick was the iron-handed editor and publisher of the Chicago Tribune. He held a commission in the U.S. Army, having served on General John J. Pershing's staff in World War I, and later as commandant of Fort Sheridan, Illinois.

Q: You had already had a demonstration of how long it took them to put in a new code.

Captain Dyer: Well, of course, they had too. They were probably trying to do better the next time around.

Q: It doesn't say too much for Japanese intelligence if they seemingly missed that article in making the connection.

Captain Dyer: Japanese intelligence sometimes was not as good as it was reputed to be. I used to say, living in Honolulu, that I didn't think much of their intelligence because if it were really as good as it was supposed to be, I ought to have been able to get a first class maid at a bargain price.

Q: Did you go through the war without a maid?

Captain Dyer: We had a maid only the first year we were out there. On the whole it was more trouble than it was worth.

Q: Were you more reluctant to have one than most naval officers were because of the nature of your job?

Captain Dyer: No, not particularly, because I never took anything home with me. I am inclined to disagree a little bit with Rochefort. He talks about his unhappiness when we picked up a Japanese code on Guadalcanal, but I don't believe, as I remember it at the time, that that code had anything to do with a change. I think the change had taken place before we picked it up; I don't know. It was very useful to have a complete code, fleet vocabulary. It settled a number of arguments as to what word was used here or there.

Q: That was the thing I didn't really understand about his description of that incident--how he would know that the Japanese knew that the code had been dug up.

Captain Dyer: I think it was a little poetic license there or a faulty memory or something.

Q: Moving then to the summer of 1942, what was the focus of your activities?

Captain Dyer: A new code and cipher went into effect the 25th of May. By the time of Midway and after Midway, we had enough material accumulated that we began to make a real attack on it. That was our focus.

We gradually built up our manpower. In addition to the California band, we got a number of brand-new recruits. A chief petty officer by the name of Rorie, later commissioned, had an uncanny knack for being able to pick good men from a new draft of recruits that had come in from the mainland. They would be lined up, maybe 100 or 150, and since they had been shipped out there under less than ideal conditions, probably looking rather scruffy.* He would go down the line and say, "I'll take you and you and you." And to the best of my knowledge, there wasn't a one of them--some of them were better than others--who didn't turn out to be perfectly satisfactory for our purposes.

Q: Was there any concern about security when he just pointed to "you, you and you?"

Captain Dyer: We needed manpower. We had to take some chances. The probability of somebody being sent down to enlist in the Navy and then being sent out there in the draft, after boot camp, for illicit purposes, was very slight.

Q: I think that carelessness would be more likely than disloyalty.

Captain Dyer: That was his genius--picking out reliable characters. I think he put the fear of God in them after he got them. But anyway, it worked.

---
*Durwood G. Rorie was commissioned an ensign in 1943.

Q: Was there any special confined living area for these men to keep them out of the general mainstream?

Captain Dyer: They built some barracks. They did live by themselves, more or less. I don't know too much about where they did live.

Q: You weren't in any sense, then, a division officer type?

Captain Dyer: No.

Q: Whom did they report to in that FRUPac organization?

Captain Dyer: Rorie sort of acted as their boss, I guess. And wherever they were assigned in the organization, they had a supervisor there. They were taught what to do.

Q: The Guadalcanal campaign was coming up that summer. How much were you involved in that?

Captain Dyer: Practically none, I would say. We knew about it. That's about all. And things did not go as well as we might have hoped for initially. We were, of course, distressed.

Q: One of the main things that they had to do was be able to contend with the raids of both ships and planes that were coming out of Rabaul. Part of that they got from coast watchers, but part also from code intercepts. Were you picking up some of that traffic?

Captain Dyer: That I can't remember. I don't think we were getting very much of it because it was too far south for us.

Q: What was your main operational focus at that point--the submarine war?

Captain Dyer: No, we had no main operational focus. It was to get the JN-25 as readable as possible.

Q: Once you had the code, you wanted to be able to read messages with it?

Captain Dyer: Yes, but we had to solve the code first. Before we solved the code, we had to solve the cipher. And it's a continuing process. If a code and cipher stay in effect in wartime conditions for two years, it's very doubtful if the cipher would be completely solved. And it's a dead certainty that the code would not be.

Q: So there was always more to do.

Dyer #5 - 276

Captain Dyer: There was always more to do. I'll just have to pull these numbers out of the air--say, about 10% of the groups in any code will read 90 to 95% of the traffic. But the most critical messages may be in the remaining 5 or 10%. It's an unending job. There's no way around that.

Q: Where were the signal interceptions themselves taking place-- in Hawaii?

Captain Dyer: In the very early days, almost simultaneously with the start of the war, the intercept stations had been on the north coast of Hawaii at Heeia, which is quite a ways from Pearl Harbor and over rather difficult roads. And we had wire lines which, thanks to the Army, sometimes broke down.

During the summer and fall of '41, a new radio station was built up on the central plateau there at Schofield Barracks, XXXXXXXXXXXXXXXXXXXXXXXX. They had built one building for a traffic center and a separate building for the intercept station. The traffic center was moved from Wailupe to XXXXXXX. This was, you might say, almost simultaneously with the attack of Pearl Harbor. It was probably planned for the week of the seventh. I'm not real sure. The district communication officer decided that since the intercept station had been built in a somewhat bombproof building, he wanted it. He pulled rank on us and he took it. He left us at the station he had built for himself. It worked out all right; we didn't need the bombproof anyway.

Q: What forms were these intercepts in when you received them and how did they physically get from an intercept station to you?

Captain Dyer: Initially they were typewritten, copied on special typewriters, and the bulk delivered by courier. Later, I can't put a date on this, a teletype line was installed from the intercept station to our place.

Q: What kind of volume were you dealing with at various phases during the war?

Captain Dyer: At peak times somewhere--around 1,000 to 1,200 messages a day.

Q: How many could you personally deal with?

Captain Dyer: It depended on what I was doing with them, which ones they were. They had to be sorted out in various systems. They were sent into the machine room, punched on cards and so forth.

In codebreaking, in the initial stages of codebreaking particularly, we might have five or six big files with maybe 500 messages in each, and we'd have an index. If such and such a group occurs, I reach over here and find it, flip open that book and see what it looks like. How many was I dealing with? Several thousand.

Q: How would you decide what sequence to take them in?

Captain Dyer: It decides itself. I'd sit there and thumb through the book and see something that ought to mean so-and-so. Look at another occurrence. Doesn't get me anywhere. Look at another one. Yes, that seems to fit. And so on.

Q: Sometimes I don't think it's a matter of hunches and intuition, but what track you follow.

Captain Dyer: A lot of it is that. A lot of it is, I'm convinced, done by the subconscious. Sometimes when people ask me how I can solve messages, I say, "Well, you sit there and stare at it until you see what it says, and then you put it down." You look--it depends on what kind of a thing you're dealing with--but you look at it until you see something that attracts your attention, your curiosity. Maybe it doesn't suggest anything at all. You go on to something else. The next day you come back and look at it again. Oh yes, that's so-and-so.

Q: Did these invade your dreams at night?

Captain Dyer: Never.

Q: That's surprising. It might have helped if they had; you might have seen solutions.

Captain Dyer: The only time I ever dreamt a solution was when I was here in Washington in the summer of '27. I saw something in my sleep, but I couldn't remember what the answer was when I woke up.

Q: Did you have a capability for intercepting the traffic in the South Pacific? You said you couldn't pick it up directly in Hawaii.

Captain Dyer: I don't know. We got some of the traffic from Bellconnen or Melbourne or whatever you want to call it.* Traffic was forwarded to Washington. It was re-enciphered to conceal the nature, and forwarded. We were information addressee on things forwarded from South Pacific, for instance, and they were information addressee on things forwarded from us. We were all working on the same things together with some duplication,

---

*Bellconnen, often called just "Bell," was the name for the naval radio station near Melbourne, Australia.

naturally. I tried repeatedly with Washington to get an agreement on some steps to eliminate some of the duplication, and they resisted. It was "father knows best."

Q: I think father would also like to be in charge, or it sounds that way.

Captain Dyer: That's right.

Q: Did OP-20G ever send you things that had been solved elsewhere as an aid to you?

Captain Dyer: There was a rather free exchange of translation. And there was a complete exchange of recoveries. If we identified a code group, we told them. If they identified one, they told us. That part went back way before the war. There was always a complete exchange of results.

Q: But it sounds as if jealousy grew. I wonder if that might have inhibited the exchange any.

Captain Dyer: No, no. Of course, they could still claim that their translation was better than ours, which they did on both Coral Sea and Midway, but they were wrong on both counts.

In the movie Midway, they have a commander, or captain, who

comes out from Washington and tries to talk Admiral Nimitz into believing that the thing's in Alaska, not Midway. I don't know whether that is historical or poetic license. Whether they sent somebody out to try to do that or not, they did try to do that. That much I know.

Q: That movie was very heavy on poetic license.

Captain Dyer: It wasn't a love affair at all.

Q: Did you have any direct contact with Admiral Nimitz?

Captain Dyer: Only once. That was, I guess, in the summer of '43. I'm not real sure. Anyway, before Wright left. I had working for me the registrar of the University of California at Berkeley, who served as a lieutenant commander. And when Admiral Nimitz had been professor of naval science at Berkeley, they had become quite good friends. One day Admiral Nimitz and Tom Steele got together.* Admiral Nimitz said, "I would like to invite the two people you consider the most key people over there to go swimming with me." And Tom Steele nominated Wright and me. We got word that Admiral Nimitz would like us to go swimming with him Wednesday afternoon, or some such day.

---

*Lieutenant Thomas Steele, USNR.

I didn't have anything to wear. I borrowed a pair of bathing trunks from Ham Wright. He was considerably larger than I was, but they worked all right. We went up and checked in along with Steele at Nimitz's quarters. And we all got in the car. There was Nimitz, and Raymond Spruance, and the aide, the three of us, and the driver. We went over to the north coast of Oahu where Nimitz had been supplied with some kind of a beach house. We got into bathing garb and went down on the beach. Nimitz said something about how he had injured his leg, and he thought he'd just sit there in the sun. I was perfectly willing to sit there in the sun with him, but Spruance suggested that we take a walk down the beach. I would have preferred to sit, but I decided that discretion was the better form of valor. So we started down the beach. It wasn't a walk; it was practically a marathon. He was putting one foot in front of the other at a very rapid pace.

Q: "He" being Spruance?

Captain Dyer: Spruance. We got down, I suppose, about a mile. I thought it was about three. And he suggested we start swimming back. We all got in the water and it was really funny. We dropped out in the order of rank. Tom Steele was the first one to give up, then Ham Wright gave up, then I gave up, and about a half a mile later, Spruance gave up. I think he only gave up just to be sociable. But we did have a very interesting talk on the walk down the beach.

Q: What was the gist of that?

Captain Dyer: We were talking about our business and the fact that the Japanese had periodic blackouts when things changed. Spruance advanced the idea that maybe they ought to plan to have operations when we thought we would be in. They did that one week later, to some extent, but they couldn't, of course, count on it.

Q: You wouldn't have an idea in advance, would you, when the blackout would come?

Captain Dyer: Not so much when it would come. You knew that it would come maybe every three or four months. It was more a question of when you lost out, how soon could you expect to be supplied some intelligence.

We went back to Pearl. That was the first day that I had been exposed to daylight, so to speak, since the war started. I got the most beautiful case of sunburn. It's the curse of my life. I've always had easily burnt skin anyway. And in addition, the trunks I borrowed from Ham Wright had chafed badly between my legs, and I was a mess. When we got out of the car,

Ham said, "We thought we'd take you out and show you how to relax so you could do better work."

The next day, I actually had to go to sick bay. I said to myself, "I don't want to be fixed up so I can do better work like this again."

Q: You had to recover from your relaxation.

Captain Dyer: I insisted that that was once that I had been injured in the line of duty. It was not a very profound afternoon, but it was a very pleasant one.

Q: You probably remember that afternoon better than many that preceded it or came after it.

Captain Dyer: Oh, yes.

Q: How much contact did you have with Commander Layton?*

Captain Dyer: Not too much, in spite of the fact that his office was about half the distance as the cottages over there are from ours.

---

*Commander Edwin T. Layton, USN, Pacific Fleet intelligence officer. His oral history is in the Naval Institute collection.

Q: So maybe a couple hundred yards?

Captain Dyer: A little less, maybe. But there wasn't much contact, unless I had something specific or he had something specific. In a sense I had more dealings with him after he moved to Guam than I did when he was right next door, because at least twice we had a secure teletype line, and we could carry on a conversation between the two places.* He got me on the teletype to ask some questions that Admiral Nimitz wanted to ask me. We had, generally speaking, a fairly long conversation.

Q: There was pretty complete confidence on the part of Admiral Nimitz and Commander Layton from about the spring of '42 on, wasn't there?

Captain Dyer: I think so. Admiral Layton is largely responsible for that picture I have up there.

Q: The autographed picture from Admiral Nimitz.

Captain Dyer: Yes. I think he said something to the admiral that he thought I would like very much to have his picture. What

---

*The Pacific Fleet staff moved from Hawaii to Guam in early 1945.

Nimitz wrote on there was his own composition.* However I got it, I'm very grateful for it.

Q: Are there any other events in 1942 that are worth discussing?

Captain Dyer: '42. That's about all.

Q: Maybe then you could go ahead and discuss some of the major milestones from the next year.

Captain Dyer: The remainder of the war constitutes almost a blur. There were 12, if I count correctly, codes placed in effect in JN-25. Twelve separate codes. There were possibly 20 or so ciphers. The ciphers gradually became more complex and required a great deal more labor in solving them. Without going into a lot of details, depending on the kind of cipher used, we had to have a number of messages that used the same cipher elements in order to recover them. The complexity was in the method of concealing which ones went together and trying to recover which ones went together. In '43, I gradually started doing more work in the machine room.

---
*The inscription reads: "25 September '45. To Captain Thomas H. Dyer, USN: With best wishes; and many thanks for the great contribution you personally made to the successful prosecution of the war against Japan /s/ C.W. Nimitz."

Dyer #5 - 287

In the summer of '43, I had a rather bad bout with some kind of a virus, thanks to a slightly run down condition. It laid me up for about two weeks--the only vacation I really got during the war. Well, I got another one. But it wasn't so much of a vacation.*

In '43, we followed various operations in the Mandate Islands, but there was no major contribution. However, we had developed a considerable capacity for getting the routings of convoys. That information supplied to the submarines resulted in a great many of the submarine sinkings. During most of that period, I would say that the information was useful but not critical.

Of course, there was the Yamamoto affair.** We decoded the message giving Yamamoto's complete itinerary on an inspection trip. We had nothing to do with any decision as to whether action should be taken or not. I think most of us thought it should be, because we felt that Yamamoto was a very critical leader in the Japanese naval effort and that there was no replacement for him. That's an opinion with which Layton

---

*This probably refers to a trip Captain Dyer made to Washington late in the war.
**Admiral Isoroku Yamamoto, IJN, Commander in Chief Combined Fleet, was killed when his aircraft was shot down by U.S. Army fighters on 17 April 1943. His detailed itinerary, which allowed for the fighter interception, had been obtained through cryptanalysis of a message received on 13 April. Lieutenant Commander Dyer was one of several cryptanalysts who broke the coded message.

apparently agreed. It was batted back and forth at the highest levels and finally decided.

There's not much point in my going into that. We know it was a successful effort. There was a leak on that--some aviator at Guadalcanal. I really can't say whether it did any damage or not.

Q: Were you ever concerned during the course of the war that all these coincidences would appear to the Japanese to be a pattern and give away your success?

Captain Dyer: Yes. But on the other hand, if you absolutely refuse to use intelligence, what the hell is the use in having it?

I want to back up and mention another gripe that I have. When I was in the hospital--but I don't think it was because I was in the hospital--they sent a reserve officer by the name of Ford out from Washington. It was unclear just what he was supposed to do. I think I saw him only once before he left, but when he got back to Washington, he submitted a very lengthy report on his inspection of the facilities at Pearl Harbor. And he thoroughly damned my running of the thing without any faint praise. This report was never referred to the officer in charge of Pearl Harbor. He was never told about it. He was never told. But people have the habit of putting things in files and forgetting them, and those things get read later. When I read it a little later, I wasn't too happy. He was very critical of things that I did personally. And I was in the hospital practically the entire time he was there.

Q: Was he even qualified to make the kind of judgments he was making?

Captain Dyer: No. He was a resident in psychology from Temple University. Whatever capacity he may have had as a cryptanalyst, I do not know, but his function in Washington was purely that of an administrator of OP-20GY, which was the processing division.

Q: That sounds like a real aberration from the normal Navy way, that is, having a junior report on seniors.

Captain Dyer: It didn't do any harm, it didn't do any good. I just want to put that in as an indication of the attitude in Washington.

When I was on Admiral Pratt's staff, I once wrote a letter, which I thought was entirely justified, criticizing the action of some captain or rear admiral. Pratt took it to the chief of staff, and the chief of staff said, "No, he's a friend of mine."

Had I been in Washington in a position of authority and received such a report from a subordinate, that subordinate would have caught holy hell. Whether he was sent out there to do that, I don't know. I strongly suspect he was told to go out there and find out what you think is wrong with the place. Now, other people came out from Washington and we got along beautifully. But the king can do no wrong.

Q: In this case, the king was named King?*

Captain Dyer: Or Wenger.

Q: As events moved along and the United States got more and more ships and planes and the Japanese forces were diminishing, you have indicated that your work was useful but no longer critical. Did the pressure on you ease up at that point?

Captain Dyer: The pressure eased up on me the day they dropped the bomb.**

Q: So it didn't help you that the Allies were doing better and better and better.

Captain Dyer: No. I said that things were routine. As for the

---
*Admiral Ernest J. King, USN, Chief of Naval Operations.
**The first U.S. atomic bomb was dropped on Hiroshima, Japan, on 6 August 1945.

sinking of Yamato, though, we supplied the information about the prospective sortie of the Yamato from the Inland Sea.*

Q: Were messages concerning the Philippine campaign handled more out of the Australia station than yours?

Captain Dyer: I would say it was a split thing. By that time, Admiral Nimitz was in Guam.

Q: That was from January '45 on, wasn't it?

Captain Dyer: Yes. When he went to Guam, we sent an advance unit out there under Lin Howeth.** It was not a complete unit, but it did some intercepting and things of that kind.

Q: You said you saw more of the admiral when you were out there. When did you make the move?

Captain Dyer: We didn't.

Q: Oh. So you didn't see him much either place.

---

*The Japanese battleship Yamato was sunk 7 April 1945 on her way to Okinawa.
**Commander Linwood S. Howeth, USN.

Captain Dyer: That was Layton I said I saw. I talked more to Layton when he was out there, but only by teletype.

Q: I see. Any other events from the war period itself that we should discuss?

Captain Dyer: I can't think of any without getting into technical details which would not help the history any.

Q: When the bomb did drop, in a sense you were suddenly a man without a job, weren't you?

Captain Dyer: We kept going until at least the second bomb--really, until the surrender, because there was quite a bit on the air to check as to whether the Japanese were doing what they said they were doing.*

Q: But it turned out that the Japanese were quite docile and cooperative.

Captain Dyer: Yes.

---
*The second atomic bomb was dropped on Nagasaki, Japan, on 9 August 1945.

Interview Number 6 with Captain Thomas H. Dyer, U.S. Navy (Retired)

Place: Captain Dyer's cottage, Sykesville, Maryland

Date: Tuesday, 20 September 1983

Subject: Biography

Interviewer: Paul Stillwell

Q: Captain, after our last meeting, you were kind enough to lend me a copy of Ladislas Farago's book The Broken Seal.* In looking at it since then, I find he makes one reference to you that I'd like to get your reaction to. He discusses a break-in at the Japanese naval attache's office in Washington in July of 1935 to examine the codes, indicating that the mastermind of this break-in was Ellis Zacharias.** He indicates also that this was done at the behest of you and Holtwick.*** So I wonder if that's an accurate portrayal.

Captain Dyer: It is inaccurate insofar as I was not anywhere in the Washington area at the time. It is accurate, to the best of my knowledge, as far as Holtwick is concerned. It's always been my understanding that he was one of the two electricians who

---
*Ladislas Farago, The Broken Seal: The Story of "Operation Magic" and the Pearl Harbor Disaster (New York: Random House, 1967).
** Rear Admiral Ellis M. Zacharias, USN, Secret Missions: The Story of an Intelligence Officer (New York: G.P. Putnam's, 1946).
***Lieutenant (junior grade) Jack S. Holtwick, USN.

Dyer #6 - 294

invaded the naval attache's apartment at the Alban Towers.

Q: As Farago described it, the electricity went out mysteriously and people were calling the repairmen. Was Holtwick one of the "repairmen?"

Captain Dyer: That's right.

Q: And with his flashlight, he would have known what to look for in the code machine.

Captain Dyer: Right. They didn't expect to get any more than a general idea of the size and shape and so forth. They did get that. What we had did have a great deal to do with the solution and reconstruction of the Japanese red machine.

Q: Also in Farago's book he talks about the Friedman achievement in breaking the Purple code.* He suggests that the Japanese denied that it could have been done, suggesting that that may have been covert also. Do you have any knowledge in that area?

Captain Dyer: That was, to the best of my knowledge, a purely analytical job. There are conflicting reports as to where the

---
*William F. Friedman, noted U.S. Army codebreaker.

major credit lies. Of course, the effort was directed under Mr. Friedman. A man named Clark contributed greatly to the solution.* That much I am aware of. But, again, I was 8,000 miles away when this was being done and I know little about it firsthand. I do know that it was not the result of any skullduggery. It was the result of analytical procedures.

Q: On the basis of your personal knowledge, would you consider Friedman's work on Purple the foremost achievement in American codebreaking?

Captain Dyer: That is probably true. It is a little difficult to sort out, because they built on the work that had been done previously on the red machine by the Navy. These things are always progressive. It was one of the finest achievements. But it's hard, also, to compare that with the early British work on Enigma, which was also unbreakable.

Q: How would it compare with Agnes Driscoll's early work on the flag officers' code?

Captain Dyer: It's so much different. There really isn't any valid basis of comparison. Considering the state of the art and

---
*Henry L. Clark.

what was known at the time, her achievement was also a very great achievement and one that was never fully recognized by the Navy. The Navy is rather guilty of maybe male chauvinism. I don't know.

Q: There seems to be some prejudice against codebreakers in general. Maybe that was the problem.

Captain Dyer: It was doubly compounded by the fact that she was a female. She was never given the status by the Navy that Friedman was given by the Army. Certainly in the Twenties and early Thirties, she was fully his equal. In the long term of history, I'd be hard put to say that one was better than the other.

Q: Several times you've mentioned Henry M. Anthony, the Coast Guardsman, and said you would discuss him when we got to the proper place. Was there more that you wanted to say about him?

Captain Dyer: He was what you think of as a natural. He was largely self-taught, as most of us were. I think I did say that he eventually took over the complete responsibility at Pearl Harbor for the Japanese maru system and did a magnificent job with it. It's always a joy, in any line of work, to have a subordinate to whom who you can turn over something and not have to give a second thought to what he's doing or how he's doing.

Q: As you indicated, that was certainly your preferred style of operating.

Captain Dyer: He was one of the shining examples of self-reliance in that respect. He had to do it.

Q: When you say he was a natural, are you suggesting that he had some innate talents, such as a musician or an athlete might?

Captain Dyer: I think that there is some mental quirk that a few people have that make them adaptable to this type of work. I may have mentioned the fact that when the Coast Guard tried to get him away from us to bring him back to Washington, the Navy Department asked how long it would take to train a relief, and my reply was, "How long would it take you to train a relief for Jose Iturbi?" I considered it in the same category. If you can find somebody with a natural talent, it won't be difficult. If you find just a reasonably intelligent individual, it may take forever.

Q: Would you consider yourself a natural in that regard?

Captain Dyer: I must be.

Q: Maybe you're the Ty Cobb of codebreakers.*

Captain Dyer: Well, I don't know.

Q: Was it exceptional for the Coast Guard to have somebody in the codebreaking program?

Captain Dyer: I don't know to what extent amongst their uniformed personnel they did, but they did have a section at headquarters, which incidentally was headed by Mrs. Friedman.** In the Twenties, when they had a great deal of activity, particularly in connection with rumrunners and such ilk, I am morally certain that Mrs. Friedman contributed to some of the success of the Coast Guard. I have no firsthand knowledge of Mrs. Friedman's ability. I believe she was employed by the Navy very briefly sometime after Mrs. Driscoll had left the Navy to work for Mr. Hebern in the matter of the Hebern cipher breaking.*** But I wasn't there, so I don't know anything about it. It's hearsay.

---

*Tyrus R. Cobb was among the greatest of all baseball players.
**Elizebeth Smith, a skilled cryptanalyst who worked on rumrunner codes for the Coast Guard, married William F. Friedman in 1917.
***Edward H. Hebern, inventor of the rotor cipher machine, developed between 1917 and 1921.

Q: When we talked last time, the war was just coming to an end. The bombs had been dropped. Did you feel any sense of letdown at that point?

Captain Dyer: Very definitely. While we continued to operate and tried to follow things, the sense of urgency had disappeared, particularly after the second bomb. We were able to sense from various things that it was only a matter of days until it was all going to be over with. There didn't seem to be much point in killing ourselves for the remaining few days.

Q: From what you were reading, did you have any sense just prior to the dropping of the atomic bombs that the war was nearly over?

Captain Dyer: No. Quite the contrary. The impression that we had from what we were reading and everything else was that they were going to continue to fight to the last Japanese. I don't know if the Japanese Navy was quite as determined as the Army. I think they were a little more realistic than the high command of the Japanese Army. But all through the Okinawa campaign, they fought just as fiercely as they had fought at any time during the war. The kamikaze threat became greater all the time. It didn't betoken any slackening.

Q: Afterward there was a school of thought that said that the bombs were really unnecessary, that the Japanese were on the point of surrender. I take it you would disagree with that.

Captain Dyer: I don't know. I know of his recent book, which I have not read, and I don't credit John Toland as being the world's greatest historian. But he recounts in his long history, The Rising Sun, how the Army high command even considered, after the first bomb, taking the Emperor into custody to prevent him from doing anything to end the war. I think there is a reasonable amount of evidence that that was true, that there was plotting against any idea of surrender. I believe--and I'm really getting out of my own depth here--that the Emperor had to resort to some sort of subterfuge when he issued the Imperial rescript that essentially brought an end to the war.

Q: Some of the U.S. military people had doubts as to whether the Japanese would really cooperate with the surrender. They thought there might be attempts at sabotage and what have you. Were you able to read anything that would allay those fears?

Captain Dyer: To a certain extent, I think that the traffic and the orders that were going out, that we were able to read, tended to show that the Japanese were going ahead in good faith doing what they were supposed to.

Dyer #6 - 301

Q: On the second of September, the surrender was signed on board the Missouri. Were you then in search of a new job?

Captain Dyer: Not immediately. I had hopes of staying in Hawaii and reorganizing a small unit XXXXXXXXXXXXXXXXXXXXXXXXXXXXXX XXXXXXX But the powers that be decided to more or less completely disband any processing effort in Hawaii. So I had to acquiesce to whatever they said.

Q: XXXXXXXXXXXXXXXXXXXXXXXXXXXXXXXXXXXXXXXXXXXXXXXXXXXXXXXXXXXX XXXXXXXXXXXXXXXXXXXXXXXXXXXXXXXXXXXXXXXXXXXX?

Captain Dyer: I prefer not to answer that.

Q: Okay. What happened next?

Captain Dyer: Before we get clear away from it, there are a few names that I would like to throw in. I have mentioned Jack Holtwick in a different connection, but he was one of the people at Pearl Harbor at the beginning of the war. When we took over part of the responsibility for JN-25, he completely organized the machine processing facilities and did an outstanding job of that. I was very grateful. He continued to be very helpful until the middle of the war, when he went out to do something else for a while.

There are several other people that I would like to mention because they contributed a great deal to the success of the Pearl Harbor unit. One was Bill Weedon, a reserve officer and professor of philosophy from the University of Virginia. He was a very dependable subordinate in handling a lot of the processing routine in connection with JN-25.*

Willis Thomas, who was commissioned locally, wound up as the officer in charge of the IBM installation and did a very fine job.

Two people in particular from the California band--the bandmaster by the name of Luckenbach, who became a commissioned officer, and one of the musicians by the name of Frank Wanat.** I somehow missed out in getting him commissioned and he should have been. That was one of the real regrets I have from the wartime period.

There were two other reserve officers who were there practically the entire war--Griff Childs and Luke Dilley.*** They were the kind of dependable people that keep things moving.

Q: What kind of support would these various individuals provide to you?

---
*Lieutenant William S. Weedon, USNR.
**Chief Lovine B. ("Red") Luckenbach, USN.
***Lieutenant Luther L.L. Dilley, USNR; Lieutenant Griffin Childs, USNR.

Captain Dyer: In some cases they would supervise other people in their work and see that the work was organized. I preferred to spend my time on strictly cryptanalytic activities rather than administration. They took over the routine of running things.

Q: You said that in one case you didn't follow through on getting a man commissioned. What was the procedure for those that you did get commissioned?

Captain Dyer: You had to send in recommendations. In the outfit we had a sort of administrative section. In this one particular case, I told them that I wanted the recommendation and somehow it didn't get carried out. I didn't want to sit down and write it myself, but I wanted it put in.

Q: Were you able to tell BuPers why you wanted these people?* How did you make the justification?

Captain Dyer: You just recommend them as qualified. There was a great deal of that.

Q: Did you have a contact in BuPers who knew what you were doing?

---

*BuPers--Bureau of Naval Personnel.

Dyer #6 - 304

Captain Dyer: No. Frankly, I don't remember what the procedures were. The front office under Commander Goggins or later, when he left, under John Harper, took care of those things.*

Q: One other junior officer who was there was Don Showers. Did you have much contact with him?**

Captain Dyer: Not very much. He worked primarily with Jasper Holmes. I knew him. I was very much impressed with his personality and ability, but he didn't work for me. He must have impressed some other people, too, because he became an admiral.

Q: We talked about Captain Rochefort's difficulties. I don't know if we mentioned it, but in his own oral history he talks about being recommended for the Distinguished Service Medal and getting instead the lower Legion of Merit. You, in fact, were awarded the Distinguished Service Medal.

Captain Dyer: That's correct.

Q: Was that by Admiral Nimitz personally?

Captain Dyer: No. I really don't understand how I got it.

---
*Captain John S. Harper, USN.
**Lieutenant Donald M. Showers, USN, later rear admiral.

At the end of the war, Washington recommended five people for Distinguished Service Medals. One was Joe Wenger, one was Howard Engstrom, who some years later he was deputy director of NSA.* One was Rosie Mason, who spent most of the war in Washington, but a little bit in Pearl Harbor. One was Jasper Holmes, who certainly deserved it, but in one sense didn't belong to us at all. And me. I think that they just didn't have the guts to keep me off the list. I think it was very unwillingly that they put my name on.

Q: So you think the politics and the jealousies were still evident at the end of the war as well?

Captain Dyer: They were evident as long as I stayed in the Navy.

Q: Did you encounter subsequent difficulties or frictions as a result of that?

Captain Dyer: Maybe I am just a little thin-skinned, I don't know. But as an example, after the war, they created the special duty only category, and it was divided into several subsets, one of which was communications. Since that was appropriate to my situation and my designation as engineering duty only was not

---

*Dr. Howard T. Engstrom.

appropriate, I requested redesignation as special duty only. Admiral Stone, the director of naval communications, called me up one day and said he was going to hold up on that recommendation because there were some other people that they would like to get into special duty only and it might crowd the field a little bit if they put my name in.* I argued, but I didn't get anywhere. Eventually I was designated as special duty only. Maybe I'd have been better off if I'd stayed in EDO; they didn't know what I was doing. Safford did until he retired.**

Q: Did you have any desire at all to go back to the seagoing line category?

Captain Dyer: I couldn't. I didn't even give it any thought, because that was a world that had passed me by. I was a battleship sailor practically all of my seagoing life, but after the war, when I went aboard the Alabama that Captain Goggins commanded, I don't think I could have even found my way around without a guide.***

Q: Do you think it was a wise move on the Navy's part to create

---
*Rear Admiral Earl E. Stone, USN.
**Captain Laurance F. Safford, USN, who had been one of the Navy's earliest codebreakers.
***Captain William B. Goggins, USN, was commanding officer of the USS Alabama (BB-60) from January through November 1945.

these special duty categories rather than to require the strict rotation policy?

Captain Dyer: Yes, I think so, for two reasons. There were a number of reserve officers that we had acquired during the war who had displayed quite a bit of ability; they would have been lost as seagoing naval officers. In later years, they were taking some people into special duty directly from the Naval Academy, and I think that was a mistake. Two or three years of sea duty were required in the past before men could go to Pensacola to become aviators. I think that it's very desirable to have that real experience. The communicators really started this special duty only outfit, but there were a lot of people climbing on the bandwagon--intelligence and public relations and law. And I'm not sure that the press agents, for instance, need to be commissioned.

Q: Maybe it's better to get them into the tent so at least they get their religion before they go out to preach it.

Captain Dyer: I don't know. I'm thinking of the time the public relations admiral did his best to get me in hot water.

Q: Can you tell that story?

Captain Dyer: That comes a lot later, but it won't hurt to put it out of order.

When David Kahn started working on his mammoth book The Codebreakers, he wrote to both Ham Wright and me and requested interviews.* We were both retired at the time. After discussing it between ourselves, we went down to Nebraska Avenue and consulted with them and went back and wrote Kahn and told him, "No soap." The next thing we knew, we got letters from the director of public information that we would grant the interview. Of course, there was some caveat in there that we would not reveal any classified information. We granted the interview, and at our insistence, a transcript of the interview was supplied to the Office of Naval Intelligence.

Very shortly thereafter, we got letters from the Director of Naval Intelligence telling us that we had been guilty of the seven deadly sins, and intimated without saying so that we might be very well subjected to disciplinary action. Having known the Director of Naval Intelligence for several years, I wrote back and pointed out to him where practically every item he had criticized was somewhere in the public record, such as the

---

*David Kahn, The Codebreakers: The Story of Secret Writing (New York: Macmillan, 1967).

congressional hearings or the Marshall-Dewey letter.* Finally, after a long lapse of time, we got letters saying that they had decided not to take action in the case. Actually, I was not very worried, but then it didn't make me think more highly of the public relations outfit.

Q: Did the public relations people come to your aid or defense at all during this time?

Captain Dyer: No.

Q: So they had gotten you into trouble and left you there.

Captain Dyer: I don't know how much they knew about it really. As I learned considerably later, Kahn did not take our first refusal lightly. He wrote to Mr. Sylvester, who was Deputy SecDef for public information.** That's how they got in the act. Kahn told the Navy.

There is one little other interesting little sidelight on the thing. There was a demand made to Kahn that he suppress and

---

*In September 1944 Chief of Staff of the Army General George C. Marshall sent by messenger a letter to New York governor and Republican presidential candidate, Thomas E. Dewey, asking him not to reveal publicly the United States's ability to decipher Japanese military codes. After several clandestine deliveries of information between the two, Governor Dewey agreed in the interests of national military security.

**Arthur J. Sylvester, Assistant Secretary of Defense for Public Affairs from 1961 to 1967.

destroy the interview. That was made through Mr. Sylvester. And he wrote back to Mr. Sylvester that he was shocked that the Director of Naval Intelligence didn't know what information was in the public record, and that he would be glad to make a special trip down to Washington and point out to the DNI just where all this material was to be found. He never got a reply to that letter at all.

Q: That's sort of the same thing that you told the DNI.

Captain Dyer: Only Kahn told it to the Assistant Secretary of Defense.

Q: Both Kahn and Farago came out with their books about the same time. How did they find out about people like you and Wright? Was it an open secret as to who had been involved in this?

Captain Dyer: I don't know how he found out about Wright. Fortunately, I appeared before only one Pearl Harbor inquiry. That was Admiral Hewitt.* At the time, he was in Pearl Harbor for one reason or another, and I was acting as officer in charge

---

*The Hewitt Inquiry was conducted from May to July 1945 by Admiral H. Kent Hewitt, USN, at the order of Secretary of the Navy James V. Forrestal.

of FRUPac. I was called as a witness, and I took over what files we had. That appears in Volume 47 of the hearings. That was an easy way for Kahn to find out. What Farago's source of his information was, I don't know.

Q: Admiral Layton took the view that the Hewitt inquiry was almost like a witch-hunt in which he didn't get a fair chance to testify. He said that the attorney, Mr. Sonnett, asked a lot of unfair questions.* Was that your impression?

Captain Dyer: I don't know that I had any particular impression of that kind. I did not come away with a troubled opinion of Sonnett. About the only thing they were questioning me about were the messages from the consulate, which had come to us from RCA. They were most interested in when they had been read. Since I had included in the papers the handwritten copy of the translation of a couple of the key messages, he made an inquiry as to whose writing it was. I wasn't sure. I thought I knew, and I went back and determined that it was Finnegan's. Since Finnegan did not start working for us until about the ninth of December, it rather conclusively established the fact that we couldn't have had the translation on the fifth or sixth to issue any warning.

---

*Lieutenant Commander John F. Sonnett, USNR. Layton discussed Sonnett's methods in his oral history.

There was no slip of paper attached to any of those messages stamped urgent; they were just routine grist for the mill. It's easy enough to say, on Monday morning, that we should have spent every effort to read them promptly. But why would they have been any more important than anything else that we had? Probably less important, because consular traffic in general was the most deadly dull thing that you can imagine.

Q: That goes along with Roberta Wohlstetter's theory that all these messages got lost in the welter of noise.* There was nothing to distinguish them as being important.

Captain Dyer: That's right. One message, a purely naval message could be from some tug saying that they needed a new bilge pump. Another message from a commander in chief could be an operation order. On first examination, there may be no way to distinguish between the two. Hopefully you are able to establish, as you go along, that one is from a higher source than the other, but you can't always be sure even of that.

Q: How did you escape testifying before the Roberts

---

*Roberta Wohlstetter, <u>Pearl Harbor: Warning and Decision</u> (Stanford: Stanford University Press, 1962).

Dyer #6 - 313

Commission?*

Captain Dyer: I think I was off that day. When the Roberts Commission was there, I guess it was the morning after they had been at FRUPac, I do remember that when I went out, Rochefort told me to get together the solution of the Mandate system I had been working on and take it over and turn it over to somebody, who was in the entourage, who would act as courier and take it back to Washington.** I had to take it over to the naval hospital, find this guy, and give it to him. That was my only contact with the Roberts Commission.

Q: Have you formed any conclusions of your own on the relative culpability, if any, on the part of U.S. officials involved in the surprise attack?

Captain Dyer: In the late winter of '40-'41 or early spring, I was standing watches, I guess they were communication watches that I got hooked into. It was a sleeping watch, but every morning, way before daybreak, you'd be awakened by the planes

---
*The Roberts Commission was held between December 1941 and January 1942 under Supreme Court Justice Owen J. Roberts, under appointment by President Roosevelt. The commission was to investigate the cause of the fleet being surprised by the Japanese attack on Pearl Harbor.
**This refers to the Central Pacific islands mandated to Japan after World War I.

taking off for the dawn patrol. When we moved to the basement, I took it for granted that they were still continuing.

Apparently they had depleted the stock of planes by sending them out so Douglas MacArthur could line them up for the Japs to destroy.* At the time it seemed to me to be culpable that no dawn patrol was flown until I found out they didn't have any planes left that could fly adequate patrol.

I don't think that I am in a position to decide whether Kimmel or Short took the messages of the war warning as seriously as they should have.** Had Kimmel been Alexander the Great or Caesar, and had a defeat of that magnitude, it would still have been imperative that he be relieved of his command. I don't think that, from any standpoint that I was able to observe, Kimmel in any sense had the abilities that Nimitz displayed. So maybe in a sense we were lucky to get rid of him.

Q: On what do you base your impressions of Admiral Kimmel?

Captain Dyer: Just items of hearsay that built up over the time that he was there. When Admiral Richardson brought the fleet to

---
*Lieutenant General Douglas MacArthur, USA, was then in command of U.S. forces in the Philippine Islands.
**At the time of the Japanese attack on Pearl Harbor, Admiral Husband E. Kimmel, USN, was Commander in Chief Pacific Fleet, and Lieutenant General Walter Short, USA, was commanding general of the Army's Hawaiian Department. Both were relieved of their commands shortly after the attack. Admiral Chester W. Nimitz, USN, became Commander in Chief Pacific Fleet.

Pearl Harbor, people I talked to seemed to have a great deal of confidence.* When Kimmel relieved Richardson, there seemed to be, amongst quite a number of people, the feeling that there was just some slacking off, some letdown. Maybe that's not true, I don't know. I have nothing concrete to go on, just impressions that I got as I go along. A cat can look at a king but he can't always form a correct opinion, I suppose.

Q: Did you have any personal contact with Admiral Kimmel?

Captain Dyer: Never. I tried to avoid it, if I could, which I did.

Q: Why? Why did you try to avoid it?

Captain Dyer: Why would I want to? I mean, I wasn't working for him. My boss was Claude Bloch.** He was captain of the flagship when I was on the staff there. I admired and respected him. I thought that he was an improvement on Murfin, though I really can't charge anything against Murfin.***

I had associated with enough admirals one way or another that

---

*Admiral James O. Richardson, USN, Commander in Chief U.S. Fleet, 1940-1941.
**Rear Admiral Claude C. Bloch, USN, Commandant of the 14th Naval District, 1940-1942.
***Rear Admiral Orin G. Murfin, USN, was Bloch's predecessor as Commandant of the 14th Naval District.

I had no particular desire to associate with any more. After all, anyone who was in the kind of business I was in should have the qualification that President Roosevelt laid down for presidential assistants--a passion for anonymity. It might be helpful if some of today's presidential assistants had that.

Q: Getting back to the part in which you were designated for special duty communications, did you then get a choice of assignments?

Captain Dyer: I never got a choice of assignments. I stayed in Washington, except when I went to Japan in late fall of '52. I didn't want to go out there. I think BuPers in all its wisdom decided that I had been in one place too long; I don't know. I enjoyed my stay out there. Don't get that wrong. But I would have preferred, since I had only three more years to serve, to do it where I was. I had a good home. When you go into special duty only or something like it, there are certain things you give up. In return, I think you're entitled to a little more permanency of location.

Q: How did the reassignment come about then from Hawaii to Washington?

Captain Dyer: By dispatch. After the war was over, Captain

Harper, not having his wife and family out there, was, of course, eager to come back to Washington.* He was ordered back and left me as officer in charge. Suddenly I got dispatch orders--no ifs, ands, buts or by your leaves--ordering me back to Washington.

My family had become somewhat complicated. In addition to our two children, my mother-in-law was living with us, as was my father who was suffering from recently diagnosed terminal cancer. It was not a desirable time to move. Having been there nine years and having bought a house, we had accumulated a lot of possessions. We managed to get things together, get rid of the house, and get everything packed up. We brought a lot of things we didn't need to bring because there wasn't time to sort them out. We had forgotten that, contrary to a good bit of the country, the Washington area houses and apartments had both stoves and refrigerators in them, so we brought our refrigerator and stove from Hawaii. I paid for 1,500 pounds of excess freight.

At that time, getting out of San Francisco was rumored to be a considerable nightmare. So I imposed on a former friendship and wrote Admiral Ingersoll, who was Commander Western Sea Frontier, with headquarters in San Francisco, and asked him if he would have one of his bright young men make train reservations.**

---

*Captain John S. Harper, USN.
**Admiral Royal E. Ingersoll, USN, with whom Dyer had served on the staff of Admiral William V. Pratt.

He wrote by dispatch telling me to be at the San Francisco station at 8:00 o'clock in the morning on New Year's Day. And he made hotel reservations for us at the St. Francis Hotel. The day after Christmas of '45, we embarked on the USS Rescue, the hospital ship.

We got about 100-150 miles out of San Francisco and ran into a thick fog. She was due in on the 31st, late afternoon. Instead, we came under the Golden Gate Bridge about 1:00 o'clock in the morning on New Year's Day. We anchored out instead of going alongside the pier as had been intended. I arranged to go ashore when they picked up the pilot, but the crew of the pilot's boat was off celebrating New Year's, and they never showed up. Finally the captain sent us ashore, and I went in to the navy landing there and called and asked them for a tug and for transport for people with baggage. I got back out to the ship about 5:00 o'clock. They had 33 pieces of baggage, a crate of dogs, two grandparents, two children and one wife, all to get down an ordinary sea ladder.

Q: It wasn't even an accommodation ladder?

Captain Dyer: No, no. No accommodation ladder. It was rough, but somehow we got everybody on the tug and took off for the pier. Then there was supposed to be a sedan there for people and a truck for the baggage. The truck for the baggage was there;

the sedan wasn't there. So we managed to get everybody loaded in the truck and took off. It was almost exactly 8:00 o'clock when we passed in front of the station. I jumped out and ran into the ticket office and sent them around to the baggage room. I won't go through all the rest of the horrible details, but I finally got the tickets and got around there and got the tickets stamped for the baggage or whatever, and walked across the platform and got on the train. I hadn't sat down and the train pulled out. I never even got a chance to call the St. Francis to tell them to cancel. I reported that in more detail than this history needs, but I think it belongs in there.

Q: Did you have any trouble finding a place to live when you got to Washington?

Captain Dyer: It happened that my mother-in-law owned a house in Kansas City, which had been rented, so we told the people to move out. We stopped in Kansas City briefly and I left the family there. I came on to Washington. They stayed there until the end of the school year in June. I bought a house on Reno Road about a mile and a half, two miles, from Nebraska Avenue.

Q: That was convenient.

Captain Dyer: I kept looking for a place within walking

distance.

Q: In many places in the country there was a general housing shortage at that time.

Captain Dyer: There weren't too many houses in Washington. I suppose I did not look at more than eight or ten houses in reasonable distance from where I wanted to be, and a couple clear out in Bethesda.

Q: How had you done in selling your house in Hawaii? Had the land boom started at all by then?

Captain Dyer: We sold it for twice what we had paid for it.

Q: You did pretty well.

Captain Dyer: It gave us enough money for a down payment in Washington.*

Q: When did you report for duty at Nebraska Avenue?

---
*This was Captain Dyer's way of saying that Washington real estate was expensive as far back as the 1940s.

Captain Dyer: About the first of February. My orders had given me 30 days' leave. They had intimated to me that they would like to have me cut that leave short, but I didn't see why I should.

Q: Especially after the previous experiences you had when you reported in at places and didn't get to take your leave. What was your new duty assignment?

Captain Dyer: We were in a state of flux there, but I became chief of production for the processing unit in Nebraska Avenue.

Q: Processing what?

Captain Dyer: Everything.

Q: Had you been promoted to captain by that point?

Captain Dyer: Yes. I was promoted to captain in the fall of '44.

Q: So you were probably in one of the pretty senior billets at Nebraska Avenue, weren't you?

Captain Dyer: Yes. We had two organizations there. We had the Naval Security Group and under that we had the Naval Security

Station. I was attached technically to the Naval Security Station. And I was number two. Bud Harper was in the class of '22.* I kept that job for about a year and a half, and then we had kind of a shake-up. I became something called technical director.

Along about '47, unification set in. We became the Armed Forces Security Agency. No, that was later. Anyway, in the annual physical examination, at the end of '47, the medicos decided that I had a couple of hernias. It never bothered me; I wasn't even aware I had them. But along in December I got written orders from the Bureau of Personnel to go to Bethesda to have them repaired.** And so we come to the genesis of the beard. I went out there. I had one on each side, so they repaired the one on the right. In those days they had not perfected spinal anesthesia. A certain number of victims got what were known as spinal headaches. As long as you lie down flat, you feel fine. The minute you sit up, you think somebody hit you in the head with a two-by-four. I had this for about a week. I did not feel like shaving during that time.

Q: Probably didn't feel like having the other hernia repaired either.

---
*Captain John S. Harper, USN.
**U.S. Naval Medical Center located in Bethesda, Maryland.

Captain Dyer: Well, I stuck with that. Somewhere along the line, one of the nurses started harassing me about the beard. I was getting amused by it a little bit. When it came time for the second operation, I had a cough that morning, so they decided to postpone that for a week. The second operation, I got by very much better. They did something a little different so that the anesthesia was not quite complete, but it was all right. Anyway, by the time I went back to duty, I had a fairly respectable looking beard.

Q: Was that virtually unheard of among naval officers of the time?

Captain Dyer: Almost unheard of among naval officers and anybody else. Hippies hadn't started yet.

Q: Admiral Reeves was . . .*

Captain Dyer: Admiral Reeves had one, and another admiral had one because he had a skin condition. The doctors told him to grow one.

---

*Admiral Joseph M. Reeves, USN, was known as "Billy Goat" because of his goatee.

Q: That was Admiral Pirie.*

Captain Dyer: Yes, Pirie. I always admired Admiral Reeves very much anyway. Somebody bet me that I would not go back to duty with the beard, and I did. Then I found out that Admiral Stone pretty much disliked it. So I decided to keep it. Now if he had ever come out and given me a flat order, I would probably have obeyed it, even though it would have been an illegal order. But the regulations at that time said hair and beard must be neatly trimmed. That's all they said. And oh, such snide things. One day we were having a bunch of visiting firemen, admirals or something, and he sent word that he didn't want anybody with a beard in the party. That's all right. I kept it.

In due course, we formed AFSA, the Armed Forces Security Agency. Earl Stone was the first director. Laurance Safford and I were--I can't remember what our title was--technical advisors or something. We shared an office, and reported directly to the director. I made a number of staff studies for the director and wrote his speeches for him. I've written speeches for a number of people, but he was the hardest person that I ever had to write speeches for. I'd write one and take it down, and he would go over it. "Don't you think we better change this to so-and-so?" And I'd go back and change it. Then change it some more. And

---

*Vice Admiral Robert B. Pirie, USN, whose oral history is in the Naval Institute collection.

almost invariably, after the seventh change, we were back almost to the identical speech I had written in the first place.

The Joint Chiefs of Staff got very concerned about having all the eggs in one basket, having all the processing units in Washington. They issued some kind of an edict to set up a stand-by unit somewhere else. I wrote a very profound staff study pointing out the impracticability and futility of trying to set up a stand-by unit, and suggesting that we should set up a functioning unit that would share the load and would be capable of taking over the full load if necessary. They bought it.

Somewhere along the line they directed me to set up a site board and go out and look around the country. I was made chairman with an Army captain and an Air Force first lieutenant. We made quite an extensive trip going as far west as Denver and as far south as Dallas. Our instructions were to find someplace with existing buildings suitable or adaptable for use by the agency and on government-owned property. Those were rather severe limitations.

Q: Did you also have to maintain proximity to antennas?

Captain Dyer: No, they didn't put that on us. The best place we could find was a former Montgomery Ward plant in Kansas City, with an eight-story building and other smaller buildings. It would have been reasonably adaptable. So we came back, and we made our recommendations. No, they didn't like that. That was too far away. They had no vision of what modern jets would do; Kansas City was only going to be an hour and a half away.

So we went out again, and we went to various places. By this time we didn't have to find buildings, so we decided to move in with the gold at Fort Knox. That met with great approval of the Joint Chiefs and the Secretary of Defense. They hired an architect and they started drawing plans. Then the Army, primarily, started screaming that you had to move everything there. You couldn't have two separate locations, which had been the modus operandi in doing anything at all. Finally the FBI and the CIA got together and went to President Truman and got him to rule that Fort Knox was too far away from the seat of the government. We had operated sort of on the precept that missiles could go 300 miles from the coast, so we were going to go a little more than 300 miles. We weren't looking too far in the future either. Finally we got orders to go look for a place within--well, not precisely, but in effect within 25 miles of the zero milestone. We scouted all around the Washington area. Fort Meade was the only place that really seemed to fit the bill. Our second choice was McLean--whatever you call where the CIA is now. There's a Bureau of Roads tract out there anyway. And the third was to stay at Arlington Hall. The first recommendation stuck, and they decided to move everything, lock, stock, and barrel to Fort Meade. Now it's doubled the size of the place out there and they're building more. In my uninformed opinion, it's become a monstrosity. But it is interesting to note how my committee, my board, selected the site of NSA, and also the site of CIA, too, because they moved to our second choice.

Somewhere along the line we had a change of directors and General Ralph J. Canine relieved Stone.* I don't know which came first, but somewhere along the line Mr. Friedman and I swapped jobs. He was head of the technical division, and I was technical advisor. After General Canine took over, he decided to change the technical division to the training division and make it responsible for the NSA school, which at that time was down on U Street, at that time a choice location.

There isn't too much to say about that job. I think my greatest accomplishment was to set up the program of academic training for agency employees. The original contract with George Washington University was to conduct a number of classes for agency employees after hours or, in some limited cases, during work hours, for agency employees partly in work related subjects and partly in non-work related subjects. It was rather a broad program. I think it's much broader now than it was.

Q: What subjects were they studying?

---

*Lieutenant General Ralph J. Canine, U.S. Army, was director of the National Security Agency from August 1951 to November 1956.

Captain Dyer: Oh, it might be some math fields or computer science or language or history.

Q: We've sort of skirted the issue of the substance of your work. Were you still intercepting signals of foreign nations and trying to decipher them?

Captain Dyer: I'd rather not answer that.

Q: All right.

Captain Dyer: It's classified information. If you don't believe me, you can read <u>Newsweek</u> or the <u>Washington Post</u>. They'll tell you what we did. I'm not allowed to say.

Q: Okay. Were there any distinguished graduates from your course, people whose names might be recognizable?

Captain Dyer: I don't think of any, no.

Q: You talked about unification breaking out. Were there ever any inter-service intelligence attempts to break the codes of other services during the war between the Navy and the Air Force?*

---
*In the formation of the Defense Department, the Air Force attempted to gain control of naval aviation.

Captain Dyer: No. At least none that I know of. I don't think we would have profited anything if we had. Any plotting that was done did not involve communications.

Q: Did unification work reasonably well in the agency you were in?

Captain Dyer: Reasonably well, yes. Neither of the directors I served under really knew beans about anything we were doing. Someone who had had a lot of experience in communications was bound to have had a certain amount of experience in intelligence. As head of the training division, I conducted a course, very unsuccessfully, trying to teach Ralph Canine the basic elements of cryptanalysis, elementary form. It disturbed him greatly if the furniture in a particular office did not match, so he wanted it shuffled around or new furniture bought. He wanted all the desks to be the same color. I think he was probably unjustly accused of trying to get only blue-eyed clerks in a given office. But there was considerably more energy wasted in that direction than I think was justified.

Incidentally, shortly after the transfer of the directorship, I decided to remove my beard.

Q: Just a coincidence, I'm sure.

Dyer #4 - 330

Captain Dyer: Just a coincidence.

Q: At some point after that you grew it back. Were you entering a Colonel Sanders look-alike contest or something?

Captain Dyer: No. It was after I retired and went to the university to teach. I have offered several explanations for that. One was that I was tired of being mistaken for a freshman on campus. But the one my daughter prefers is the fact that the math department is devoted to inculcating precision of expression, and it disturbed me that when students referred to "that son of a bitch in the math department," it was very indefinite. But when they referred to "that bearded son of a bitch in the math department," there was no question as to whom they meant. That worked all right until we got a head of the department who also had a beard. I really kind of liked it and I thought maybe it made me look a little more professorial; I don't know.

Q: Did you have any contact with Admiral Hillenkoetter when he came back to head the CIA?*

---

*Rear Admiral Roscoe H. Hillenkoetter, USN, first director of the Central Intelligence Agency.

Dyer #6 - 331

Captain Dyer: I never saw Roscoe once.

Q: He was assigned to sea shortly after the Korean War broke out. When he was at the CIA, there was a sort of minor league version of the repercussions that had been seen after Pearl Harbor. Did that spill over on to your organization at all?

Captain Dyer: I wasn't aware if it did.

Q: Were you surprised when the North Koreans attacked South Korea?

Captain Dyer: Yes. Incidentally, that was coincidental with my taking off on the first site board trip. They did that the same day we started out.

Q: So you had the day off again as you had when the Roberts Commission was there. Was your relocation to Japan related to the Korean War?

Captain Dyer: All three services had activities in and around Tokyo. At least a couple of years before I went out there, they had set up what was known as the Armed Forces Security Agency Far East. Just before I went out, Ham Wright was chief of AFSAFE. I was sent out to relieve him. I guess while I was en route they changed the charter and made it the National Security Agency. So we became NSAFE. When I got there, Ham had been shipped back to the States because all of a sudden they thought he had stomach cancer. Fortunately, it was a false alarm, but I did not have the value of person-to-person relief at NSA. I stayed there about 15, 16 months. I came back in January of '54.

Q: Where were you located physically when you were in Japan?

Captain Dyer: In Tokyo. At General Clark's headquarters, he having relieved as Supreme Commander.*

Q: I think it was Supreme Commander Allied Powers.

Captain Dyer: I saw him only once, I think, his New Year's reception.

Q: Did you have any ties with the Commander Naval Forces Far East?

Captain Dyer: Not really. He had been in Tokyo until just about

---

*General Mark W. Clark relieved General Matthew B. Ridgway, as Supreme Command Allied Powers in Tokyo in May 1952. Ridgway had replaced General MacArthur who was "fired" by President Truman in April 1951.

the time I arrived. He moved his headquarters to Yokosuka. I saw him a few times. I went down to a cocktail party he gave for Mick Carney when he was Chief of Naval Operations.* But I really didn't see him very much.

Q: Were you sort of independent from the Navy by that point?

Captain Dyer: For administrative action I was under the naval attache. He paid me and things of that kind. I had no real contact with the Navy except to go down to Yokosuka for an annual physical examination or something like that.

Q: Did you have any activities in connection with General Eisenhower's visit to Korea?

Captain Dyer: No.

Q: What are your recollections of the Japanese people from that period?

Captain Dyer: I was very pleasantly surprised and impressed by most of them. I think that I received more little acts of

---
*Admiral Robert B. Carney, USN, Chief of Naval Operations from August 1953 to August 1955.

spontaneous courtesy and consideration there than I ever had anyplace in my life. I got along very well with the Japanese.

To back up here a good many years, when I was still a midshipmen, I joined the Masons. And shortly after graduation I entered the Scottish Rite as far as the 18th degree. When I came to Washington after the war, I transferred my Scottish Rite membership from Long Beach, California, to Washington and finished the 32nd degree and became very active in the activities there.

My family did not go out to Japan because our boy was in his last year of high school and planning to enter the Naval Academy. It didn't seem the wise thing to do. So, not having a family with me, I spent a lot of my free time at the Masonic Temple taking part in their activities. A number of Japanese had become members of the Masons. That was one thing that MacArthur did. Before the war that was forbidden, but he told the Emperor to allow it. And so I got acquainted with a number of Japanese--not a close acquaintance, but a reasonably social one.

Q: Many of the naval officers who were involved in the war described the breaking down of hostilities that occurred and the formation later of some genuine friendships.

Captain Dyer: There's one man that was very active in the lodge there, a Rotarian. He had been president of the Japanese-American

Friendship Society. He was a very fine gentleman.

The six Tokyo universities had English-speaking societies, and they held an annual play competition in English. There was another naval officer there; I don't know how he met up with them to begin with, but he was coaching the people in Kao University to put on their play. He asked me if I'd like to go along, so I used to go with him fairly regularly. That was quite an experience. These were 19, 20, 21-year-old Japanese lads. They were quite young when the war ended. This was some eight years later. And they were a very nice bunch of boys. They didn't win; I was very unhappy about that.

Q: Did you ever have an opportunity to compare notes with the Japanese naval officers who had been involved in cryptography on their side during the war?

Captain Dyer: No. In fact, I made every effort to conceal the fact that I knew anything about that.

Q: I wonder why there wasn't any effort to interrogate them on cryptography, as there was in the things that were involved in the strategic bombing survey?

Captain Dyer: I think there was some, but it's awfully hard to ask too much without disclosing how much you know. Even at the time I was out there, the bars were still sky high on revealing things. Sometimes the bars were ridiculous.

When the Armed Forces Security Agency was first formed and Earl Stone was designated first director, the Joint Chiefs of Staff themselves originated a press release: "Admiral So-and-So is relieving Admiral Stone as Director of Naval Communications," blah, blah, blah. Last sentence: "Admiral Stone is going to duty under the Chief of Naval Operations."

Q: So they were deliberately very vague.

Captain Dyer: That was decided at the very highest level of the armed services. Four-star generals and admirals decided that that's the way it should be.

Q: Did you have any contact during that period with Arthur McCollum, a Japanese language officer and intelligence specialist?*

Captain Dyer: No. I've met Mike a time or two somewhere, but I've never had any real contact with him.

It's odd the way people are. When I met Sebald once, I made

---
*Captain Arthur H. McCollum, USN, later rear admiral. His oral history is in the Naval Institute collection.

the mistake of saying something like, "I almost feel as if I know you, I've heard so much about you."* And then he tried to pin me down as to what. I said, "Well, language students who were there with you and knew you have mentioned your name and I've heard it." One of the things that I did remember very distinctly, and one of the first things I heard about him, was that he married a Japanese girl. That I didn't dare say. That was the kind of thing that stuck in my mind. Major Sullivan, a Marine officer, was the first one I heard talk about Sebald. Other language students that I knew also had mentioned him. But that was before he became ambassador.

Q: Destroyermen and aviators and submariners like to get together and spin yarns about their deeds. Was that discouraged among intelligence officers and cryptanalysts?

Captain Dyer: I don't know that it was discouraged, but it certainly wasn't encouraged. To a limited extent there was some encouragement of your socializing with your own kind, so if you did happen to say something you shouldn't, there would be less

---

*Ambassador William J. Sebald, was a graduate of the Naval Academy, class of 1924, returned to active duty to serve as an intelligence officer during the war, retiring as captain, U.S. Naval Reserve. He served as deputy for Supreme Commander for Allied Powers in Japan from 1947 to 1952 and was acting, and then appointed U.S. political advisor for Japan with the rank of ambassador from 1947 to 1950. He is the subject of a three-volume Naval Institute oral history.

harm done. But never any organized effort in that regard.

Q: You mentioned your son was going into the Naval Academy. Did you give him any assistance or encouragement along those lines?

Captain Dyer: The decision was entirely his, but yes, I gave him some encouragement. He was too short. I called up a captain in the Medical Corps, whom I knew and with whom I had served when we were both lieutenants, and told him what the problem was. He recommended a civilian doctor, an endocrinologist, who might be able to help. I spent some $1,700 trying to get him a little taller, almost to no avail. When he took his physical examination, I was in Japan. In my day only about 20 of us reported on a given day, sort of a lackadaisical physical exam. But in the modern salt mines approach, they get 800 or 1,000 or whatever number they have, and run all of them through the mill the same day. They have them do various things. As you probably know, but maybe you don't, you're taller when you first wake up in the morning.

Q: No, I didn't.

Captain Dyer: We even tried to get him to take a taxi cab over from Carvel Hall to Bancroft Hall, but he pooh-poohed that idea. As luck would have it, the first thing he had to do was run the obstacle course. It was about as well calculated as anything could be to jar you down. He got up there and was a full half-inch short. He had to go in and see the captain. The captain says, "Well, son, it looks like you're standing in a hole."

And Ted said, "It would seem so, sir." Afterward, he kind of halfway thought that that "sir" was . . .

Mrs. Dyer: I think that did it.

Captain Dyer: Anyway, he got a waiver. He says, "You're young, you'll grow." He didn't grow. But in the irony of fate, before the next class came in, they lowered the height requirement by two inches.

Q: How tall was your son?

Captain Dyer: 5' 5 1/2". 5'6" was the limit, and then they lowered it to 5'4".

Q: When did you come back from Japan and resume your duties in this country?

Captain Dyer: In mid-January of '54.

Q: Did you then go back to Nebraska Avenue?

Captain Dyer: Oh, yes. And I was made historian. Now, since you're a historian, I probably shouldn't say that I rebelled violently. But General Canine and I argued the question for, I guess, over an hour. His three stars won over my four stripes. I became a historian--the first one they'd had. I was not denigrating the importance of history or anything else, but I thought in what small amount of time remained to me that my abilities could be better used, than in trying to set up a history organization, which would not get very much done in the time that remained to me anyway.

Q: What was his rationale?

Captain Dyer: He didn't have any, except that history was important and he thought I would do a good job. I think Bill Friedman sold him a bill of goods. I don't know. But he didn't like the idea of a subordinate disagreeing with him. He thought, I guess, he had me across a barrel.

Sometime before unification came in, there had been a previous organization that he had recruited around 1930, the Three Musketeers, Kullback, Sinkhov, and Rowlett.* All were commissioned during the war and reverted afterwards to civilian status. In the unification, each one of them was more or less

---
*Solomon Kullback, Abraham Sinkhov, and Frank B. Rowlett.

head of an important element of the organization. And Canine decided he wanted to switch them around. He wanted to put Rowlett in where Sinkhov was or something. Rowlett, being a civilian, balked at it and went down and got a job working for the CIA. That did not set very well with the general. And then I came along in uniform and didn't want to take the job he wanted to assign me.

Q: You perhaps got some of the animosity that was intended for the other fellow.

Captain Dyer: Could be. I started looking around for a way of getting out myself and didn't have much luck. This was the spring of '54, and I knew I would retire in the summer of '55. The dean of the College of Arts and Sciences at the University of Maryland was a reserve captain I had gotten acquainted with. He came to work with us, came on active duty every summer. We were having lunch together. I said, "I'm going to be looking for a job. How about giving me a job out at the university?" I was just kidding as much as anything else.

Q: Was it your intention at that point to stay in intelligence-- perhaps the CIA or something?

Captain Dyer: No. If they had offered me a job, I did consider that briefly. But I wasn't set on it. My intent was to go out and make a million dollars.

I was kidding with the dean about going to work for him. He said, "You know, I think maybe we could use you in the math department. We've got a couple of retired officers over there now." I sort of dismissed it, and then I followed up several leads. I arranged an interview with the local head of IBM. I had a very pleasant but not very productive interview. When I left I found out that he had been living on crackers and milk for two years. That didn't sound like an outfit I wanted to get into.

The bridge and poker expert, Os Jacoby, who had worked for me at Pearl Harbor, was by profession an insurance actuary.* He made some contact with New York Life for me, and I went up there for an interview. It sounded good and yet it sounded bad. So actually, I was kind of relieved when they turned me down.

The more I thought about it, the more I thought this teaching racket might be just what I'm looking for. I won't get rich, but if it makes up the difference in present pay and retired pay, I won't be too bad off. So I called up Dean Leon Smith and said, "If you weren't kidding, I'd like to look into it."

He said, "Well, come on out and I'll take you over and introduce you in the math department."

---

*Oswald Jacoby was a lieutenant in the Naval Reserve at Pearl Harbor.

We went over. The head of the math department said, "I've got everything filled up for this year." He was very nice, very pleasant. He took my name and so forth. About a month or two later I got a call from him. He said, "One of our younger people is going to leave at the end of this semester. Would you like the job?" This was about the first of December.

I said, "I sure would if I can get retired by that time." I knew the aide in the Secretary's office. I called him up and asked, "Do you think you can get my retirement papers through by the first of February?"

He said, "Sure." And so I retired the 31st of January and went to work for the university the first of February in an academic rank that no one had ever heard of. I was a junior instructor teaching primarily remedial math. Finally I got to be an instructor, and miracle of miracles, though it was contrary to all the canons of the department, they made me an assistant professor. I think it was largely because I'd taken sort of a half-time administrative job and they figured if I was going to try to administer a bunch of professors and associate professors, I ought to at least be an assistant professor.

Q: Did you do any advanced course work yourself toward a degree?

Captain Dyer: I took advanced course work but not particularly toward a degree. I kept the option sort of halfway open. But in the first place I didn't want to waste a lot of time on languages unless I had to. And the courses I took were probably not well integrated for a degree program as far as that goes.

It was really funny. The first course I took was advanced calculus. And for the first time in the history of the department they had too large an enrollment for a single section. So they had to divide it. They did a very logical thing. Since advanced calculus can be either a graduate course or advanced undergraduate, they put undergraduates in one section and graduates in the other section. Unfortunately, I was a graduate. I was with math and physics majors who had somehow managed to escape advanced calculus. I've forgotten my exact mark on the first exam--44, I think, or something like that. But I got a "B" for the course.

Q: When you were taking these various job interviews, were you again at a disadvantage in that you couldn't tell employers what you had been doing?

Captain Dyer: Pretty much so, yes. The president of New York Life was on some presidential board for which he had a different kind of clearance which was just as high as mine, but . . .

Q: But you still couldn't talk to each other.

Captain Dyer: His clearance had to do with nuclear energy. Just why, I don't know.

Q: Did you feel any regrets at your naval service coming to an end, or were you sort of relieved since you had this kind of sour note with the general over your job?

Captain Dyer: On the whole, I think that I was relieved, looking forward to a new career, and so on.

Q: Did you enjoy teaching, once you got into it?

Captain Dyer: Once I got over being scared.

Q: What were you scared of?

Captain Dyer: Kids. College students and bluejackets are two different breeds of cats.

Q: And they were tamer then than they are now, probably. How long did it take you to feel comfortable in that environment?

Captain Dyer: Oh, I think about half the semester. I guess I knew more than they did about most things.

Q: You must have liked it since you wound up staying there quite a while.

Captain Dyer: I stayed there about 12 years. Somewhere in mid-course or a little after, I moved into the front office half-time. The department was continually expanding. When I went to the department, if I remember correctly, there were 31 on the staff including regular assistants and secretaries. When I left, it was 170-some. It makes a difference. I guess the last two years I had only large lecture sections, 175 to 200 students with six graduate assistants to take the drill part of the course and mark papers.

Q: You stayed there until 1967?

Captain Dyer: June of '67.

Q: Looking back over your naval career, what would you pick out as your biggest satisfactions and your biggest disappointments?

Captain Dyer: I don't think it can be pinned down any more closely, but overall the war years were the biggest satisfaction. You can't pin it down any closer than that, but certainly throughout the war I felt that I personally was doing just about as much toward winning the war as any other single individual.

Q: Do you think you reached the limit of your potential during those years?

Captain Dyer: I must have. Certainly, looking back on it. I don't think I was particularly aware of it at the time, but when I came back to Washington after the war, there was a certain degree of burnout. I had worked at my utmost capacity over the better part of four years. I didn't have a great deal of concern as to whether school kept or not. I had to more or less force myself to do many of the things that needed to be done.

Q: You mean professional things or household things?

Captain Dyer: Professional things around the office.

Q: Did you seek any medical help in relieving this burnout and bouncing back?

Captain Dyer: No. It just took time.

Q: Were there any forms of recreation that served as useful outlets?

Captain Dyer: Nothing very specific. In the summertime, trying to get grass to grow where there was 12 big oak trees. Things like that. Trying not exactly to garden, but trying to do things of that kind that I wanted to do. We had what I considered a very lovely place to live, but it was not adapted to anything of that kind.

Q: You grew orchids, didn't you?

Captain Dyer: Not then.

Q: That was later?

Captain Dyer: I didn't grow orchids until after I went to the university. I retired in January of '55, and we lived in Washington until the summer of '57. After we moved out to Maryland, we had a large basement. I experimented a little with growing this and that under artificial lights. I had gotten interested in orchids in Hawaii because I was close friends with one of the leading growers. Garden Magazine had an ad for three orchids for some ridiculously low price. I sent and got them, and they at least lived. Finally I sent out to my friend in Hawaii. There was at that time, still is, an orchid which was named after our daughter when she was born. I said I wanted an Ann Dyer, and he sent me one as well as some other things. Over the years I got orchids from other places. I would send him maybe $50 and tell him to send me a $50 orchid because he knew what I liked as well as I did. And I built up to where I had about 400 plants under lights.

Q: Did you have a business?

Captain Dyer: Oh, no.

Q: Did you give them away?

Captain Dyer: Just enjoyed them, except for a while when we were having a coed class luncheon every three months. I would cut a dozen or so orchids, and my wife would make up corsages. We would take them out there and have a drawing for them. They went over pretty well, too.

When I finally got crippled up with arthritis and couldn't really take care of them anymore, we had to consider getting rid of them. I decided I wanted some way of getting rid of them quickly. At that time I was treasurer of our little church, and I told the vestry, "If you arrange to bring most of my orchids up here and put them out on tables, we'll have an orchid sale and sell them for $5 a plant and the church can have all the money." There were plants that were worth up to $40 or $45. Others were worth all of $5. Maybe a couple of them weren't even worth $5, I'm not sure. We took 256 plants up there. I had already gotten rid of some, and I was keeping a few. The sale was scheduled to start at 1:00 o'clock and go to 5:00 o'clock. And I said to myself that if by 3:30 or 4:00 o'clock they're not all gone, I'll cut the price in half. The sale lasted 19 minutes.

Q: I guess there were some buyers there.

Captain Dyer: They began lining up at 10:00 a.m. outside the door in the boiling sun. It was a day about like today. I didn't have all the money in 19 minutes, but all the plants were gone.

Q: Elbowing each other aside.

Captain Dyer: Those four orchids sitting outside the French on that little table on the patio are all that are left. Three are Ann Dyers and the fourth one is an Edith Dyer.

Q: How did they happen to get named for family members?

Captain Dyer: That's the advantage of knowing an orchid grower. Anyone who develops a new orchid or breeds a new orchid and blooms it, has the privilege of registering it with the Royal Horticultural Society in London and giving it a name. The Ann Dyers were named at the time she was born so that we could give the obstetrician who delivered her, who was also an orchid grower, an orchid in gratitude. The Edith Dyer was named for my wife after I began growing orchids.

Q: And that orchid wallhanging--is that an Ann Dyer?

Captain Dyer: No, that isn't even the right kind. That's a paphiopedilium. An Ann Dyer is a cattleya. It is the shape of the one in the other hanging. But not that color. Ann Dyer is lavender and Edith is a white.

Q: Can you still find that name in orchid catalogs today?

Captain Dyer: Probably not in catalogs, but Sanders in London publishes a book, a big thick book of all the orchid hybrids. On the average, there are about 200 hybrids named and registered every month. Their books now form a stack about a foot high. But they're both still listed in there.

Of all the thousands and thousands and thousands of orchid hybrids, probably about 3,000 developed every year, there are probably not more than six which receive the highest award and not more than 100 the next highest award. Neither of these happen to be awarded plants and, of course, it's awarded plants that are propagated and more widely available.

Q: That's one way of leaving a legacy, though, and oral history is another.

You told me before that you were not disappointed that you were not selected for flag rank. Do you think that having been in that very specialized, secretive category worked against you in that regard?

Captain Dyer: No, it was just really a question of timing and fate. Up to the time I retired there had been only one SDO in communication selected for admiral. That was Joe Wenger. And he was a class senior to me, class of '23. On the record, I have to agree that probably any selection board would have no reason whatsoever to pass over him to go down to get me. His record on paper is probably better than mine. But whether it is or not, even supposing I was only very slightly better, it has to be materially better for them to say, "We're going to pass him up and go get Dyer." The only other SDO who had been selected was Eddie Layton in intelligence. We were not in direct competition because the selection board was told the first time to select a communication SDO. The second time, they were told to select an intelligence SDO. Even had I been in direct competition with Eddie, I think he would have been selected. After all, he was the intelligence officer for the fleet commander the entire four years of the war.

Q: And you were the cryptanalyst.

Captain Dyer: Which one is more vital?

Q: I'm wondering . . .

Captain Dyer: No details of anything I did--maybe Bill Goggins did write on a report that he's the Navy's best cryptanalyst. But what's that mean to a guy who doesn't know what a cryptanalyst is?

Q: That was my suggestion, that perhaps your specialized profession did work against you in the sense that there was not an appreciation for what you did.

Captain Dyer: Layton was theoretically in the same field. Although as a cryptanalyst, I know I'm better than he is--was. He's dead. But then why should I bemoan the fact that I didn't get to be an admiral? Wenger was selected; he's dead. Jeff Dennis was selected; he's dead.* Somebody else was selected; he's dead. I'm still alive and kicking. Kicking rather loudly at times.

Q: Any other thoughts to wrap it up? Reminiscences or sum-ups or what have you?

---
*Rear Admiral Jefferson R. Dennis, USN.

Captain Dyer: I think this is a life history in a way. I mentioned my Masonic connection, and I think the fact that in 1971 I received the 33rd degree is worthy of note.

From the time I retired from teaching in 1967 until I was laid up with arthritis in '77, I was treasurer of my church and in order to get money to pay the bills, I gave dinners once a month, where I did all the buying and cooking myself. When I took the job, they were definitely in the red to the extent of $300. When I gave up the job, they were definitely in the black to the extent of $2,000. I think that is a reasonably valid accomplishment.

Q: Then your commissary experience in destroyers paid off.

Captain Dyer: No, it had very little to do with it. I also did a great deal of cooking for the Scottish Rite, but that was more fun because I didn't have to do the buying and we could spend a lot more money.

I seem to be a prime victim for the surgeons to play with at times. In 1970 I had a prostate operation, and in 1977 they replaced both my knees. And in 1980 we decided to give up living on our own and we moved into Fairhaven, which is a total life-care community. The first six months were a depressing period because of the serious illness and death of our son. But on the whole it has been a very satisfactory move, and we are quite content to live life as it comes day by day.

Q: And do your kicking as necessary.

Captain Dyer: Oh, sure.

Q: I appreciate your many recollections. Certainly this is a valuable contribution to naval history.

Captain Dyer: I hope there isn't too much persiflage in it.

Index

to

Reminiscences of

Captain Thomas H. Dyer

U.S. Navy (Retired)

Adams, Charles Francis
    Secretary of the Navy, 1929-1933, described as ordinary individual who did not stand on ceremony, pages 106-107

Aircraft Carriers
    U.S. fleet problem in 1929 was one of earliest uses of carriers as part of the battle fleet, page 90

Antares, USS (AG-10)
    Flagship of Train Squadron One, the logistical supply unit of the Atlantic Fleet in the late 1920s, pages 68-75

Anthony, Lieutenant Commander Henry M., USCG
    As chief radio electrician in Coast Guard during search for Amelia Earhart in 1937, page 194; innate ability for cyptanalysis, pages 226-227, 296; assigned to Fleet Radio Unit Pacific in World War II, Anthony took over work on maru code and did a magnificent job, pages 257, 296; considered invaluable as part of the codebreaking team at Pearl Harbor, pages 226, 297

Armed Forces Security Agency (AFSA)
    Formation shortly after World War II, pages 322, 324. See also: National Security Agency.

Arkansas, USS (BB-33)
    Battleship which visited Europe during midshipman training cruise in 1923, pages 39-40

Asiatic Fleet, U.S.
    Reliance on codebreakers in the Philippines in the 1920s and 1930s, pages 129-130

Australia
    Hospitality offered by the Australians in Sydney during the visit by U.S. Fleet in 1925, pages 61-62; Australians visited U.S. ships, pages 63-64

Badger, USS (DD-126)
    Four-stack destroyer in which Dyer performed a variety of duties in the early 1930s, pages 109, 111-117

Batterton, Ensign Henry D., USN (USNA, 1923)
    Persuaded Dyer in the mid-1920s to go into the radio department of the USS New Mexico (BB-40), page 53

Battleship Division Four
    Commanded by Rear Admiral William Pratt in the mid-1920s, pages 55-58

Baumberger, Ensign Walter H. (Red), USN (USNA, 1934)
    When on the USS Pennsylvania (BB-38) in the mid-1930s, assessed as a good junior officer, page 158

Berkey, Lieutenant Russell S., USN (USNA, 1916)
    As flag secretary on Vice Admiral William V. Pratt's staff in the late 1920s, page 81; described as "one of the boys" until he got his stars when he turned a bit stuffy, page 104

Best, Commander Charles L., USN (USNA, 1908)
   As commanding officer of the USS Badger (DD-126) in the early
   1930s, assessed as excellent shiphandler, pages 113-114, 159

Birtley, Commander Thomas B., Jr., USN (USNA, 1923)
   Student in Navy codebreaking course in 1927, pages 76-77;
   Japanese language officer in OP-20GX in early 1930s, page 146;
   relieved Gill Richardson at Pearl Harbor unit in 1939, page
   197; worked on Japanese machine cipher, page 257

Bloch, Admiral Claude C., USN (USNA, 1899)
   Brought Wilfred J. Holmes on active duty as part of staff of
   the 14th Naval District shortly before World War II, assessed
   favorably by Dyer, pages 214, 315; Dyer felt historians were
   too tough on Bloch, pages 213-214

Bogel, Klaus
   Former actor and Library of Congress staffer who served as
   instructor in Navy codebreaking course in the late 1920s,
   pages 76-77

Bureau of Navigation
   Functioned as Navy personnel office in the 1930s, page 138;
   without first checking with Bureau of Medicine, issued order
   disqualifying officers with visual problems, page 152

Burnette, Malcolm
   Top Singapore officer never gave any indication that British
   could have tipped off U.S. about the 1941 Japanese attack on
   Pearl Harbor, page 231

California, USS (BB-44)
   Served as flagship for Admiral William V. Pratt in the late
   1920s, pages 84, 93-94; members of the California's band were
   recruited for codebreaking work in Hawaii during World War II
   and performed well, pages 234-235, 272

Campbell, Lieutenant Charles W.A. (Jimmy), USN
   Argued violently with Admiral William V. Pratt in the presence
   of junior officers, pages 57-58, 105; extremely pleasant
   personality, page 104

Canine, Lieutenant General Ralph J., USA
   Director of the National Security Agency, 1951-1956, pages
   327, 329; assessed as not knowing anything about the work of
   the organization, page 329; Dyer unsuccessful in teaching
   Canine basic elements of cryptanalysis, page 329; insisted
   that Dyer become NSA's first historian, pages 340-342

Caribbean
   Battleship Delaware (BB-28) visited Panama, Virgin Islands, and
   Martinique during midshipman training cruise in 1922, pages
   37-38

Cavite, Philippine Islands
   Site of U.S. Navy radio intercept station in the 1930s, pages 129-130; comparison of facilities of its navy yard with those of Pearl Harbor, pages 187-188; assigned to work on Japanese naval code JN-25, page 196

Chicago Tribune
   Newspaper which on 7 June 1943, reported that the U.S. Navy knew in advance about the planned Japanese attack on Miday, pages 269-270; Dyer's very negative assessment of the story and the people responsible for it, page 270

Childs, Lieutenant Griffin, USNR
   Assessed as dependable officer who contributed a great deal to the success of the Pearl Harbor unit, page 302

Coast Guard, U.S.
   Description of codebreaking program in the 1920s, headed by Elizabeth Friedman, page 298

Codebreaking
   Enciphered crossword puzzles published in the Navy communications bulletin in the mid-1920s, pages 53-54; training of U.S. naval officers in the late 1920s, pages 76-77; connection between skill at bridge and codebreaking, page 83; codebreaking experience gained in the U.S. fleet problem in 1929 proved invaluable, pages 85-90; codebreakers have often been considered "blue sky merchants"--crazy, harmless, and useless, pages 125, 139, 228, 296; need to be able to study easily all previous uses of a given code group, page 141; relationship between codebreaking and the characteristics of a language, page 143; need for a large volume of messages on which to work, page 225; codebreaking a scientific endeavor, page 226; codebreakers need the ability to see things in messages that others cannot, pages 227, 278; codebreakers need extreme patience, page 227; affinity between musical ability and codebreaking, page 235; codebreakers break systems, not messages, page 256; description of the initial stages of codebreaking, pages 277-278; William Friedman's work on the Japanese purple code was one of the foremost achievements in U.S. codebreaking, page 295; most good codebreakers have innate ability and are self-taught, pages 296-297; See also: Codes; Combat Intelligence Unit; Fleet Problems; IBM; Japanese Codebreakers; Japanese Diplomatic Codes; Japanese Naval Codes; Willson, Russell

Codes
   OP-20GX had responsibility for in U.S. Navy in the late 1920s, page 75; Dyer assessed 1929 U.S. Navy codes as fairly good, page 85; use of cipher devices in 1929 fleet problem, pages 85-86, 88; coding practices in 1931, page 120; See also: Codebreaking; Combat Intelligence Unit; IBM; Japanese Codebreakers; Japanese Diplomatic Codes; Japanese Naval Codes; Willson, Russell

Combat Intelligence Unit, Pearl Harbor, Hawaii
  Characterized as chaotic, page 142; agreement between Chief of Naval Operations and Commandant of 14th Naval District to set up unit at Pearl Harbor in the late 1930s, pages 186, 188; Yarnell's chief of staff unsympathetic to setting up unit and makes Dyer assistant war plans officer, pages 188, 190-191; physical locations and setup, pages 191-193, 199, 201, 219, 276; assigned to work on Japanese flag officers' code while Washington and Cavite worked on JN-25, pages 202, 296-297; history of names of unit, pages 197, 200; personnel broadly divided into cryptanalysis and traffic analysts and language and non-language officers, pages 221-222; recriminations against unit for not predicting Japanese attack on

Pearl Harbor, page 224; only outfit to go to around-the-clock watches prior to the war, page 215; after war began, worked 24 hours, off 24 hours, pages 233-234, 248-249, 250, 261; main operational focus in summer of 1942 was to get JN-25 as readable as possible, page 275; after atom bombs were dropped, continued to work until the surrender to check to make sure Japanese were doing what they said they were doing, pages 292, 300; personnel, pages 94-95, 194, 197, 199, 200, 205, 212, 218, 226, 231, 242-244, 247-248, 253-254, 257, 265-267, 291, 296-297, 302, 304-305, 311-312, 317, 342, 353

Communications Course
  Description of Navy's 1927 course, pages 75-78, 81

Cook, Captain Harold E., USN (USNA, 1901)
  Captain of the USS Antares (AG-10) in the late 1920s assessed as nervous, picayune type, page 71

Cooley, Commander Hollis M., USN (USNA, 1906)
  Made an alteration around 1930 to his USS Texas (BB-35) stateroom that resulted in a complaint letter supposedly from Bureau of Construction but in reality a joke played on him by Admiral William Pratt and his staff, pages 95-96

Crossword Puzzles
  Dyer solves 90% of the enciphered crossword puzzles published in monthly Communication Division Bulletin which led to his being ordered in 1927 to Navy communications course, pages 53-54

Delaware, USS (BB-28)
  Made a midshipman training cruise to the Caribbean in 1922, pages 37-38

DeMolay, Order of
  Initiated in December 1919, Dyer became first member to go to any of the service academies or to become a commissioned officer, page 46

de Steiguer, Rear Admiral Louis R., USN (USNA, 1889)
　　As Commander Battleship Division Four in the mid-1920s, assessed as having a good albeit somewhat gruff personality, page 65

Destroyers
　　Operations of the USS Badger (DD-126) in the early 1930s, pages 109, 111-117; role of destroyers in the early 1930s, page 116

Dilley, Ensign Luther L.L., USNR
　　Assessed as dependable officer who contributed a great deal to the success of the Pearl Harbor unit, page 302

Disarmament
　　Scrapping of U.S. warships as the result of international treaty in 1922, page 35

Driscoll, Agnes Meyer
　　Worked with students in Navy codebreaking course in the late 1920s, pages 78-80; discovered in the early 1930s Japanese naval code was a new code composed of four kata-kana groups, page 126; part of small staff in OP-20GX, page 128; work on flag officers' code assessed as very great achievement never fully recognized by the Navy, pages 295-296

Drugs
　　Navy physician prescribed phenobarbital and Benzedrine sulphate for Dyer's inflammatory colitis during World War II, page 206; Dyer denied that he kept pills on his desk in a candy dish, page 207; Dyer continued use of Benzedrine throughout the war and did not worry about possible impact on his health, page 249

Dyer, Edith Beatrice Miller
　　Met Dyer in 1918 when they worked together on high school yearbook, page 3; married and honeymoon in 1930, pages 102-103; did not know what Dyer did during the war until after publication of The Codebreakers in 1967, pages 207-208; children, pages 29, 185-185, 212, 217, 317-318, 334, 338-339, 348, 350-351, 354

Dyer, Lieutenant Robert A. III, USN (USNA, 1914)
　　At the Naval Academy in the early 1920s, Robert Dyer could always remember Thomas Dyer and would put him on report when others escaped, pages 48-49

Dyer, Commander Thomas E., USN (USNA, 1957)
　　First piano recital at age six resulted in his father being at Pearl Harbor the morning of 7 December 1941, page 217; difficulty meeting height requirements to enter the Naval Academy in the early 1950s, pages 334, 338-339

Dyer, Captain Thomas H., USN (USNA, 1924)
　　Birth in 1902 and early years, pages 1-18; parents, siblings, and ancestry, pages 11-12, 43, 51, 317-318; intention to

become a physician, pages 4, 9-10, 40; academic ability, pages 4, 11, 15, 20, 25-26; steps toward attending the Naval Academy, pages 3-4, 11, 13-15; Naval Academy years, 1920-1924, pages 6, 16-50; served as assistant manager for the Lucky Bag, pages 30, 41-45, 52; wife and children, pages 3, 29, 98-99, 101, 103, 112, 184-185, 207-208, 212, 217, 239, 249, 317-319, 330, 334, 338-339, 348-349, 350-351, 354; health, pages 24, 37, 40-41, 98, 151-152, 206, 221, 249-250, 287, 322, 333, 349, 354; beard, pages 322-323, 329-330; duty in battleship USS New Mexico (BB-40) in the mid-1920s, pages 51-66; Submarine School, New London, Connecticut, pages 65-66; duty in USS Antares (AG-10) in the late 1920s, pages 67-75; communications course, Washington, D.C., 1927, pages 75-81; duty in battleship USS West Virginia (BB-48), pages 83, 93, 107; duty on USS California (BB-44) in the late 1920s, pages 84-85, 90, 92-94, 96-97, 103, 107, 108, 213; duty on USS Texas (BB-35), pages 90-94, 99-100, 105, 107; duty on USS Pruitt (DD-347), pages 99-100; duty on USS Badger (DD-126), pages 100-101, 103, 109-116; OP-20G, Washington, D.C., 1931-1933, pages 118-179; duty on board the battleship Pennsylvania (BB-38) in the mid-1930s, pages 147-184; 14th Naval District, Pearl Harbor, 1936-1945, pages 186-317; Naval Security Station, Washington, D.C., 1945-1947, pages 320-322; Armed Forces Security Agency, Washington, D.C., 1947-1952, pages 322, 324-330; Armed Forces Security Agency Far East, Tokyo, later National Security Far East, 1952-1954, pages 332, 334-337; National Security Agency, 1954-1955, pages 339-340; post-retirement job as assistant professor, University of Maryland, 1955-1967, pages 31, 341-346; interest in gardening and orchids, pages 347-350

Earhart, Amelia
Dyer spent 4 July 1937 at radio station in Hawaii trying to find trace of lost aviator, page 194; Dyer skeptical about legend that Japanese seized Earhart or that she was a spy, pages 202-203

Engineering Duty
In the 1930s some U.S. Navy codebreakers were spuriously designated EDOs to facilitate promotion, pages 209-211

Espionage
U.S. Navy borrowed and copied Japanese naval codes in the early 1920s, page 80; U.S. Navy inspected coding machine at the Japanese Embassy in Washington in 1935, pages 293-294

Ethier, Radioman Second Class Henry E. (Tony)
On duty with Dyer during the December 1941 Pearl Harbor attack, page 218; became an expert in weather systems which he handled very effectively, page 257; took over work on maru code and did a magnificent job, pages 257, 296

Farago, Ladislas
Author whose book The Broken Seal described break-in at the Japanese naval attache's office in Washington, July 1935, page 293

Finnegan, Lieutenant Joseph, USN (USNA, 1928)
   Highly competent linguist with whom Dyer made bets on codebreaking in World War II, pages 143-144; translation of Japanese diplomatic messages received through RCA made in Finnegan's own handwriting proved they could not have been done until after Pearl Harbor attack, pages 205, 311-312; credited by Dyer with brilliant piece of work in hitting upon the systematic structure of the internal day code used by Japanese to discuss the Midway operation, page 244; assessed as very good translator given to wild flights of fancy, page 266

Fitness Reports
   Dyer felt reports written by Captain Russell Willson in the mid-1930s led to his failure of selection and that of the chief engineer of the battleship Pennsylvania (BB-38), page 174; fitness report procedures, page 173

Flagships
   Requirement for spit and polish on board the USS Pennsylvania (BB-38) in the mid-1930s, pages 160-161; some officers thought it good to serve on flagships, other did not, page 163

Fleet Problems
   Spring 1928, Dyer tried by himself to decode the enemy's communications but had no luck, pages 83-84; Navy Department offered Laurance Safford, Joseph Rochefort, and Dyer as officers available to form a communications intelligence or coding unit, page 85; 1929, Dyer and Rochefort read every enemy message intercepted, page 86; 1929, at critique, Dyer had chance to tell of successes, pages 89-90; 1929, earliest use of carriers as part of battle fleet, page 90; spring 1930, Dyer worked with Wesley Wright for the first time but unsuccessfully, page 97; spring 1930, Dyer went to the Scouting Force and was again successful but turned down opportunity to make critique, page 99; spring 1937, intercept station at Heeia and Dyer played the role of Japanese intercept station, pages 189-191

Food
   Poor quality on Naval Academy midshipman cruises in the early 1920s, page 33; various uses of tomatoes to feed Navy men, page 117

Foreign Languages
   Dyer's inability to learn foreign languages, pages 26, 110-111; Dyer takes Russian because of his estimate that Russia posed great threat to U.S., page 137; discussion of usefulness for codebreakers, page 143

Fourteenth Naval District, Pearl Harbor, Hawaii
   See: Combat Intelligence Unit

Friedman, Elizebeth Smith
   Skilled cryptanalyst who headed Coast Guard codebreaking program, page 298

Friedman, William
> His <u>The Elements of Cryptanalysis</u> used as textbook for 1927 Navy communications course, page 76; did not think well of Herbert Yardley, page 217; his breaking of the Japanese Purple code was a purely analytical job, not the result of espionage, pages 294-295

Goggins, Captain William B., USN (USNA, 1920)
> As head of Combat Intelligence Unit at Pearl Harbor in World War II, supported Dyer in his dispute with Washington over the solving of two-part unnamed Japanese tactical code, pages 253-254; Dyer initially believed that Goggins was in on plot to remove Rochefort in 1942, but concluded he was innocent bystander, pages 265-266; although in charge of Combat Intelligence Unit and Fleet Radio Unit Pacific (FRUPac), he was a communicator, not a codebreaker, page 267; commanding officer of the USS <u>Alabama</u> (BB-60), January-November 1945, page 306; assessed Dyer as the Navy's best cryptanalyst, page 353

Guam
> Location of radio intercept station before World War II, pages 129, 230; radio operators captured in December 1941 and interned as prisoners for duration of the war, page 232; Pacific Fleet headquarters moved to Guam in 1945, pages 291-292

Gunnery - Naval
> Improper procedures for handling broken powder bag in the battleship <u>Pennsylvania</u> (BB-38) in the mid-1930s, pages 153-157; duties of turret officer, pages 155, 158

Hawaii
> Various duties performed by Dyer while on the staff of Commander 14th Naval District in Hawaii from 1936 to 1942, pages 187-240; living conditions in the late 1930s and early 1940s, page 211; buying a house saved Dyer from having to have his family evacuated after World War II began, page 212; <u>See also</u>: Combat Intelligence Unit

Hepburn, Captain Arthur J., USN (USNA, 1897)
> Invited very junior officer Dyer to give eight-minute presentation during critique of codebreaking following 1929 fleet problem, page 89; qualities assessed as Admiral William Pratt's chief of staff around 1930, pages 103-104

Hewitt, Admiral H. Kent, USN (USNA, 1907)
> Conducted inquiry in 1945 about the 1941 Japanese attack on Pearl Harbor, page 310; Dyer's testimony at Hewitt inquiry concerning RCA messages from Japanese consulate, pages 311-312

Hillenkoetter, Captain Roscoe H., USN (USNA, 1920)
> Headed up intelligence center in Hawaii in World War II, pages 263-264; assessed as being out of his element but with some experience in intelligence, page 266; first director of the Central Intelligence Agency in the late 1940s, pages 266-330

Holmes, Lieutenant Wilfred J., USN (USNA, 1922)
　　Selected shortly before World War II to be combat intelligence officer on the staff of the 14th Naval District commandant, pages 199-200; claimed credit for concocting strategy of asking Midway to send message about broken evaporators in order to prove that AF meant Midway, page 242; mistakenly gave Dyer credit for solving internal time and day code in relation to Japanese Midway operation, pages 243-244; Dyer felt that Holmes's description of him in Double-Edged Secrets had a bit of poetic license but could have been true, pages 247-248; took over communicating with Edwin Layton after Joseph Rochefort's departure from Pearl Harbor in 1942, page 265; gradually slid from being solely with Combat Intelligence Unit to being almost entirely with ICPOA, page 267; awarded Distinguished Service Medal, page 305

Holtwick, Lieutenant Jack S., Jr., USN (USNA, 1927)
　　Given credit by both Ladislas Farago and Dyer as being one of the "electricians" involved in break-in of Japanese naval attache's office in Washington in July 1935, pages 293-294; after reporting to Combat Intelligence Unit in Hawaii in 1941, did an outstanding job of completely organizing the machine processing facilities, pages 221, 301

Hoover, President Herbert
　　Served as host in the White House at annual reception for Army and Navy in 1931, pages 121-122

Howeth, Commander Linwood S., USN (USNA, 1925)
　　Headed advance unit of Combat Intelligence sent to Guam in 1945 to work with Admiral Chester Nimitz, page 291

Huckins, Lieutenant Commander Thomas A., USN (USNA, 1924)
　　Relieved Dyer as head of OP-20GX in 1933, pages 146-147; ordered to codebreaking unit in Hawaii shortly before World War II, page 197

Hypo
　　Explanation of name of World War II codebreaking unit in Hawaii, page 197; See also: Combat Intelligence Unit

IBM
　　Installation of IBM machines to help U.S. Navy in analytically recovering new Japanese code in the early 1930s, pages 126-127; Dyer designed operating procedures, page 128; description of machine operation, pages 128-129; fact that Japanese code had changed was major selling point in getting IBM installation, page 140; system proved its worth almost immediately, page 140; machines not used for attacking ciphers, page 141; invention of additional machine allowed for better indexing, page 141; indexing procedures, pages 141-142; IBM machines installed in Pearl Harbor by 1938, page 196; Japanese blue code being key punched in both Washington and Hawaii, page 196; gradual buildup of new equipment after World War II began, pages 235-236; latter part of the war Dyer spent practically entire time in IBM room operating and using

machines, pages 256, 258, 286

Ingersoll, Admiral Royal E., USN (USNA, 1905)
    Work on fleet battle plans in late 1920s, page 91; described by Rochefort as a great flag officer but overly modest, page 92; assessed by Dyer as never too busy to stop and treat junior officers as equal, page 92; sparkplug for Admiral Pratt's plan to reorganize the fleet more along ship type lines and commands around 1930, page 105; as Commander Western Sea Frontier in 1945, immediately responded to Dyer's personal request for assistance with travel arrangements after the war, pages 93, 317-318; Dyer asked Ingersoll's help in becoming EDO in the late 1930s since Ingersoll knew about Dyer's codebreaking specialty, pages 210-211

Intelligence
    Duties of combat intelligence officer compared to district intelligence officer in Pearl Harbor at the beginning of World War II, page 201; discussion of "need to know," the guiding principle in intelligence, page 160; a military attache at a major embassy is a creature of the intelligence organization, page 266; assessment of intelligence officers' responsibilities and possibility of being able to predict Japanese attack on Pearl Harbor in 1941, pages 224-225; Dyer questioned purpose of intelligence if not used, page 288; See also: Combat Intelligence Unit

Intelligence Center Pacific Ocean Areas (ICPOA)
    Rochefort served as acting head after establishment in 1942, pages 263-264; relationship between ICPOA and Combat Intelligence Unit, pages 264, 267; See also: Joint Intelligence Center Pacific Ocean Area

Intercept Operators School
    Description of first class and training in late 1920s, pages 130-131; students chosen based on radio proficiency and high character, pages 131-133; Dyer left operation to competent chief petty officer, pages 129, 130, 134-135; See also: On the Roof Gang; Radio Intercept; Radio Operators

Jacob Jones, USS (DD-130)
    Involved in a collision with another ship in the early 1930s, page 112

Japan
    U.S. expectation in the 1930s that there would be war with Japan, pages 137, 206, 215-216; viewed 1924 U.S. Oriental Exclusion Act as insult since they had already voluntarily agreed in 1907 not to immigrate to the United States, page 137; shooting down of Admiral Isoroku Yamamoto, Commander in Chief Combined Fleet, in 1943, pages 287-288; prior to atomic bomb in 1945, Japanese gave no impression of slacking off, page 299; during 14-month tour in the 1950s, Dyer favorably impressed with Japanese, pages 316, 333-335

Japanese Army
   Author John Toland recounted how Japanese high command wanted to take the Emperor into custody to prevent him from doing anything to end the war in 1945, page 300

Japanese Codebreakers
   During 1950s tour in Japan, Dyer concealed his identity as American codebreaker, page 335; Japanese codebreakers probably not interrogated because it was hard to ask very much without disclosing how much U.S. knew, which would be a security violation, pages 335-336

Japanese Diplomatic Codes
   Subsequent to someone "borrowing" a copy of the fleet code (red) in the early 1920s, U.S. Office of Naval Intelligence undertook its translation, pages 80, 124; 1931, Dyer assigned to recover new ciphers on 1919 code, pages 124, 126; recovery of new ciphers not considered important by those who could have made personnel available, page 125; Agnes Driscoll determined that there was a new code (blue, 1929) composed of four kata-kana characters instead of three, pages 126, 194-195; new code enciphered in two forms: confidential and secret, pages 126; 90-95% of ciphers recovered in form of code but progress on code solution minimal, page 135; most of blue code recovered, page 195; break-in of Japanese naval attache's office in 1935 helped in solution and reconstruction of red machine, pages 293-294; comparison of red one-part code with blue two-part code, pages 144-145; in 1937-1938, change of code from blue book to black book, pages 194-195; designation of codes by colors referred to color of binders, page 195; Dyer and Wesley A. Wright collaborated to get firm entry into black book code, pages 195-196; in 1939, introduced new and different system which became known as JN-25, solution of which was assigned to Cavite and Washington while Pearl Harbor continued work on black code, page 196; in 1940, flag officers' code replaced black book code, pages 196-197; author John Costello asserted that December 1941 change in JN-25 so moderate that the Combat Intelligence Unit should have been back in to produce intelligence by 7 December 1941, page 225; Dyer disputed Costello's assertion because of limited volume of traffic, page 225; system used to communicate with Mandate Islands, pages 202, 218; explanation of geographical code, page 241; JN-25 change planned for 1 April 1942, not actually made until 25 May 1942, pages 244, 272; Dyer surmised that internal place and date codes were used so that lower echelons would not know what plans were, pages 246-247; solution of unnamed two-part tactical code in 1943, page 254; copy of Japanese code picked up on Guadalcanal, page 272; maru code or merchant ship code, similar to JN-25, pages 257, 296; daily volume of messages intercepted, page 277; number of codes and ciphers in JN-25, page 286

JN-25
   See: Japanese Naval Codes

Joint Intelligence Center Pacific Ocean Areas (JICPOA)
   Staffed by both Army and Navy in Hawaii in World War II, Combat Intelligence Unit initially shared space but did not fraternize because JICPOA did not need to know what they were doing and vice versa, pages 259-260. See also: Intelligence Center Pacific Ocean Areas (ICPOA)

Joslin, Captain Harold E., USN
   As enlisted man served as radio intercept operator on Guam, was captured at the beginning of World War II and held prisoner, page 232

Kahn, David
   His interview of Dyer and Wright while doing research for his 1968 book, The Codebreakers, resulted in Dyer and Captain Wesley Wright being threatened with disciplinary action by the Office of Naval Intelligence, pages 308-310

Kimmel, Admiral Husband E., USN (USNA, 1904)
   Commander in Chief Pacific Fleet at the time of Pearl Harbor attack and relieved of command shortly thereafter, pages 314-315

Lasswell, Captain Alva B., USMC
   In work with Pearl Harbor unit, assessed as very good translator, precise and methodical, pages 197, 265

Layton, Captain Edwin T., USN (USNA, 1924)
   Dyer's shipmate in the USS Pennsylvania (BB-38) in the mid-1930s, page 165; warm and friendly relations with Rochefort, despite rumors to the contrary, pages 214, 263; in spite of close physical proximity, Dyer did not see much of Layton because of schedules, pages 215, 284-285; not privy to private cryptographic system used by Wenger and Redman, page 263; responsible for Dyer receiving autographed picture from Admiral Nimitz, pages 285-286; as Nimitz's intelligence officer for four years, deserved flag rank, pages 352-353

Leave
   Dyer's leave periods as a midshipman in the early 1920s, pages 42-43; Dyer requests 30 days' leave to get married and is told "leave in excess of 15 days can be granted only for urgent personal or business reasons," pages 100-101; Dyer's 30 days of leave between Badger and assignment in Washington cancelled so regularly assigned Navy Department personnel could take leave, page 119

Lee, Commander Willis A., Jr., USN (USNA, 1908)
   An Olympic gold medalist, Willis taught his officers how to handle a .45 while he was executive officer on the USS Antares (AG-10) in the late 1920s, pages 71-73;

Lewin, Ronald
   Did not agree with revisionist theory on attack on Pearl Harbor, page 231; in this book, The American Magic, rated Dyer as one of the top codebreakers in the U.S. Navy, page 251

Liberty
    Dyer returned late from liberty in Scotland in 1923 because streetcars stopped running, and lost later liberty in Lisbon and Gibraltar, pages 27, 40

Liquor
    One drink violation of Prohibition after Naval Academy graduation in 1924, page 50; ships present at Guantanamo in the late 1920s challenged to a drinking contest, pages 68-69; naval officers' patronage of speakeasies during Prohibition, pages 180-182; use of liquor aboard ship, page 182

Luckenbach, Chief Lovine B., USN
    Bandmaster of the USS California (BB-44) band, he contributed a great deal to the success of the Pearl Harbor codebreaking unit, pages 235, 302

Lucky Bag
    Naval Academy yearbook for which Dyer served as assistant manager of the 1924 edition, pages 30, 41-45, 52

MacDougall, Rear Admiral William Dugald, USN (USNA, 1889)
    Relieved Admiral William Pratt as Commander Battleship Division Four in the late 1920s, page 59; assessed as prissy old son of a bitch, pages 59-60; MacDougall's relationship with Admiral Hugh Redman, who failed to vote for selection of MacDougall, pages 60-61

McClaran, Commander John W., USN (USNA, 1911)
    Delivered speech at fleet problem critique in 1930, page 99; as head of OP-20G, in the midst of the Depression, succeeded in getting $5,000 for the first year's rental of IBM machines for use in codebreaking, pages 118, 124, 127, 140; Dyer feels McClaran may have helped in getting Dyer classified as EDO, page 211

McCormick, Colonel Robert R.
    Dyer claimed he would have shot this editor and publisher of the Chicago Tribune responsible for publishing story detailing Navy's advance knowledge of the planned attack on Midway, page 270

Magic"
    Term used by President Franklin Roosevelt to describe the decoding of intercepted Japanese diplomatic messages, subsequently taken as general name for all American breaking of Japanese codes, page 226

Male Chauvinism
    Codebreaker Agnes Driscoll never given appropriate recognition by Navy because she was a woman, page 296

Maloney, Commander James D., USN (USNA, 1909)
    Captain of the USS Badger (DD-126), assessed as "back seat driver" who issued constant stream of criticism, pages 114-115

13

Mason, Commander Redfield (Rosie), USN (USNA, 1925)
   Collaborated with Captain Earl Stone in writing letter sent to Captain William Goggins in World War II, complaining that Dyer was responsible for confusion on unnamed two-part Japanese tactical code solution, page 254; Dyer lost no love for Mason, beginning with early acquaintance at the Naval Academy in the 1920s, pages 254-255; assessed as good intelligence officer with some cryptanalytic ability, page 255; spent most of war in Washington and recommended by them for Distinguished Service Medal, page 305

Masons
   Dyer joined Annapolis Lodge upon turning 21 (1923) and coached other midshipmen in ritual, pages 46-47; picked the Annapolis Lodge because he thought he would be stationed there the majority of his time in the Navy, but never served one day there, page 47; remained an active Mason his entire life, becoming a 33rd degree Mason in 1971, pages 334, 354; since his family did not accompany him to Japan in 1950s, spent much of his free time at the Masonic Temple in Tokyo, page 334

Midway Island
   Early indications in 1942 that Japanese geographical code AF meant Midway, pages 240-242; ruse concocted to prove that AF meant Midway by asking Hawaii to send a message in plain language that their evaporators had broken down, page 242; scope of operation, page 243; Wesley Wright and Joseph Finnegan determined systematic structure of day code, page 244; good luck for U.S. that Japan was not able to change JN-25 code until 25 May, page 244; night after Battle of Midway, Dyer attempted to solve message in tactical code but was unsuccessful, page 245; Chicago Tribune published front-page story on Navy's advance knowledge of attack, pages 269-270

Miller, Donald
   Reserve officer and professor of mathematics who worked on machine cipher in Hawaii in World War II, page 257

Minnesota, USS (BB-22)
   Battleship used for midshipman training cruise to Europe in the summer of 1921, pages 31-36

Morse Code
   Dyer never became proficient in Morse, page 110; Japanese developed their own Morse code equivalent to accommodate 48 characters to 26 in American Morse, page 131; personnel selected for intercept school had to have outstanding proficiency in American Morse code, pages 131-132

Murfin, Rear Admiral Orin G., USN (USNA, 1897)
   As commandant of 14th Naval District, Pearl Harbor, in the late 1930s, relieved Dyer of all "extraneous" duties after Dyer complained that he'd been sent to Pearl Harbor a year before to do a certain job and was unable to do it, pages 191-193; Murfin assured Dyer that failure of his selection to lieutenant commander in the late 1930s was not due to any

differences of opinion between them and recommended that Dyer go to sea, page 208; Murfin's qualities assessed, pages 212-213

National Security Agency (NSA)
Armed Forces Security Agency became National Security Agency in the late 1940s, page 332; Howard Engstrom, deputy director, page 305; NSA School, program of academic training for agency employees, pages 327-328; description of site selection process in 1950s that resulted in NSA being located at Fort Meade, Maryland, pages 325-327, 331; Dyer made first NSA historian, pages 339-340

Naval Academy, U.S.
Dyer describes circumstances around his entrance into USNA in 1920, pages 3-4, 11-15; assessment of quality of education and instructors in early 1920s, pages 20, 26, 28-29; smoking as an illegal privilege, pages 21-22; midshipman summer cruises, pages 27, 31-40, 74; new uniforms without stand-up collars introduced by Superintendent Henry Wilson in 1923, pages 47-48; activity of the midshipman theatrical group, pages 20-21, 23-24; The Log magazine put out by the midshipmen, pages 21-22; Dyer's work as assistant manager of the 1924 Naval Academy yearbook Lucky Bag, pages 30, 41-45, 52; Class of 1924, pages 29, 164-165, 188, 349

Naval Security Station, Washington, D.C.
Did not come into picture until well into World War II, page 132; divided into Naval Security Group and under that, Naval Security Station, page 321

Navigation, Bureau of
See: Bureau of Navigation

Nebraska Avenue
See: Naval Security Station

New Mexico, USS (BB-40)
Junior officers in the battleship in the mid-1920s, pages 51-52; radio communications setup, pages 53-55; took part in U.S. Fleet cruise to Australia and New Zealand in 1925, pages 61-64

New Zealand
Port on the 1925 cruise of U.S. Fleet, hospitality offered in Auckland, pages 62-63

Nielson, Lieutenant Henry S., USN (USNA, 1920)
Assessed as a good executive officer on the USS Badger (DD-139) in the early 1930s, page 115

Nimitz, Admiral Chester W., USN (USNA, 1905)
Acted in the spring of 1942 on information that AF meant Midway by getting the USS Yorktown (CV-5) back from the Battle of the Coral Sea and getting repairs made in record time, page 243; had complete confidence in Combat Intelligence Unit after spring of 1942, page 285; as Commander in Chief Pacific Fleet,

wanted to know how long it would take for Combat Intelligence Unit to get back in after a change in Japanese code, page 225; invited Dyer to go swimming in the summer of 1943, and Dyer ended up so sunburned, he was ill for several days, pages 281-284

Nitro, USS (AE-2)
   Ammunition ship in which Dyer stood watches while a passenger in 1927, pages 82-83

Norway
   Visited by Naval Academy midshipmen during training cruise in 1921, pages 32-33

Office of Price Administration
   Irritates Dyer by suggesting that he could carry passengers in World War II despite his long and irregular work hours, page 262

On the Roof Gang
   Organization of radio operators trained at the intercept operators school at the Navy Department in Washington, D.C., in the 1930s, page 132; a rather select group, about half were commissioned during World War II and another quarter achieved warrant rank, pages 133, 232

OP-20G
   Description of in late 1920s, page 75; very few people knew about its activities in the early 1930s, page 125; generally calm atmosphere in early 1930s, page 142; physical setup, page 142; in winter 1931-1932, Dyer became officer in charge, page 126; development of electrical cipher machine, page 135; Huckins relieved Dyer in 1933, pages 146-147; personnel, pages 76, 78, 80, 124-126, 142, 145-146; assigned to work on JN-25, page 196; did not believe that designation AF meant Midway, pages 243, 280-281; said in spring of 1942 that unnamed two-part Japanese tactical code could not be solved, then disputed Dyer's solution of it, pages 252-254; outlined a procedure for machine cipher and said no other method was to be used, pages 257-258; resisted attempts to eliminate duplication between Pearl Harbor and Bellconnen units, pages 279-280; exchange of translations and recoveries with Combat Intelligence Unit, pages 280-281; sending out reserve junior officer to report on senior officers an indication of their "we know best" attitude, pages 288-289; at end of war, recommended five people, including Dyer, for Distinguished Service Medal, page 305; See also: IBM

Pearl Harbor
   Conditions of the navy yard in the late 1930s, pages 186-187; Dyer's personal reaction to the Pearl Harbor attack of December 1941, pages 217-219; Dyer did not subscribe to revisionist school of "conspiracy," pages 229-231; small Japanese air attack on Oahu in March 1942, page 239; originally thought U.S. culpable because no dawn patrol was flown until he found out there were no planes left to fly,

page 314; not in a position to decide whether Admiral Husband Kimmel or General Walter Short took messages warning of war seriously enough, page 314

Pennsylvania, USS (BB-38)
   Incident of broken powder bag results in Dyer's being relieved as turret officer, pages 153-158; Dyer was the ship's service officer in the mid-1930s, responsible for laundry, tailor shop, barbershop, and store, pages 148-150; bridge watches stood by officers of the deck, pages 159-160; as U.S. Fleet flagship, pages 160-161, 167; mishandling of funds in ship's cigar mess in the mid-1930s, pages 169-170, 174-175; Dyer as the ship's secretary, pages 176-177; ship's communications in the mid-1930s, pages 179-180; operations off the West Coast in the 1930s, pages 181-183

Prange, Gordon W.
   In his At Dawn We Slept, thoroughly dispelled revisionist school of thought on Pearl Harbor conspiracy in Dyer's opinion, page 231

Pratt, Rear Admiral William V., USN (USNA, 1889)
   Commander of Battleship Division Four, ordered to become president of the War College in June 1925, pages 53, 56-58; argued so violently with his flag lieutenant, Jimmy Campbell, that Dyer was afraid he would have to be a witness at a court-martial, page 58; invited Admiral Hugh Rodman to sail with flag staff on Great Cruise to Australia in 1925, pages 58-59; moved up to Commander Battle Fleet, page 84; promoted to Commander in Chief U.S. Fleet, page 90; in Dyer's opinion, Pratt was loyal to Admiral Henry Wiley but thought him stupid, pages 91-92; invited Dyer and another junior officer to eat in the cabin with the admiral and his staff giving Dyer the most rewarding year in his life in the Navy, page 94; able to participate in jokes on staff, pages 95-96; description of Pratt's fleet staff around 1930, pages 103-105; wanted to reorganize fleet along ship type lines, ship type commands, and tactical organization, page 105; applied for the job of CNO, which he shortly got in 1930, page 106; sold on necessity of air cover for fleet operations and the need for carriers, page 109; friend of Japanese Admiral Nomura, pages 136-137; taught Dyer the impropriety of criticizing the actions of a senior officer, page 289

Promotion of Officers
   Dyer and chief engineer of the USS Pennsylvania (BB-38) were passed over in the mid-1930s because of skipper's fitness reports, pages 170-173; difficulty of codebreakers being promoted in the 1930s because of secrecy of their work, pages 208-211

Radio Intercept
   Description of intercept network, page 129; training of intercept operators, pages 129-130; form of intercepts and typewriters used, pages 130-131, 177; location of intercept stations, pages 129, 205, 276-277, 279, 291; See also: On the

Roof Gang

Radio Operators
Dyer never able to learn how to be radio operator, pages 55, 110, 224; operators demonstrated outstanding proficiency chosen for intercept school, page 132; operators on Guam captured and imprisoned through the war, pages 232-233

RCA
Office in Hawaii turned Japanese commercially-sent messages over to U.S. Navy Combat Intelligence Unit in 1941, pages 203-204; RCA messages discussed during Hewitt inquiry in 1945, pages 311-312

Radio Corporation of America
See: RCA

Rawson Strateford de Chair, Sir Dudley
Governor of New South Wales at time of visit by U.S. Fleet in 1925, page 63; son Rodney asked Admiral William D. MacDougall if he could bring a few schoolmates to visit the ship, subsequently found to have asked each admiral, thus having enough ships to parcel out every child from King School to one of them, pages 63-64

Redman, Captain John R., USN (USNA, 1919)
After 1942 Battle of Midway, came out to Hawaii to be communication officer on Admiral Chester Nimitz's staff, bringing Rochefort's not very diplomatic reply to Washington's offer to help as proof of Commander Joseph Rochefort's inadequacies, pages 262-263; had a private cryptographic system to communicate with Joseph Wenger using Navy radio, page 263; felt he should have control over FRUPac even though they still belonged to Commandant 14th Naval District, page 263; reported friction between Edwin Layton and Rochefort, page 263; interested in claiming glory and honor for something that Dyer felt he had nothing to do with, page 268; assessed as better politician than Rochefort, page 268

Redman, Lieutenant Joseph R., USN (USNA, 1914)
Communication officer on Wiley's staff in the 1920s following his having been radio officer of the USS New Mexico (BB-40), although he still seemed to think he was radio officer, pages 53, 269; Dyer felt he was interested in claiming glory and honor for something he had nothing to do with, pages 268-269; assessed as better politician than Rochefort and hard to get along with, pages 268-269

Roberts Commission
Description of 1941 investigation of attack on Pearl Harbor, pages 312-313; Dyer's only contact was to ask someone in entourage to act as courier to take solution of Mandate system back to Washington, page 313

Rochefort, Commander Joseph J., USN
   Officer in charge of OP-20GX in Washington, D.C., in the late 1920s, pages 75-78; member of communication intelligence unit for 1929, pages 85-86; as Japanese language student, felt that codebreakers needed to know the characteristics of Japanese, pages 87, 143; relieved Thomas Birtley in summer of '41 to become head of Combat Intelligence Unit, page 198; held low opinion of Herbert Yardley, page 217; Rochefort was calm when told of bombing at Pearl Harbor in December 1941, pages 219-220; felt he was a failure as an intelligence officer if he could not tell his boss today what the enemy was going to do tomorrow, page 224; work schedule during World War II, pages 233-234, 261; did not take credit for concoting strategy of asking Midway to send message in plain language about broken evaporators, thus proving that AF meant Midway, page 243; unhappy about copy of Japanese code dug up on Guadalcanal, because he thought the Japanese would find out, page 272; warm and friendly relationship with Edwin Layton despite rumors to the contrary, pages 214, 263; in fall 1942, appointed temporary head of ICPOA, received orders to Washington for temporary duty and predicted he would never return, pages 263-264; circumstances surrounding Rochefort's departure from Pearl Harbor in 1942 and the gap it made in the Combat Intelligence Unit, pages 262, 264-265; assessed as a good cryptanalyst, outstanding leader, and superior intelligence officer and analyst, pages 85-87, 247, 251; creature of both naval communications and intelligence, pages 267-268; although recommended for the Distinguished Service Medal, received the Legion of Merit instead because of professional jealousies, page 304

Rodman, Rear Admiral Hugh, USN (USNA, 1880)
   Unpleasant view of Rear Admiral William Dugald MacDougall in the 1920s, pages 60-69

Rorie, Durwood G. (Tex)
   Chief petty officer in Hawaii in World War II had an uncanny knack for being able to pick good men for codebreaking from the new drafts of recruits coming in from the mainland, pages 272-274

Rowlett, Frank B.
   Recruited by Ralph Canine in 1930, Rowlett objected to Canine's switching him in the early 1950s to a new job and left NSA to go work for CIA, pages 340-341

Russia
   In Dyer's estimation, after Japan, Russia posed the greatest threat to the United States in the 1930s, pages 137-138

Sadler, Captain Frank H., USN (USNA, 1903)
   Qualities as commanding officer of the battleship <u>Pennsylvania</u> (BB-38) in the mid-1930s, pages 159-160

Safford, Laurance F., USN (USNA, 1916)
   While in charge of OP-20GX in the mid-1920s, began putting cryptograms in the monthly Communication Division Bulletin as a way of identifying possible candidates for training, page 53; suggested by Navy Department to be a member of communications intelligence unit for 1929 fleet problem where he worked on traffic analysis and call identification, page 85; suggested Dyer as one to set up unit in Pearl Harbor in response to Dyer's request for help to get non-Washington billet in 1936, page 186; did not become SDO but remained EDO until he retired, page 306

Sea Duty
   Dyer always enjoyed sea duty but had to give it up when he became EDO, pages 34, 250, 306; Rear Admiral Orin Murfin advised Dyer to go to sea in the mid-1930s when he was not selected for lieutenant commander, page 208; Dyer felt that his greatest contribution to war would be to continue what he was doing rather than go to sea, page 250

Sebald, Ambassador William J. (USNA, 1922)
   Dyer made social comment in the early 1950s about feeling he knew Sebald, and Sebald grilled Dyer as to what he had heard, pages 336-337

Security
   The offices of OP-20G were under security during codebreaking raining in the late 1920s, page 79; success of 1929 fleet problem codebreaking due largely to lack of proper security considerations, page 90; Dyer could not ask IBM for help in using their machines because of secrecy of work so couched questions in hypothetical business or accounting terms, page 127; in order to improve security, Admiral Frank B. Upham removed Dyer's name from Navy Directory, pages 138-139; concern that operators in outlying stations could be captured and tortured to reveal information about the system, pages 232-233; radio operators on Guam were captured but never revealed anything, pages 232-233; no one chosen by Chief Durwood Rorie's personnel selection process ever violated security, pages 272-274; Japanese codebreakers not interrogated after war probably because it was hard to ask very much without disclosing what U.S. knew, which would be a security violation, pages 335-336; Dyer could not tell his wife what he was doing, page 207; because codebreakers' work is so secret, they are often not acknowledged or selected because no one knows what they do, page 209; idea of formal security clearance a late development, page 133; Dyer never cleared until 1946, page 133; announcing that Stone was going to duty under the CNO when he was actually going to be first director of AFSA an example, in Dyer's mind, of ridiculous security, page 336; security concerns made it difficult for Dyer to discuss what he could do or had done when looking for post-retirement job, page 344; Dyer and Wright threatened by Office of Naval Intelligence disciplinary action for granting interview to David Kahn, thus creating security violation, pages 308-310

Scotland
    Site of liberty for Naval Academy midshipmen on training cruise in 1923, page 27

Selection Boards
    Description of the Navy officer selection process in late 1930s, pages 208-209; because codebreakers' work was so secret, they were often not selected, page 209; Rodman states that if he had continued on selection board, William D. MacDougall would never have been selected for admiral, pages 60-61; as ship's secretary, Dyer notified people privately if they were not on selection lists, pages 171-172; Dyer not disappointed at not being selected for flag rank and does not think secrecy of work was an issue so much as timing and fate, pages 352-353

Sellers, Admiral David F., USN (USNA, 1894)
    Commander in Chief U.S. Fleet, 1933-1934, assessed as being too detail conscious and not up to the level of his predecessor, pages 162-163

Short, Lieutenant General Walter, USA
    Commanding General of the Army's Hawaiian Detachment at time of Pearl Harbor attack and relieved of command shortly thereafter, page 314; Dyer unable to assess whether Short took messages warning of war seriously enough, page 314

Showers, Lieutenant Donald M., USN
    Dyer very impressed with the personality and ability of this young officer who worked with Holmes, page 304

Smoking
    Midshipmen asked to turn in cigarettes upon reporting to the Naval Academy in 1920, pages 16-17; extending the illegal privilege of smoking to Dyer when he was a plebe in 1920-21 encouraged him to take up a bad habit, pages 21-22

Special Duty Officers
    Description of special duty officer category and subsets, page 305; Dyer redesignated as SDO (communications), page 306; creation of SDO assessed as wise move, page 307; Dyer believed that SDO should have permanency of location to make up for loss of other things, page 316; up to January 1955, Layton the first SDO in intelligence to receive flag rank, page 352

Spruance, Admiral Raymond, USN (USNA, 1907)
    Led walk up the beach and swim back at Admiral Chester Nimitz's swimming party in 1943, pages 282-284; assessed as cold and methodical, page 103

Stark, Captain Harold R., USN (USNA, 1903)
    Destroyer force chief of staff who helped Dyer get leave for marriage in 1930, page 101

Steele, Lieutenant Thomas, USNR
Friend of Admiral Nimitz from their University of California days and member of Dyer's staff, Steele was responsible for Nimitz's inviting Dyer to go swimming in the summer of 1943, pages 282-284

Stone, Captain Earl E., USN (USNA, 1918)
A communication specialist, Stone wrote letter to Captain William Goggins during World War II, saying that Dyer was responsible for confusion over the two-part unnamed tactical Japanese code, page 254; Dyer's adverse feelings toward Stone began in earnest after Stone transferred Wright back to Washington in 1943, page 254; first director of Armed Forces Security Agency, page 324; Director of the National Security Agency, 1949-1951, page 254; as director of naval communications, denied Dyer's request to be redesignated as Special Duty Only, pages 305-306; did not approve of Dyer's beard, page 324; Dyer wrote and rewrote speeches for Stone, who was never satisfied with them, page 324; assessed as not knowing anything about the job, page 329

Submarines
Information supplied by Combat Intelligence Unit to submarines during World War II resulted in a great many sinkings, page 287

Submarine School, New London, Connecticut
Nominated to attend, Dyer stayed only three weeks in the late 1920s before being notified that he couldn't see well enough to be a submarine officer, pages 66-67

Sylvester, Arthur J.
Assistant Secretary of Defense for Public Affairs to whom David Kahn appealed in the 1960s for reversal of denial to interview Dyer and Captain Wesley Wright, pages 309-310

Texas, USS (BB-35)
Flagship for Admiral William V. Pratt as Commander in Chief U.S. Fleet in 1930, pages 94-97, 107

Thomas, Ensign Willis L., USNR
Commissioned locally, wound up as the officer in charge of the IBM installation used in codebreaking at Pearl Harbor and did a very fine job, page 302

Tobacco
See: Smoking

Toland, John
Historian, whose revisionist view of 1941 Pearl Harbor attack was not shared by Dyer, pages 229-231

Traffic Analysis
Explanation of what a traffic analyst does in examining the enemy's radio communications, page 222; Dyer spent virtually no time in traffic analysis because it didn't interest him,

page 223

Training
U.S. Navy instruction in codebreaking in the late 1920s, pages 76-77

Turrets
Powder-handling accident in 14-inch gun in the battleship Pennsylvania (BB-38) in the mid-1930s, pages 153-157

Underwood Typewriter Company
Developed typewriter in the 1920s that could print Japanese kata-kana characters, pages 130-131

Uniforms, Naval
In 1923, Superintendent Henry B. Wilson introduced a new style uniform for Naval Academy midshipmen, pages 47-48

Upham, Admiral Frank Brooks, USN (USNA, 1893)
Impressed with potential importance and value of the work of OP-20GX, Upham removed Dyer's name from Navy Directory to improve security in the early 1930s, page 138

U.S. Navy Codes
In early 1930s, operational traffic sent in confidential, E code, or secret, A code, page 120; protection of U.S. codes an assigned function of the OP-20GX, page 135; development of electrical cipher machine, page 135

Wanat, Frank
One of the musicians of the California (BB-44) band who contributed a great deal to the success of the Pearl Harbor codebreaking unit in World War II and who missed getting commissioned when he should have been, page 302

Ward, USS (DD-139)
Dyer made sure that the Ward's message announcing sinking of midget submarine on 7 December 1941 was passed along to the commandant, page 218

Washington, D.C.
Living conditions and off-duty activities available in early 1930s, pages 121-122; high cost of real estate in 1940s, page 320

Weedon, Lieutenant William S., USNR
Contributed a great deal to the success of the Pearl Harbor codebreaking unit during World War II by being a very dependable subordinate in handling a lot of the processing routine in connection with the JN-25, page 302

Wenger, Commander Joseph N., USN (USNA, 1923)
Had private and personal cryptographic system during World War II, using Navy radio, to communicate with Commander John Redman, page 263; suspected by Dyer of sending out junior officers to write critical report on Combat Intelligence Unit,

23

page 290; recommended by Washington to receive Distinguished Service Medal, page 305; up to January 1955, only SDO in communication to be selected for admiral, page 352

Wiley, Admiral Henry A., USN   (USNA, 1888)
   Assessment of while commanding the U.S. Fleet in the late 1920s, pages 90-92

Willson, Russell   (USNA, 1906)
   Received $15,000 in the 1930s for designing a cylinder coding device although Dyer wrote a letter disapproving idea of award, pages 120, 168-169, 174; while commanding officer of the USS Pennsylvania (BB-38) in the mid-1930s, reacted negatively to Dyer's uncovering embezzlement in wardroom cigar mess, pages 169-170, 174-175; inventor of course angle card, page 172; chief engineer who won the engineering "E" for the year not selected because of Willson's inadequate writeup of the engineer's fitness report, pages 170-171; Dyer felt that his failure to be selected for lieutenant commander was due largely to negative statements on his fitness report made by Willson, pages 172-173; although considered by others to be a genius, assessed by Dyer as overrated as a shiphandler and open to question as a leader, pages 170, 172

Wilson, Rear Admiral Henry B., USN   (USNA, 1881)
   In 1923, while Naval Academy Superintendent, introduced new uniforms without the stand-up collar of the cadet-type uniform, pages 47-48

Woodward, Chief Radioman Farnsley C., USN
   Having worked on diplomatic systems in Combat Intelligence Unit, Japanese consulate messages received through RCA were passed along to Woodward in 1941, pages 203-204; announced Japanese attack on Pearl Harbor to Dyer in December 1941, "There are planes flying around dropping things," page 219

World War I
   Dyer's brother served in the same Army artillery battery with future President Harry Truman, page 12

Wright, Captain Wesley A. (Ham)   (USNA, 1926)
   Background as codebreaker, page 97; made first entry into black-book Japanese fleet code in 1937-38, page 195; ordered to fleet staff at Pearl Harbor but works in Hypo office, pages 197-198; hitting upon the systematic structure of the internal day code used by Japanese to discuss the Midway operation credited by Dyer as a brilliant piece of work, page 243; did initial work with Dyer on maru code, page 257; invited together with Dyer to go swimming with Admiral Nimitz, lends Dyer a pair of too-large swim trunks, page 281; considered by Dyer to be his greatest support, Wright transferred back to Washington in 1943 and replaced by a junior officer, page 254; as Chief of Armed Forces Security Agency Far East in Tokyo in the 1950s, was relieved by Dyer, page 331; threatened by Office of Naval Intelligence with disciplinary action for granting interview with David Kahn after being ordered to by

Office of Information, pages 308-310

Yamamoto, Admiral Isoroku, IJN
   Commander in Chief Combined Fleet of the Japanese Navy shot down by U.S. Army Air Forces fighters in 1943 after Combat Intelligence Unit decoded message concerning his itinerary, page 287

Yamato
   Japanese battleship sunk 7 April 1945, based on information provided by Combat Intelligence Unit, page 291

Yardley, Herbert O.
   State Department code clerk who had been in charge of "The American Black Chamber" was in favor of giving cryptographic aid to the Chinese during their fight with Japan in the late 1930s, page 216; not well respected by professional cryptanalysts, page 217

Yarnell, Rear Admiral Harry E., USN   (USNA, 1897)
   As Commandant of the Navy Yard at Pearl Harbor in the 1930s, Dyer was favorably impressed, pages 188, 212

Zacharias, Rear Admiral Ellis M., USN   (USNA, 1912)
   Credited by Ladislas Farago as the mastermind behind the break-in at the Japanese naval attache's office in July 1935, page 293

www.ingramcontent.com/pod-product-compliance
Lightning Source LLC
Chambersburg PA
CBHW080621170426
43209CB00007B/1484